D1526487

KEEPING
TITO
AFLOAT

LORRAINE M. LEES

KEEPING
TITO
AFLOAT

THE
UNITED STATES,
YUGOSLAVIA,
and the
COLD WAR

The Pennsylvania State University Press
University Park, Pennsylvania

Library of Congress Cataloging-in-Publication Data

Lees, Lorraine M., 1946–
    Keeping Tito afloat : the United States, Yugoslavia, and the Cold
War / Lorraine M. Lees.
        p.   cm.
    Includes bibliographical references and index.
    ISBN 0-271-01629-9 (alk. paper)
    1. United States—Foreign relations—Yugoslavia.   2. Yugoslavia
—Foreign relations—United States.   3. United States—Foreign
relations—1945–1989.   4. Cold War.   I. Title.
E183.8.Y8L44   1997
327.730497—dc20   96-9159
                                                                                  CIP

Copyright © 1997 The Pennsylvania State University
All rights reserved
Printed in the United States of America
Published by The Pennsylvania State University Press,
University Park, PA 16802-1003

It is the policy of The Pennsylvania State University Press to use acid-free
paper for the first printing of all clothbound books. Publications on uncoated
stock satisfy the minimum requirements of American National Standard for
Information Sciences—Permanence of Paper for Printed Library Materials,
ANSI Z39.48-1992.

For Bill
and
To the memory of James J. Lees

CONTENTS

ACKNOWLEDGMENTS

I am grateful to the many individuals and institutions who sustained me in the twenty years I have spent on this project. Robert J. Maddox first suggested the topic to me when I was pursuing my doctorate at Penn State in the 1970s, and I thank him for his continued support and guidance. The History Department at Penn State provided me with initial funding in the form of a Hill Dissertation Fellowship. The late John Moors Cabot graciously agreed to an interview while I was still working on my thesis and gave me access to his diary as well. In 1976, a grant from the Harry S. Truman Library Institute assisted me in first expanding my work for publication. In recent years, travel funds and a research leave supported by the Department of History at Old Dominion University as well as a number of research grants from the College of Arts and Letters enabled me to put the manuscript in its present form.

During a year in the Office of the Historian at the Department of State in the late 1970s, I profited from the expertise of the historians who compile and edit the *Foreign Relations* volumes. After joining the faculty at Old Dominion, I attended several conferences in Yugoslavia and I wish to acknowledge Arthur Funk and the American Committee for the Study of the Second World War, the Matici Iseljenika Hrvatske, and John R. Lampe and the East European Program at the Woodrow Wilson Center for Scholars for making those trips possible. I am particularly grateful to Leo Mates and Vladimir Velebit for consenting to be interviewed and to the many Yugoslav scholars I met who shared their views with me. I hope they have survived the carnage visited on their land in the wake of the Cold War.

The expertise of many librarians and archivists, from Pattee Library at Penn State, to the Old Dominion University Library's interlibrary loan and acquisitions staff, to the archivists at the Seeley G. Mudd Manuscript Library at Princeton, has been most important to me. Special thanks must go to John Taylor and Dean Hartgrove of the National Archives, Dennis Bilger and Liz Safly at the Truman Library and David Haight at the Eisenhower Library. They provided not only documents but the good cheer and kind attention that a weary researcher needs to plod on.

Numerous colleagues and friends assisted me as well. Robert McMahon and Russell Buhite provided valuable comments on conference presentations as this project moved into the Eisenhower years. H. W. Brands and Wilson Miscamble were both generous in their praise and constructive in their criticism of the final manuscript. Editors Peter Potter and Cherene Holland of Penn State Press have been patient and supportive companions in the publication process, while Andrew Lewis acted as a thorough and astute copyeditor. Over the years, John Treadway repeatedly shared his knowledge of the Balkans and put me in touch with others in the field. Paul B. Harvey listened to tales of Tito since my days at Penn State, and more recently, Steve Lofgren contributed his views and doubts about Eisenhower revisionism. Carolyn Colwell, the best friend any historian could have, gave me food and shelter on trip after trip to the National Archives.

To my family I owe the greatest debt; the love and support of my parents, Caroline and the late James Lees, and, most of all, my husband William Rodner have made everything possible.

Yugoslavia

International boundary
Republic boundary
Autonomous area boundary
★ National capital
⊙ Republic or autonomous
    area capital
╪╪╪╪ Railroad
Road

0   25   50   75   100 Kilometers
0   25   50   75   100 Miles

INTRODUCTION

During the early years of the Cold War, Yugoslavia was the focal point of an attempt by the United States to promote fissures within the communist world. The "wedge" strategy, identified by John Lewis Gaddis in *The Long Peace* as a crucial and innovative aspect of the foreign policies of Harry S. Truman and Dwight D. Eisenhower, relied on nationalism and a combination of U.S. pressure and support to create divisions between the Soviet Union and other communist states.[1] Although developed for use in both Europe and Asia, the wedge received its most sustained application in U.S. policy toward Yugoslavia, where it also revealed its greatest strengths and weaknesses.

In the immediate post–World War II period, the Truman administration nursed the hope that nationalism would eventually propel the Soviet satellites in Eastern Europe and the Balkans to resist Soviet rule. But Truman, more concerned with keeping vital areas such as Western Europe free of Soviet control, did not translate that hope into policy. The break between Yugoslavia and the Soviet Union in 1948 not only came as a surprise to the United States but was caused by a dispute between Josip Broz Tito and Josef Stalin, not by the West. After the split, the Truman administration adopted a policy of "keeping Tito afloat" in order to sustain the damage his defection inflicted on the Kremlin rather than to achieve any immediate "Titoist" gains in the satellites. By 1950, Tito's survival demonstrated the feasibility of challenging Soviet control and gave credence to George F. Kennan's theory that the communist regime in China might break with Stalin

---

1. John Lewis Gaddis, *The Long Peace: Inquiries into the History of the Cold War* (New York: Oxford University Press, 1987), 152–94.

as well; however, the Korean War rendered a Chinese version of the wedge strategy impractical.[2]

The war in Korea also caused the political utility of Titoism to be overshadowed by the need to provide Tito enough economic and military aid to forestall a Soviet or satellite attack on Yugoslavia, assumed by many in the West to be Stalin's next target. The Truman administration's willingness to extend secret and then open military assistance as well as economic aid to one communist country while waging war against another is one of the more remarkable episodes of the history of the wedge strategy. By 1951, the Truman administration had concluded that the immediate danger of Soviet military action against Yugoslavia had passed. U.S. diplomatic efforts were then concentrated on promoting Tito's influence among the satellites and persuading him to affiliate Yugoslavia with NATO.

It was Eisenhower and his secretary of state, John Foster Dulles, however, who made these two considerations the goal of their more elaborate and sustained application of the wedge. Yet Tito resisted Eisenhower's attempts to entice him into NATO and Dulles's plan to use him to liberate the satellites. His growing commitment to the nonaligned movement and his willingness to reestablish relations with the Soviets made it difficult for the Eisenhower administration to obtain congressional support for military aid for Yugoslavia, since such aid had always been viewed as contingent on Tito's cooperation with Western defense plans. The United States and Yugoslavia agreed to end the program in 1958, but the administration continued its economic and hence its political support for Titoism as a long-term alternative to Soviet domination.

The flow of economic and military aid to Yugoslavia during these perilous Cold War years is evidence that both Truman and Eisenhower realized the "monolithic international communist movement" was filled with tensions that could be exploited to the West's advantage. My analysis of their wedge strategy sustains the positive reassessments of both administrations that have appeared in recent foreign relations scholarship; yet the story of U.S.-Yugoslav relations during the Cold War does more than illuminate one of the United States's more successful and bipartisan foreign policies.

U.S. foreign policymakers, as Melvyn Leffler recently noted,[3] fol-

2. Ibid., 164–67; Alan G. Kirk to Dean Acheson, 13 August 1949, U.S. Department of State, *Foreign Relations of the United States, 1949* (Washington, D.C.: U.S. Government Printing Office, 1976), 5:923 (hereafter cited as *"FRUS,"* by year, volume, and page).

3. Melvyn Leffler, *The Preponderance of Power: National Security, the Truman Administration, and the Cold War* (Stanford: Stanford University Press, 1992).

lowed a geopolitical imperative during the Cold War by trying to deny the Soviets the resources that would enable them to threaten U.S. security. Assistance to communist but renegade Yugoslavia not only fit that approach superbly, but demonstrated one of the tenets essential to the wedge strategy: mere adherence to communist ideology, absent allegiance to Soviet imperialism, did not render a state an unsuitable ally. Still, the Cold War was an ideological struggle as well as a geopolitical one. Both sides motivated their populations to fight on by predicting the eventual triumph of their belief system over that of their adversary. This divergence of rhetoric and policy posed an intriguing question: what most reflected each administration's sentiments—the assistance given to Tito's communist state or the words, particularly those verbal missiles launched by Dulles, positing the defeat of the ideology to which that regime adhered? Richard Immerman raised this point in a critique of *The Long Peace* published in 1988 by claiming that while Dulles may not have believed that communists were monolithic, he was certain that "communism" was and would have sought "to conquer" those who broke away from the Soviets as a result of the wedge strategy.[4]

I agree that neither the Truman nor Eisenhower administrations was entirely comfortable with the relationship between the United States and communist Yugoslavia and jeopardized it in futile attempts to alter Tito's ideology. But both also repeatedly did battle with Congress on Tito's behalf, with Dulles serving as the Yugoslav's greatest champion. However, Eisenhower and Dulles, after years of striving to embellish the policy they had inherited from Truman, eventually acknowledged that the wedge strategy raised too many questions about the ties that could exist between communist, noncommunist, and neutral states, while providing results too intangible to merit congressional sustenance. By the end of the 1950s, Tito had not thrown his lot in with the West and had derived more in material terms from the wedge strategy than his patron had. The Eisenhower administration, unable to reconcile the contradictions between its geopolitical and ideological impulses, finally accepted Tito's continued absence from the Soviet orbit as victory enough.

During the Truman and Eisenhower eras, the United States directed its Yugoslav policy toward the central entity that Tito ruled, not its ethnic components. The wedge strategy relied on the force of nationalism, in this case Yugoslav nationalism, to disrupt the at-

---

4. Richard H. Immerman, "In Search of History—and Relevancy: Breaking through the 'Encrustations of Interpretation,'" *Diplomatic History* 12 (1988):341–56.

tempts at control exercised by the Soviets. Yugoslavia's short and turbulent history filled with ethnic tensions and its recent reunification after Axis partition played little part in Truman or Eisenhower's Cold War strategy. During World War II, the communist movement in Yugoslavia had based its appeal in part on the idea of a multiethnic but unified Yugoslav state. In creating the "Second Yugoslavia" at war's end,[5] Tito and his Partisans continued to appeal to all of Yugoslavia's peoples to join them in their revolution.

Before Stalin threated Yugoslavia's very survival, U.S. policymakers surveyed Yugoslavia's ethnic groups only to ascertain if any could serve as a viable option to Tito's communist regime. After Tito defied Stalin in 1948, to avoid the creation of a Yugoslavia subservient to Moscow, the United States championed the survival of the new Yugoslavia that Tito had created, with Tito at its head.

Throughout his years in power, Tito never presented himself as the leader of the Serbs, Croats, or Slovenes, but as the leader of the nation of Yugoslavia, claiming the right to govern his country free from Soviet domination. The wedge strategy employed by the Truman and Eisenhower administrations sought to defend this national freedom and to promote it as an example for other similarly threatened states to emulate.

Josip Broz Tito died in 1980. Yugoslavia and the Cold War survived him by less than a dozen years. In the 1950s, the members of the Western Alliance debated how much they would do to defend Yugoslavia from a Soviet or satellite attack. In the 1990s, the fate of Yugoslavia was debated once again, but the focus shifted to limiting the effects of that country's dissolution. The geopolitical landscape had changed; the Soviet-led communist bloc waiting to profit from Yugoslavia's demise was no more. The United States had declared Yugoslavia's own slow collapse a European problem. The Europeans proved impotent; the result was four years of barbarity of an order not seen in Europe since World War II.

The wars of the former Yugoslavia have ceased at this writing; the fragile peace, brokered in the end by the United States, will survive only through the resolution of ethnic issues, a factor neither Truman nor Eisenhower had to consider. The wedge strategy also never required the United States to defend Yugoslavia—only to furnish the Yugoslavs with the means to defend themselves. Whether the wedge strategy shortened the Cold War is arguable; that neither the Cold

5. Lenard J. Cohen, *Broken Bonds: Yugoslavia's Disintegration and Balkan Politics in Transition* (Boulder, Colo.: Westview Press, 1995), 21–28.

War nor Yugoslavia still exist but U.S. forces are stationed where Yugoslavia once stood is ironic.

Several authors have analyzed postwar U.S.-Yugoslav relations, but there has been no recent monograph on U.S. foreign policy toward Yugoslavia during the crucial Truman and Eisenhower period. John C. Campbell's classic *Tito's Separate Road*[6] is still valuable, since Campbell participated in so many of the policy decisions he described; however, the majority of documents dealing with U.S. foreign relations were still classified when Campbell published his analysis, causing him to omit or make only passing reference to many of the more sensitive aspects of the topic. Scholarly studies completed in the late 1980s by H. W. Brands and Beatrice Heuser[7] benefited from the greater availability of documentary material but were limited in scope. Brands for example, covers the Truman and Eisenhower period but explores the relationship between the United States and Yugoslavia only as part of an overview of the U.S. attitude toward neutralism in the third world. Heuser, who deals in detail only with the Truman administration, concentrates on the policymaking process of the Western powers but focuses more on Britain than on the United States. Both works have also been outdated by the continuing release of classified material and the end of the Cold War.

Keeping Tito Afloat represents the most comprehensive and recent study of this subject and is based on several years of research and interviews, as well as newly released archival material. I explore the U.S.-Yugoslav relationship from the mutual hostility of the immediate postwar period, to the decision to assist Tito in his quarrel with Stalin, to the hopes for a Yugoslav association with NATO and the contagious effects of Titoism. Sources include official and private papers and oral histories on deposit in the Roosevelt, Truman, and Eisenhower libraries as well as several record groups, some only recently declassified, from the National Archives in Washington, D.C. I consulted the George F. Kennan and John Foster Dulles collections in Princeton and other private manuscript sources as well. I was also fortunate to be able to interview John Moors Cabot, the chargé d'affairs in Belgrade in 1947; Vladimir Velebit, one of Tito's most trusted officials; and Leo

---

6. John C. Campbell, *Tito's Separate Road: America and Yugoslavia in World Politics* (New York: Harper & Row, 1967).

7. H. W. Brands, *The Specter of Neutralism: The United States and the Emergence of the Third World* (New York: Columbia University Press, 1989); Beatrice Heuser, *Western "Containment" Policies in the Cold War: The Yugoslav Case, 1948–1953* (London: Routledge, 1989).

Mates, Yugoslavia's ambassador to the United States in the 1950s. Their recollections added an invaluable and unique dimension to my study of U.S.-Yugoslav relations during the early years of the Cold War.

CHAPTER ONE

1945–1947
THE MOST LOYAL SATELLITE

In December 1945, Josip Broz Tito proclaimed the Federated People's Republic of Yugoslavia. During World War II, Tito and his multiethnic Partisans had fought Yugoslavia's Axis occupiers more effectively than the royalist and Serb-dominated Chetniks. As a result, Tito had gained the military support, if not the political confidence, of the members of the Grand Alliance. Tito forced the exiled Yugoslav king to abdicate and reunited the country under the leadership of the Yugoslav Communist Party. Both Great Britain and the Soviet Union immediately established diplomatic relations with the new Yugoslavia; the former because it hoped to broaden the political base of Tito's regime and the latter because it sought to reduce it to a satellite.

The United States, the third major member of the Grand Alliance, had more reservations about Tito and his government than its wartime partners did. Formal diplomatic relations, once established, did little to lessen U.S. concerns about the repressive nature of Tito's regime or his role within the emerging Soviet system. Tito and his supporters, preoccupied with solidifying their revolution at home and extending their influence into the Balkans, were no more kindly disposed toward the United States. Although one of the U.S. diplomats stationed in Belgrade attempted to improve U.S.-Yugoslav relations in 1947, he had little success. The animosity between Yugoslavia and the United States continued unabated until Yugoslavia's break with Moscow.

Although the United States had been the first country to recognize the new Kingdom of the Serbs, Croats, and Slovenes in 1919, that country remained on the periphery of U.S. interests. During the 1920s and 1930s, the United States provided most of Yugoslavia's foreign capital but, because of various U.S. trade and loan restrictions, Germany and Italy and then Germany alone were Yugoslavia's largest trading partners. When war broke out in Europe in 1939, Yugoslavia attempted to buy arms from the United States, but because Yugoslavia had defaulted on its World War I debt, the United States government could not extend the necessary credit.[1]

Franklin D. Roosevelt became more actively involved in Yugoslavia only because of his resolve to help Great Britain keep the Balkans free of Axis control. In January 1941, FDR began his ultimately fruitless attempts to convince the Yugoslav regent, Prince Paul, to resist Adolf Hitler's demands that he sign the Tripartite Pact and allow German troops transit rights through his country.[2] Prince Paul signed the pact in late March, but was immediately overthrown by members of the Yugoslav armed forces, who proclaimed the underage Peter king and declared Yugoslavia's neutrality. Within a few weeks, Germany and Italy had invaded and partitioned Yugoslavia, and the king had fled into exile. The United States refused to acknowledge the partition and announced that it recognized only King Peter and the Royal Yugoslav Government-In-Exile as the legitimate government of Yugoslavia.[3]

When the United States entered the war, the Roosevelt administration committed itself to self-determination for the peoples under Axis control. Yet the existence of two resistance groups within Yugoslavia, the Royalist Chetniks led by Draža Mihailović and the more broadly based but communist-led Partisans of Josip Broz Tito, who opposed the return of the monarchy, complicated the question of who would govern Yugoslavia when the war ended. The United States extended Lend Lease to the Royal Yugoslav Government-In-Exile in 1942. By 1943, because of British pressure, reports from his own military on the Partisans' strength, and rumors of Mihailović's collaboration with the Axis, FDR agreed to assist Tito's forces as well; however, the United

1. Linda Killen, *Testing the Periphery: US-Yugoslav Economic Relations in the Interwar Years* (Boulder, Colo.: Eastern European Monographs, Columbia University Press, 1994), 13, 150–51, 173, 182, 209.

2. Arthur Bliss Lane to Cordell Hull, 25 January 1941, *FRUS, 1941*, 2:939.

3. Hull to Constantin Fotic, 28 May 1941, *FRUS, 1941*, 2:980–81.

States continued to recognize King Peter as Yugoslavia's ruler.[4] The Soviets provided even less material assistance to the Partisans. According to Vladimir Dedijer, the USSR usually denied Tito's repeated requests for medicines, ammunition, weapons, and uniform cloth from the USSR on the grounds of "technical differences." The Soviets also admonished Tito to minimize the communist affiliation of the Partisan movement and to reach an accommodation with the Royal Government, all in the name of the "common struggle" against the invaders.[5]

After the Partisans created their own acting government in late 1943 and repudiated the royal government-in-exile, the British brokered a coalition agreement between Tito and Ivan Šubašić, the former governor of Croatia, who represented the interests of the king. The Tito-Šubašić agreement recognized Tito's group (the Anti-Fascist Council for the National Liberation of Yugoslavia or AVNOJ) as the only legitimate political authority within Yugoslavia, but called for the establishment of a united government and for a postwar plebiscite to determine the monarchy's future.[6] FDR, who had previously declared himself "delighted" with Winston Churchill's mediation, and Stalin, who had urged the Partisans to hold talks with the king on the grounds that Tito's control of Yugoslavia "cannot be recognized right away" supported the settlement.[7]

Secretary of State Cordell Hull, less willing than the president to compromise, labeled the Tito-Šubašić agreement "an almost unconditional acceptance of Partisan demands."[8] However, as Cavendish Cannon, chief of the Division of Southern European Affairs and later ambassador to Yugoslavia advised in January 1945, the United States had little power to influence events in Yugoslavia. He added that the USSR "has shown no particular interest in learning what the United States thinks" concerning the situation in Yugoslavia and Great

4. Walter R. Roberts, *Tito, Mihailovic, and the Allies, 1941–1945* (New Brunswick: Rutgers University Press, 1973), 152, 167, 170, 172; R. Harris Smith, *The OSS: The Secret History of America's First Central Intelligence Agency* (Berkeley and Los Angeles: University of California Press, 1972), 140–57.

5. Vladimir Dedijer, *Tito Speaks: His Self Portrait and Struggle with Stalin* (London: Weidenfeld & Nicolson, 1953), 175–78.

6. Roberts, *Tito, Mihailovic, and the Allies*, 231; Barbara Jelavich, *History of the Balkans Twentieth Century* (Cambridge: Cambridge University Press, 1982), 2:270–71.

7. Franklin Delano Roosevelt to Winston Churchill, 18 May 1944, in Warren F. Kimball, ed., *Churchill and Roosevelt: The Complete Correspondence* (Princeton: Princeton University Press, 1984), 3:131–33; Milovan Djilas, *Conversations with Stalin* (New York: Harcourt Brace Jovanovich, 1962), 74.

8. Hull to Selden Chapin for Robert Murphy, 8 July 1944, *FRUS, 1944*, 4:1386–88.

Britain was only trying to maintain its power there vis-à-vis the Soviets.[9]

Yet the Soviets appeared to have the edge. In briefing books prepared for the Yalta Conference in February 1945, the State Department acknowledged that "the general mood of the people of Europe is to the left and strongly in favor of far-reaching economic and social reforms," but that there was "no sentiment for totalitarianism." The interim regimes established in liberated Europe had to "be sufficiently left to satisfy the prevailing mood in Europe and to allay Soviet suspicions" but could not be "preludes to a Communist dictatorship."[10] Although "the Soviet Union will exert predominant influence" over areas like the Balkans, the United States would demand "equal opportunity in trade, investment and access to source of information."[11]

The question of how much of a U.S. presence the Soviets would tolerate was not FDR's to ponder. By the spring of 1945, Roosevelt had died and the war-inspired cooperation of the Grand Alliance was quickly fading. One of the major points of friction between the United States and the USSR centered on the conflict between U.S. insistence on self-determination in Eastern Europe and the Soviets' security needs in the same area. By early April, the Soviets' policies in Eastern Europe had prompted W. Averell Harriman, the U.S. ambassador to the Soviet Union, to counsel FDR that the Soviets should be told "they cannot expect our continued cooperation on terms laid down by them."[12] A few weeks later the ambassador, giving early voice to the geopolitical principles on which Harry S. Truman was to base his containment policy, informed a group of foreign policy experts that the dispute between the United States and the Soviet Union sprang from the latter's desire "for its own security to see Soviet concepts extend to as large an area of the world as possible." The Soviets would look first to Eastern Europe and then to adjacent states; the establishment of Soviet satellites in these areas would threaten both world stability

---

9. Cavendish Cannon, memorandum, 29 January 1945, *FRUS, 1945*, 5:1192–94.

10. Briefing Book Paper, "Liberated Countries," undated, *FRUS, Malta/Yalta*, 102–3.

11. Position Paper, "Reconstruction of Poland and the Balkans: American Interests and Soviet Attitude," January 1945, Franklin D. Roosevelt Papers, Papers as President (PAP), President's Secretary's File (PSF) 6, Franklin D. Roosevelt Library, Hyde Park, New York.

12. W. Averell Harriman to Edward R. Stettinius, 6 April 1945, *FRUS, 1945*, 5:821–24.

and U.S. security. The Soviets would not use force to achieve their gains, but "will take control of everything they can by bluffing."[13]

George F. Kennan, counselor in the U.S. Embassy in Moscow, echoed his superior by picturing Yugoslavia as one of the Soviets' "newly won areas." According to Kennan, Tito, who was installing only communists in office and allowing only communists or their sympathizers to run for the elections called for in the Tito-Šubašić agreement and scheduled for November 1945, employed the kinds of political tactics that would become common in areas under Soviet control. U.S. recognition of these puppet regimes as independent states would only serve to sanction the fiction by which such areas were governed. Rather than cooperate, Kennan suggested that if the United States stood firm against Soviet expansion, the USSR would not be able to control the satellite states for any length of time. Such pressures in the East would cause the Soviet government to provoke unrest in the West; but if the United States resisted this as well "Moscow would have played its last real card" and "would have no further means with which to assail the western world." In his opinion the Soviet Union had based its global policies on the belief that the West would not resist its moves.[14]

Although President Truman would not fully accept Harriman's advice concerning the Soviet Union for some months, his Yugoslav policy closely followed Kennan's reasoning. He was supported in his approach by Richard C. Patterson, a Democratic party fundraiser and businessman who had been appointed ambassador to Yugoslavia by FDR, and who continued to serve under Truman as the U.S. representative to the Tito-Šubašić government. Throughout the spring and early summer of 1945 Patterson's dispatches from Belgrade portrayed Yugoslavia as being "under almost complete Soviet control." Patterson, after meeting with Šubašić, repeated his claim that "no freedom of speech or press" existed in Yugoslavia and that Tito had established a "complete dictatorship."[15]

When he returned to the United States for consultations and met with Truman in August, Patterson told the president that Tito, though

13. Minutes of the Secretary of State's Staff Committee, 20 April and 21 April 1945, *FRUS, 1945*, 5:839–46.

14. George F. Kennan, memorandum, undated, *FRUS, 1945*, 5:853–60; Roberts, *Tito, Mihailovich, and the Allies*, 231; Jelavich, *History of the Balkans*, 271; Rudolf Schoenfeld to Hull, 4 July 1944, *FRUS, 1944*, 4:1384–86.

15. Richard C. Patterson to Stettinius, 9 April 1945, *FRUS, 1945*, 5:1218; Patterson to Stettinius, 6 June 1945, ibid., 1236.

"dynamic, hospitable, a military genius" was a "thorough Communist, and his economic and political philosophy is not ours." Patterson had informed Tito that he would receive "no economic help . . . whatsoever" unless he changed his policies. The president, according to Patterson's account of the meeting, agreed with his stance and instructed him to use "a two-fisted, tough policy with Tito."[16]

Harold Shantz, who served as Patterson's counselor in Belgrade and as chargé d'affaires in his absence, closely monitored the election campaign throughout the summer and fall of 1945. Despite his own hostility to the Tito regime, Shantz perceived no viable opposition. The Croats had adopted a "passive attitude," and the Serbs, though more active, had little power.[17] By September, Shantz urged the administration to issue a statement declaring that conditions in Yugoslavia, which he likened to a "ruthless totalitarian police regime," made it impossible for the scheduled elections to express the free will of the people. As proof, he cited a number of incidents, ranging from Milovan Djilas's statement that the election's only real purpose was to continue the "national liberation struggle" to reports of opposition leaders being beaten on the streets.[18] Once back in Yugoslavia, Patterson sought a postponement of the balloting on the grounds that Šubašić had resigned from the government, thus negating America's commitment to the Tito-Šubašić agreement.[19] As Patterson told the president's secretary Matthew Connelly, he was attempting to follow Truman's "two-fisted policy" with Tito, but he could "only go so far. It is action and not words that count with him."[20]

Much to Patterson's dismay, the State Department instructed him only to express its concern to Tito about the manner in which the elections were being conducted. This led Patterson to lament, in a letter to George E. Allen, also on the White House staff, that "once a week I talk with Tito about his failure to carry out his solemn commitments to us. . . . He understands only one thing: force and action." In a comment similar to that made to Truman, Patterson

16. Patterson, memorandum of meeting with the President at twelve o'clock, August 31, 1945, at the White House, Richard C. Patterson Papers, File: Belgrade Correspondence T, Harry S. Truman Library, Independence, Missouri.

17. Harold Shantz to James F. Byrnes, 19 and 22 August, *FRUS, 1945*, 5:1250–52.

18. Shantz to Byrnes, 27 September 1945, RG 59, no. 505, 860H.00/9-2745 National Archives, Washington, D.C.; Shantz to Byrnes, 7 September 1945, *FRUS, 1945*, 5:1254–55; Shantz to Byrnes, 21 September 1945, ibid., 1258–59.

19. Patterson to Byrnes, 13 October 1945, *FRUS, 1945*, 5:1267–68.

20. Patterson to Matthew J. Connelly, 26 October 1945, Patterson Papers, File: Belgrade Correspondence C.

acknowledged to Allen that he liked Tito but "he has been indoctrinated with communism, and you know what that means."[21]

To no one's surprise, the November elections resulted in a victory for Tito's followers. Samuel Reber, acting chief of the State Department's Division of Southern European Affairs, advised Secretary James F. Byrnes that while the balloting had been held "under conditions that make it difficult for us to admit that they constitute the free choice of the people," no useful purpose would be served by withholding recognition of the soon-to-be-proclaimed republic. The United States did recognize the new Yugoslavia but it also declared officially that recognition did not imply acceptance of the regime's policies and that economic aid would be forthcoming only if conditions within the country improved.[22]

The United States followed similar policies of recognition coupled with disapproval in the other eastern European and Balkan states where communists had come to power with the support of the USSR. Patterson, however, continued to question this approach to Yugoslavia; by recognizing Tito's regime, he claimed, the United States was "undermining American prestige by abandoning the agreements we have made and the issues on which we fought the war." The administration's policy toward Tito "may be only a small part in the greater problem of American relations with Russia" but Patterson counseled that "from the standpoint of the situation in Yugoslavia itself, it is time to act" and withhold recognition.[23] The State Department's decision stood; Patterson presented his credentials and the accompanying caveat to Tito's government in late December.[24]

The issue of how to deal with what Patterson described as "the greater problem of American relations with Russia" and how to maintain a U.S. presence in Eastern Europe preoccupied Washington policymakers in the winter of 1945–46. Kennan advised in the famous "Long Telegram" of February 1946 that the Soviet Union did not base its policy "on any objective analysis of situation beyond Russia's border; that it had indeed little to do with conditions outside of Russia." At the core of that policy instead lay the need to advance the strength and prestige of the Soviet state and correspondingly to

21. Patterson to J. B. Tito, 6 November 1945, *FRUS, 1945*, 5:1281–82; Patterson to George E. Allen, 14 November 1945, Patterson Papers, File: Belgrade Correspondence A.

22. Samuel Reber to Byrnes, 24 November 1945, *FRUS, 1945*, 5:1289–91.

23. Patterson to Byrnes, 29 November 1945, *FRUS, 1945*, 5:1292–94.

24. Patterson to Byrnes, 26 December 1945, *FRUS, 1945*, 5:1302–3; *Department of State Bulletin*, 23 December 1945, 13:1020–21 (hereafter cited as *"DSB"* by date, volume, and page).

weaken the power of the West. Kennan predicted that "all Soviet efforts on unofficial international plane will be negative and destructive in character, designed to tear down sources of strength beyond reach of Soviet control." The instruments the Soviets would use included the "inner central core of Communist Parties in other countries" and "governments or governing groups willing to lend themselves to Soviet purposes in one degree or the other, such as the present Bulgarian and Yugoslav Governments." Such countries would not only give propaganda support to Russia, but the "actual policies of these regimes can be placed extensively at disposal of USSR."[25]

However, as John Lewis Gaddis explains in *The Long Peace*, Kennan also warned that the Soviet empire, like so many in the past, was overextended and vulnerable. Soviet ideology did not suit the histories or circumstances of other countries; the repugnant methods used to keep their puppet regimes in power might generate resistance. By 1947, what Gaddis labeled as "anticipations of fragmentation within the international communist movement" led the Truman administration to begin to develop a strategy "aimed at driving a wedge" between the Soviets and their allies.[26] After his break with the Kremlin, Tito became a vital component of that strategy; but in the first years of the Cold War, U.S. policymakers considered him an instrument of Soviet power and sought ways to force him to alter his government's practices.

In early 1946, Yugoslavia adopted a federal constitution and formed a new government to replace the partisan provisional government in existence since the war. The United States viewed the change to a formal structure as little more than a "sop to public opinion at home and abroad" and labeled the government, despite its recent election victory, as one with "no general representation of the will of the Yugoslav people."[27] Nevertheless, when the mercurial Ambassador Patterson returned to the United States for consultations and an extended leave in March 1946, he characterized the situation in Yugoslavia as "hopeful." Although the communists' control of Yugoslavia had not lessened, Patterson described the regime's efforts to feed and care for its people sympathetically. He viewed Tito as "a great personality, easy to like and extremely friendly to the United States."[28]

25. Kennan to Byrnes, 22 February 1946, *FRUS, 1946*, 6:696–709.
26. Gaddis, *Long Peace*, 150–52.
27. Summary, 8 February 1946, Harry S. Truman Papers, Naval Aide Files/State Department Briefs, File: State Department Briefs, January–May 1946, Truman Library.
28. "Patterson Back, Sees Hope for Yugoslavs," *New York Times*, 19 March 1946, 3.

While on leave Patterson made a series of public speeches, usually under the title "Behind Tito's Iron Curtain," depicting Tito as an "agent of Moscow" and the regime as one that denied its people basic liberties.[29] He also wrote to Charles Murz, editor-in-chief of the *New York Times*, to suggest the paper print an editorial on Yugoslavia that would illustrate "the truth about the Balkan situation in general." He claimed that Western reporters either were denied access to Belgrade or choose to write less than the truth in order to remain in the country. Patterson hoped to remedy that by "briefing, off-the-record, bank boards, legislators and clubs concerning the facts of the Communist regime in Yugoslavia," which he likened to a "reign of terror." He told Murz he had assured Tito that he could expect no assistance from the United States until conditions changed: "I have been as tough as a diplomat can be without the Tito Government asking for my recall." Patterson claimed that he had returned to Yugoslavia only because Truman had insisted that he alone had the requisite knowledge of the "Tito set-up" but he planned to stay only for a "limited time."[30]

Like Patterson, the United States considered Yugoslavia a repressive state, but Washington appeared even more concerned about Tito's role as an agent of Soviet imperialism. War Department intelligence reviews completed in the spring and summer of 1946 placed Yugoslavia, once oriented toward the West, as "fully within the pro-Russian bloc of States." The Soviets' control of Yugoslavia "increases the opportunity for the Soviets to spread Communism to Italy and Greece" and to create a Balkan federation "closely aligned to the U.S.S.R." Yugoslavia also added to the Soviets' overall military potential, since unlike the other satellite states in Eastern Europe, it was a victorious ally and had no limitations on the postwar size of its armed forces.[31] The Yugoslav army, the "largest and most effective army of any Balkan country," was still in the process of modernization, but the "officer corps makes up in fanaticism what it lacks in military skill." Both the army and air force were currently receiving training in the Soviet Union.[32]

29. Copies of these speeches are in Patterson's papers at the Truman Library.

30. Patterson to Charles Murz, 20 May 1946, Patterson Papers, File: Belgrade Correspondence M.

31. Department of State, Bureau of Research and Intelligence, "Situation Report USSR," 6 February 1946, RG 59, R & A no. 1785.62; War Department, Intelligence Review, "Significance of Yugoslavia to the USSR," 7 March 1946, Truman Papers, Naval Aide Files, File: War Department Intelligence Review March 1946.

32. Military Intelligence Division, Intelligence Review 17–20, "Yugoslavia's Armed Forces–Strength and Capabilities," 13 June 1946, Truman Papers, Naval Aide Files, File: War Department Intelligence Review June 1946.

All of Yugoslavia's policies appeared to validate U.S. assessments. Economically, Yugoslavia surpassed other states in Eastern Europe in its adoption of Soviet planning and development models. In 1946, Yugoslavia created a Federal Planning Commission to develop the country's first five-year plan. Tito also initiated a comprehensive nationalization scheme, the first of its kind in Eastern Europe, and achieved impressive results. Seventy percent of Yugoslavia's nonagricultural enterprises had been nationalized or put under some form of state control by the end of the year. By 1947, the country, which had seen 40 percent of its industrial capacity destroyed in the war, had recovered to 1938 production levels. Only Bulgaria, with much less war damage, had a comparable record.[33] Ironically, the Soviets, while supplying credits to assist Yugoslavia's economic development, did not support the intent of Tito's economic schemes. Stalin preferred that Yugoslavia depend on the Soviet Union for industrial goods and concentrate on developing its mineral resources for Soviet use.[34]

Politically, Tito limited the power of his most visible opponents. In September of 1946, the government arrested Archbishop Alojzije Stepinac, the Roman Catholic primate of Yugoslavia, for war crimes. He was accused of having collaborated with the Ustasha and their leader Ante Pavelić. Within weeks, Stepinac had been tried, convicted, and sentenced to sixteen years in prison, prompting members of the United States Congress to insist that diplomatic relations be severed with Yugoslavia in protest. Truman resisted these demands but Acting Secretary of State Dean Acheson expressed the "concern and deep worry" of the administration over Yugoslavia's disregard for its citizens' civil and human rights. The administration also promised to continue to hold Yugoslavia accountable for these and other violations of its commitments as a member of the United Nations.[35]

However, it was the earlier capture and trial of Chetnik leader Draža Mihailović that generated the largest number of protests involving Yugoslavia in 1946, and demonstrated how little leverage the

---

33. John R. Lampe, Russell O. Prickett, and Ljubiša S. Adamović, *Yugoslav-American Economic Relations since World War II* (Durham: Duke University Press, 1990), 20–21.

34. Stephen Clissold, ed., *Yugoslavia and the Soviet Union, 1939–1973: A Documentary Survey* (London: Oxford University Press, 1975), 43.

35. "Yugoslav Primate Seized as Traitor," *New York Times*, 19 September 1946, 1, 2; "Tito Disclaims Aim to Persecute Church," ibid., 27 September 1946, 12; Arthur M. Brandel, "Stepinatz Declared Guilty: He Gets 16 Years in Prison," ibid., 12 October 1946, 1, 7; "U.S. Voices Worry at Yugoslav Trial," ibid.; "U.S. Envoy Doing All He Can For Stepinatz," ibid., 24 October 1946, 14. The undersecretary of state served as acting secretary of state when the secretary of state was out of the country.

United States actually had in Belgrade. During the war, evidence of Mihailović's collaboration with the Axis had been an important factor in the Allied decision to extend assistance to Tito and the Partisans. After the war, Mihailović had become a fugitive in the mountains of Bosnia and Serbia, refusing escape in the hope that the Serbs would rebel against Tito and ask Mihailović to lead them. Tito remained equally determined that Mihailović be apprehended and tried in order to expose his collaboration and discredit the Chetnik movement.[36] On 24 March 1946, the Yugoslav government announced Mihailović's capture and stated that he would be tried for treason.

The United States immediately reminded Yugoslavia that despite the controversies surrounding Mihailović, he and his followers "without adequate supplies and fighting under the greatest hardships contributed . . . materially to the Allied cause." Tito in turn charged that the Chetniks had rescued U.S. airmen only to obtain U.S. supplies, while the Partisans had saved them out of a sense of duty.[37]

The Chetnik leader's plight quickly became a public issue in the United States. A group of prominent Americans led by George Creel and including Ray Brock, Sumner Welles, John Dewey, Norman Thomas, Clare Booth Luce, John Dos Passos, Senators Robert LaFollette and Robert Taft, and Congressmen Jerry Voorhees and Mike Mansfield formed a "Committee for a Fair Trial for Draza Mihailovic."[38] A number of airmen rescued by the Chetniks during World War II organized another group called the "National Committee of American Airmen" to aid Mihailović and petitioned Yugoslavia for permission to testify at his trial. On 1 May 1946 a delegation of these men called on Acheson, who assured them of the United States's interest in Mihailović but did not allow them to see President Truman.[39] Numerous Slavic groups and their congressmen also petitioned the administration to aid Mihailović.[40] In June, Yugoslavia agreed to accept the veterans' testimony and assured the United States that it would be used.[41] Nonetheless, Mihailović was found guilty of treason and executed on 17 July 1946.

Yugoslavia's internal policies, which the United States viewed as coercive, would have earned Tito the opprobrium of the Truman

36. Phyllis Auty, *Tito: A Biography* (New York: McGraw Hill, 1970), 267.

37. *DSB*, 21 April 1946, 14:634, 669–70.

38. Ray Brock to Byrnes, 19 June 1946, RG 59, 860H.00/6-1946.

39. Acheson, memorandum of conversation, 1 May 1946, RG 59, 860H.00/5-1946; Jeanne Perkins, "Fight for Mihailovich: U.S. Airmen Try to Help," *Life*, 10 June 1946, 17, 18, 20, 23, 24.

40. See Box 6427 and Box 6428, R6 59, 860H.00 file.

41. Byrnes to Shantz, 6 June 1946, *FRUS, 1946*, 6:898–99.

administration in almost any context. However, by the time of Mihai-lović's execution, the context had become highly charged as Truman implemented a containment policy designed to resist the growth of Soviet influence. When a series of international crises erupted involv-ing Yugoslavia and the United States, the latter based its policy decisions not only on the merits of the issue at hand, but on its continuing belief that Yugoslavia was an agent of the Kremlin's imperial design. In truth, it was Tito who was the more ambitious. He sought to fix socialism on the Balkans by extending his own borders, supporting the communist revolution in Greece, and establishing control over Albania and a federation with Bulgaria.[42] The Western allies challenged him in the first two areas; the Soviets rendered him little or no support in any of them.

The border dispute between Italy and Yugoslav in the Julian Region was one of the most serious points of early conflict between the emerging blocs of East and West. Claimed by both Italy and Yugosla-via, the area had a mixed population of Italians, Croats, and Slovenes, but had been liberated mostly by the Partisans. Tito had demanded the right to occupy it until its final disposition could be settled, but the United States and Great Britain had insisted that the area be placed under an Allied command. In September 1945, when the Council of Foreign Ministers (CFM) met in London to begin drafting the Italian and Balkan peace treaties, both Italy and Yugoslavia submitted claims to the city of Trieste. The Soviets supported the Yugoslavs, whereas the West seconded Italy's demand that the city remain under Italian control. Secretary of State Byrnes finally suggested that a four-power commission be established to study the ethnic and economic questions involved in the boundary dispute and that the final recommendations concerning the Italo-Yugoslav frontier be based on the commission's findings. The CFM agreed and further suggested that Trieste be declared a free port.[43]

The CFM reconvened in Paris in April 1946 to consider the experts' report, only to find that each of the powers had put forth a different boundary line. The deadlock on both the border and the Italian treaty therefore continued, with the Soviets also demanding that the Italians pay billions of dollars in reparations to the USSR and the Balkan states.[44] The West refused, and the United States, by then fully

---

42. Clissold, *Yugoslavia and the Soviet Union*, 44.

43. Roberto G. Rabel, *Between East and West: Trieste, the United States, and the Cold War* (Durham: Duke University Press, 1988), 2–16, 87.

44. Ibid., 89; George Curry, *James F. Byrnes* (New York: Cooper Square, 1965), 213–19.

committed to a policy of containing Soviet influence, remained steadfast in its support of the Italian position. Charles E. Bohlen, who served as Byrnes's press spokesman at the Paris meeting, later recalled that the United States saw the Italian territorial claim as more valid, since most of the inhabitants of the area were Italian. In addition, the United States believed "the Soviets and the Yugoslavs were as one" and was certain that the Soviets intended to use the dispute to "extend their control into the Mediterranean and westward into Europe."[45]

As the weeks wore on, Soviet foreign minister V. M. Molotov argued Tito's claim, telling Byrnes that his government would be very embarrassed if it could not assist Tito in obtaining his demands. The Americans remained steadfast. Molotov finally proposed, in response to a Western suggestion to internationalize Trieste, that the city be made an autonomous district, governed by international laws drafted by the Big Four but subject to the sovereignty of Yugoslavia. He also hinted that the Soviets might be willing to modify their reparations demands if Trieste were settled. Byrnes agreed to discuss the first part of this offer, but insisted that the area be under the jurisdiction of the United Nations. The ministers finally compromised and created the Free Territory of Trieste (FTT), which included some Italian land, but which would be ruled by a governor appointed by the Security Council of the United Nations.[46] This solution was presented to the Yugoslavs at the Paris Peace Conference in August. Before an agreement could be reached however, an even more serious crisis occurred between the United States and Yugoslav governments.

Since the end of the war, Yugoslav and U.S. authorities had been discussing the question of U.S. aviation rights over Yugoslavia. The Yugoslavs at first requested of the Civil Aeronautics Board that Belgrade be made a stop on the Balkan route to Turkey, but then declined to begin formal negotiations for a bilateral aviation agreement with the United States. By the late summer of 1945, the Yugoslavs had placed more and more obstacles in the way of regular air traffic from Belgrade to Vienna. Yugoslav fighter planes simulated air attacks on transport planes and practiced strafing runs on U.S. ground installations. The Yugoslav government also requested that U.S. and British personnel withdraw from the Zemun airdrome and turn over all their equipment to Yugoslavia. Both countries refused, and the

45. Charles E. Bohlen, *Witness to History, 1929–1969* (New York: W. W. Norton, 1973), 253–54.
46. Rabel, *Between East and West*, 91–92; Curry, *James F. Byrnes*, 228, 230–31.

Yugoslavs announced in effect that continued flights of foreign aircraft into the country were not required and that immediate withdrawal from the installation was necessary.[47] Harassment of U.S. diplomatic flights intensified; the baggage of all Foreign Service personnel was searched, and people leaving and entering aircraft in Yugoslavia were escorted by armed Yugoslav guards. The United States government protested such treatment, but the Yugoslavs claimed it justified by continued U.S. violations of Yugoslav airspace.[48]

Tensions deepened on 9 August 1946, when Yugoslav fighter planes approached a U.S. C-47 air transport on a regular flight from Vienna to Udine and forced it down in a field twelve kilometers from Ljubljana. The Yugoslavs, who claimed that the plane had violated Yugoslav airspace and refused repeated requests to land, detained the passengers and crew and denied them access to U.S. consular officials.[49] The United States, in a strongly worded protest, denied all charges and maintained that the plane, an unarmed passenger flight, had only lost its bearings in bad weather.[50]

On 19 August, while the passengers and crew from the first plane remained in custody, Yugoslav fighter planes attacked a second C-47 bound for Vienna. The plane crashed in an unidentified area with the loss of all aboard.[51] Ambassador Patterson, who had returned to Belgrade on 16 August, reported to the State Department that while the Yugoslavs regretted the second incident and the loss of life it involved, they assigned responsibility for the tragedy to the United States government "since Yugoslav Government has repeatedly drawn attention to unauthorized flights and consequences which might arise."[52] In Paris, Secretary of State Byrnes met immediately with Yugoslav vice-premier Edvard Kardelj to demand an explanation. The Yugoslavs again responded by charging that the planes had violated Yugoslav airspace.[53]

On 21 August, the United States, in protest of the "outrageous acts" committed by the Yugoslavs, delivered an ultimatum to the Yugoslav government that demanded the release of the occupants of the planes

47. U.S. Department of State, *Policy and Information Statement on Yugoslavia*, 30 July 1946, James F. Byrnes Papers, Clemson University, Clemson, South Carolina.
48. Shantz to Byrnes, 9 August 1946, *FRUS, 1946*, 6:913–14.
49. Acheson to Shantz, 13 August 1946, *FRUS, 1946*, 6:920.
50. Acheson to Shantz, 14 August 1946, *FRUS, 1946*, 6:920–21; *DSB*, 1 September 1946, 15:415–16.
51. *DSB*, 1 September 1946, 15:415, 417–18.
52. Patterson to Byrnes, 20 August 1946, *FRUS, 1946*, 6:925.
53. Byrnes to Acheson, 20 August 1946, *FRUS, 1946*, 6:925–26.

within forty-eight hours. If Yugoslavia did not comply, the United States planned to bring the matter before the United Nations Security Council.[54] The next day, when Patterson met with Tito, the latter informed the ambassador that the people on the first plane had been released, and a search for the occupants of the second was under way. Tito granted Patterson's request to allow U.S. representatives to accompany the search teams and to communicate with any survivors found. Tito also gave his assurance that no foreign planes would be fired on in the future, but again charged the United States with "deliberate flaunting of Yugoslav sovereignty."[55] After the bodies of the occupants of the second plane were found, the Yugoslav government, "inspired by human feelings towards the innocent families of the crashed airplane," agreed to pay a total indemnity of $150,000.00 to the next of kin, while continuing to reject any responsibility for the incidents.[56]

After the attacks, the United States temporarily suspended service on the Vienna-Udine route. On 22 August, Byrnes recommended resumption, but urged that the pilots be instructed to "carefully avoid" Yugoslav territory and the flights be escorted by fighter planes. He asked Acheson to obtain consent for this proposal from the Joint Chiefs of Staff (JCS).[57] The JCS considered it preferable that armed bombers rather than transport planes with fighter escorts take over the route on the grounds that "any action by such armed bombers will be clearly defensive." Bombers were also more likely to remain on course. The military predicated their advice on the assumption that Byrnes wished to resume the flights for "reasons other than military necessity" and that the president approved the use of combat aircraft.[58] Admiral William Leahy, who conveyed these suggestions to President Truman on board the USS *Williamsburg,* recommended that Byrnes "be given authority in advance for any action in this matter that he considers necessary."[59] On 23 August, the president approved both the JCS recommendation and Leahy's suggestion.[60] The flights resumed a few days later.

54. *DSB*, 1 September 1946, 15:417–18.
55. Acheson to Byrnes, 24 August 1946, RG 59, no. 4359, 740.00119/8-2446; *DSB*, 1 September 1946, 15:418.
56. Patterson to Byrnes, 20 September 1946, *FRUS, 1946*, 6:955–56; Shantz to Byrnes, 10 October 1946, ibid., 966–67.
57. Byrnes to Acheson, 22 August 1946, *FRUS, 1946*, 6:927.
58. Acheson to Byrnes, 22 August 1946, *FRUS, 1946*, 6:927–28.
59. William Leahy to Truman, 22 August 1946, with enclosures, Robert L. Dennison Papers, File: White House Message Traffic 1946, Truman Library.
60. *FRUS, 1946*, 6:928 n. 34.

At the end of August, Patterson again met with Tito and discussed a wide range of subjects, including the air attacks. In a letter to a friend a few days later Patterson characterized the fatal airplane attack as "first degree murder" and claimed he had said the same to Tito; however, the documents sent to the State Department from the embassy do not contain such an exchange. In these accounts, which serve as a good indication of the sterile verbal sparring so characteristic of the U.S.-Yugoslav relationship, Patterson said only that he informed Tito that he could expect no aid from the United States under existing circumstances, that the recent elections in Yugoslavia had been "fraudulent," and that his government did not enjoy genuine majority support. Tito would never gain the good will of the United States "by shooting down American planes." Tito responded by cataloguing the "bullying attitude" of some of the Great Powers toward smaller states such as Yugoslavia. In the end, Patterson characterized the interview as "intense" but "salutary." In the letter noted above, Patterson claimed that Tito appreciated such "blunt talk" but he also confided that his own family was in Switzerland because the State Department considered it unsafe for them to be in Yugoslavia.[61]

The attacks on U.S. aircraft created a furor in the United States. Most newspaper and editorial opinion concluded that the incidents were not isolated occurrences but part of a pattern of hostility by Tito, geared to force the United States to consent to his demands for Trieste. The great majority of newspapers commenting on the attacks also saw them as being supported by the Soviet Union and believed that U.S.-Yugoslav relations on such issues were part of the larger picture of "American relations with Russia and her satellite bloc in Eastern Europe."[62]

Administration officials, equally in the grip of containment's tunnel vision, also credited the Soviet Union with a major role in the air attacks. In his memoirs, Secretary Byrnes wrote that after the delivery of the U.S. ultimatum, he saw Molotov and Kardelj "in a huddle and suspected what they were discussing."[63] A few months after the episode, Averell Harriman told a meeting of State Department bureau

61. Patterson to George Howard, 6 September 1946, Patterson Papers, File: Belgrade Correspondence H; Patterson to Byrnes, 31 August 1946, *FRUS, 1946*, 6:942–43; Patterson to Byrnes, 31 August 1946, ibid., 943–45.

62. American Opinion Report, 4 September 1946 and 31 August 1946, Bureau of Public Affairs, U.S. Department of State, Washington, D.C. (hereafter cited as "AOR" by date).

63. James F. Byrnes, *All in One Lifetime* (New York: Harper & Brothers, 1958), 364–65.

chiefs that each time the Soviets made a move "such as they undoubtedly did in letting the Yugoslavs shoot down our pilots, our reaction should be immediate, sharp and firm."[64] Patterson, in an October letter to his friend Pierre Cartier, founder of the famed New York jewelry store, claimed that in Yugoslavia "all roads lead to Moscow." He speculated that Yugoslavia's hostility toward the United States "was calculated in advance to test the reaction of the American government and the American public. No one believes the downing of the American planes was spontaneous truculence."[65] Dean Acheson thought that the air attacks were linked to the Trieste issue and may have been Tito's way of testing the reaction of the West to a planned aggression in the Julian Region. Acheson theorized that Tito complied with the U.S. ultimatum because he realized that the United States would stand firm and because the Soviets urged him to compromise.[66]

The Yugoslav view was rather different; in his writings Vladimir Dedijer, long a member of Tito's inner circle, treated the incident as one example of the pressures exerted on his country by the West. In the summer of 1946 the situation in Trieste "was extremely tense"; the sacrifices the Yugoslavs had made in the war were not being recognized at the Paris Peace Conference and in fact "those efforts were belittled." U.S. planes continually flew over Yugoslav territory, despite the presentation by the Yugoslavs of over a dozen diplomatic notes to the U.S. government protesting these violations. Eventually "one plane was compelled to land and regretfully another was shot down." Dedijer, though, did not link the attacks directly to the wrangle over Trieste, nor did he mention any complicity by the Soviet Union. Milovan Djilas has alluded to a stronger, but after-the-fact connection, claiming that Molotov "almost embraced" Kardelj in Paris when he heard of the attacks, but warned the Yugoslavs not to continue them.[67]

The assessments of Acheson and the memoirs of Dedijer and Djilas all provide bits of the truth. The Yugoslav government objected to the presence of U.S. planes in and above Yugoslavia, but the timing of the attacks suggested that they represented more than a vivid protest against violations of Yugoslav airspace. The Yugoslavs probably aimed their show of force at the Soviet Union as well as at the West, to

64. Walter Millis, ed., *The Forrestal Diaries* (New York: Viking Press, 1951), 212.

65. Patterson to Pierre Cartier, 4 October 1946, Patterson Papers, File: Belgrade Correspondence C.

66. Dean Acheson, *Present at the Creation: My Years in the State Department* (New York: W. W. Norton, 1969), 194–96.

67. Vladimir Dedijer, *Tito* (New York: Simon & Schuster, 1953), 250–52; Djilas, *Conversations with Stalin*, 119.

indicate that the Yugoslavs would act unilaterally to secure their territorial demands if the Soviets did not adequately support them. In his published account of the Paris Conference, Kardelj detailed his anger over Molotov's compromises on Trieste. Although he also acknowledged the Soviets' justifiable concern with a whole range of issues at Paris, it is clear that he believed Molotov too eager to bargain away Yugoslavia's interests. But Kardelj also maintained that he knew nothing about the air attacks until Byrnes told him of them and restated his conviction that the attacks had occurred by accident or because of U.S. violations of Yugoslav airspace.[68]

In any case, the attacks were an unsuccessful gamble. All Tito achieved was a deepening of the hostility felt by the U.S. government and people for his regime.[69] This animus, which would complicate later U.S. attempts to assist Tito in his defiance of Stalin's control, also affected the U.S.-dominated aid program from which Yugoslavia benefited in the years after World War II. At the time of the air attacks, Yugoslavia was receiving United Nations Relief and Rehabilitation Administration (UNRRA) aid. In the words of *Newsweek*, the aircraft shot down in Yugoslavia had been fired upon by the very nation which "American food, supplied through UNRRA, saved from starvation last winter."[70] As a result of the air attacks, the question of U.S. participation in the UNRRA program in Yugoslavia quickly become a topic of national debate.

UNRRA distributed food and other supplies to war-ravaged nations under the auspices and financing of the United Nations. The United States was the largest single contributor to the UNRRA fund, but from its inception critics of the program had charged that the recipient regimes, which were mostly in eastern and central Europe and leftist in nature, used UNRRA supplies to solidify their political power rather than to alleviate their peoples' suffering.[71]

During the years it operated in Yugoslavia, UNRRA fed millions of people, served as the only source for civilian clothing and medical supplies, and provided livestock and farm implements to assist the country in its own food production. By the time the program ended in the summer of 1947, UNRRA had spent $415.6 million in Yugoslavia,

68. Edvard Kardelj, *Reminiscences, the Struggle for Recognition and Independence: The New Yugoslavia, 1944–1957* (London: Blond & Briggs in Association with Summerfield Press, 1982), 80–82.

69. AOR, 4 September 1946.

70. Editorial, "Yugoslavia: Biting the Hand," *Newsweek*, 26 August 1946, 36.

71. John C. Campbell, ed., *The United States in World Affairs, 1945–1947* (New York: Harper & Brothers, 1947), 331–33.

which represented one-fifth of its total budget and the largest amount distributed to any single European country.[72] Much suffering occurred even with UNRRA assistance, but as Dedijer later wrote: "There is no doubt that the aid UNRRA extended to Yugoslavia during those days played an enormous role in alleviating hardship. It was sent urgently, when it was most required."[73]

Yet critics in the United States, as well as in the U.S. Embassy in Belgrade, claimed that the Yugoslav regime distributed goods not to the civilian population but to the army and the secret police and administered the program to augment Tito's control over the country. The Yugoslav government added to the controversy by handling the distribution of all UNRRA material and usually refusing to allow UNRRA officials to inspect the factories that were to be restored to peacetime production with UNRRA equipment.[74]

Truman had limited power to deal with these complaints. UNRRA was an international program, administered by a United Nations committee of which the United States was only one member. Even though an American chaired the UNRRA committee, the United States could not unilaterally determine the disposition of UNRRA material. To delete communist nations from the list of recipients would leave the United States vulnerable to charges of linking humanitarian commitments with political concerns.

Nonetheless, the attacks on U.S. aircraft in August 1946 increased the volume of criticism leveled against the UNRRA program in Yugoslavia, with Secretary of State Byrnes joining the fray. A week after the second attack, even though the Yugoslav government had met the demands of the U.S. ultimatum, Byrnes instructed the State Department that in light of "recent developments" he wanted to "do everything we properly can to stop further shipments of supplies of any sort by UNRRA for Yugoslavia."[75] Acting Secretary of State Dean Acheson and Assistant Secretary of State for Economic Affairs William Clayton advised against this. They acknowledged there had been much public discussion of the UNRRA program, but they reminded Byrnes that the program worked "on the basis of need without political consideration" and that a request for cessation of aid would

72. Stevan K. Pavlowitch, *Yugoslavia* (New York: Praeger Publishers, 1971), 188; Lampe, Prickett, and Adamović, *Economic Relations*, 21.

73. Dedijer, *Tito Speaks*, 251.

74. George Woodbridge, ed., *UNRRA: The History of the United Nations Relief and Rehabilitation Administration* 3 vols. (New York: Columbia University Press, 1950), 1: 167; Shantz to Byrnes, 9 March 1946, RG 59, no. 287, 863.24/3-946.

75. Byrnes to Acheson, 28 August 1946, *FRUS, 1946*, 6:930.

seem to demand that UNRRA take punitive action against Yugoslavia. They counseled that if any action were deemed necessary, "it would be preferable for the United States to impose economic sanctions on Yugoslavia" but they advised Byrnes not to do so.[76] When Clayton informed Byrnes in early September that Secretary of the Navy James Forrestal and Secretary of War Robert P. Patterson had protested UNRRA's continuation of shipments to Yugoslavia,[77] Byrnes replied that he agreed with their views. He told Clayton that if anyone in the State Department could "think of some other reason which would make it possible for us to stop shipments without having our good faith questioned, I will be happy to consider it."[78]

Some Americans refused to wait. In September, New York longshoremen declined to load a UNRRA ship with goods bound for Yugoslavia. A spokesman for the men said that they would "rather see the cargo going to Greece or any other country that gave us some help in the war." The American Federation of Labor and the International Longshoremen's Association sympathized with the work stoppage, as did numerous veterans groups, who issued statements to the effect that supplies should not be sent to a country which "shot down Americans."[79]

In the end, as Acheson and Clayton had predicted, no method of terminating aid proved acceptable. In a final press statement issued in mid-September, the United States announced that it could not retaliate for the attacks by withholding UNRRA aid. The UNRRA governing council had authorized the shipment of goods to Yugoslavia, and the United States could not cease to contribute to these shipments without abandoning its commitment to international agreements.[80] An investigatory body created by UNRRA director Fiorella LaGuardia to probe reports of irregularities in Yugoslavia issued a report a few weeks later which declared that "UNRRA principles were scrupulously observed by the Yugoslav government."[81]

The United States had received enough information of its own to question LaGuardia's statement. Acheson found the report to be "a substantial whitewash of the Yugoslavian Government and its cooperation with UNRRA," but also noted that this problem was "more than

76. Acheson to Byrnes, 29 August 1946, *FRUS, 1946*, 6:931–33.
77. William L. Clayton to Byrnes, 4 September 1946, *FRUS, 1946*, 6:946–47.
78. Byrnes to Clayton, 11 September 1946, *FRUS, 1946*, 6:950–51.
79. "Workmen Refuse to Load UNRRA Ship," *New York Times*, 6 September 1946, 1, 2.
80. Clayton to Byrnes, 13 September 1946, RG 59, no. 4817, 740.00119/9-1346.
81. Woodbridge, *UNRRA*, 1:165.

a question between the United States and Yugoslavia." If the United States acted unilaterally to cease shipments it would precipitate an "issue between East and West."[82] For the first time in the postwar period, but certainly not the last, the question of whether Yugoslavia deserved Western economic assistance had become entangled in Cold War politics.

Once the crisis occasioned by the aircraft incident had subsided, the CFM resumed its discussion of Trieste. The ministers agreed to the compromise reached in August, only to have the Yugoslavs reject the boundary settlement and refuse to withdraw their troops from the area now designated as the Free Territory of Trieste. The ministers in turn informed Yugoslavia that it would receive no benefits from the peace treaties, such as reparations from Italy, if it did not agree to the compromise accord.[83] The impasse continued until the foreign ministers reconvened in November. The United States, Britain, and France then repeated their resolve to deny Yugoslavia reparations, and this time Molotov joined them. Yugoslavia's minister for foreign affairs Stanoje Simić attempted to compromise by suggesting that if the boundary lines were modified his country would reduce its reparations demands, but Byrnes refused to discuss any such changes. Molotov appealed privately to Byrnes on the grounds that the Soviets "had a very difficult problem with Yugoslavia," but he agreed to consent to the Paris accords, with slight modifications. These modifications represented only a few changes in the language of the accord, changes Byrnes construed as face-saving for the Soviet Union. The secretary assumed that Molotov agreed because he realized that nothing more could be gained by delay.[84] The Trieste compromise became part of the Italian peace treaty, signed in February 1947.

The Yugoslavs remained dissatisfied, and in September of 1947, as the treaty came into force, threatened to move their troops beyond their assigned zone. The United States, in the midst of reorganizing its national security and defense structure, pledged action against Yugoslavia if it did not withdraw.[85] The president, aboard the USS *Missouri*, also discussed accelerating the swearing in of James Forrestal to the newly created post of secretary of defense.[86] Neither the

82. Record of the Meeting of the Secretaries of State, War, and Navy, 16 October 1946, *FRUS, 1946*, 6:967–68.

83. Curry, *James F. Byrnes*, 278.

84. Byrnes, *All in One Lifetime*, 382–83; Curry, *James F. Byrnes*, 286–87.

85. Clark M. Clifford to Truman, 15 September 1947, Dennison Papers, File: White House Message Traffic 1947.

86. Truman to Clifford, 16 September 1947, Dennison Papers, File: White House Message Traffic 1947.

State Department nor Forrestal agreed with this suggestion, confident that the Yugoslavs, who "were probing for a soft spot" would take no aggressive action,[87] which proved to be the case.

Yugoslavia's support for the communist faction in the Greek civil war also increased tensions between Yugoslavia and the West. By the spring of 1946, Greece rivaled Eastern Europe as a symbol of the antagonism between the former members of the Grand Alliance. In late February, the British had informed the United States of their inability to continue assisting the Greek government against the rebels. Truman, fearing the increase of Soviet influence throughout the Mediterranean, not only assumed the British burden but promised, in a speech to Congress in mid-March, to resist any Soviet attempt at subversion or aggression wherever it occurred.[88]

Although assisted by Bulgaria and Albania, Yugoslavia provided most of the material and expertise used by the Greek guerrillas.[89] After complaints from the Greek government, the United Nations Balkan Commission concluded in May 1947 by an eight to two vote that Yugoslavia, Albania, and Bulgaria were guilty of supporting the rebellion. In the UN debates that followed, the United States attempted to have the General Assembly pass a resolution citing the three nations for conduct that threatened the peace of the world. Secretary of State George C. Marshall, in his instructions to the U.S. Delegation to the UN, directed that principal criticism should be directed against Yugoslavia, who along with Albania and Bulgaria had carried on these activities "under the direction of the USSR." The United States further asserted that Yugoslavia, as a member of the United Nations, had violated its charter commitments.[90]

The final resolution passed by the UN declared only that Bulgaria, Albania, and Yugoslavia had given assistance to the rebels and must immediately cease to do so; the UN also created a special commission to observe the three nations' compliance with this directive.[91] Yugoslavia objected to these actions and to the role of the United States in the affair, while attempting to rally support for its own defense. In September 1947, Yugoslav ambassador Sava Kosanović asked former

87. Clifford to Truman, 16 September 1947, Dennison Papers, File: White House Message Traffic 1947.

88. Ralph B. Levering, *The Cold War: A Post–Cold War History* (Arlington Heights, Ill.: Harlan Davidson), 34.

89. Clissold, *Yugoslavia and the Soviet Union*, 47–48.

90. George C. Marshall to Warren R. Austin, 26 June 1947, *FRUS, 1947*, 5:866–68; Marshall to Herschel Johnson, 30 July 1947, ibid., 875–77.

91. Campbell, *United States in World Affairs, 1947–1948*, 399.

secretary of state Byrnes to join a group of prominent Americans invited by the Yugoslav government to inspect conditions along the Greek frontier. Byrnes, although encouraged by Tito's willingness to allow such an investigation, refused on the grounds that the matter was then before the United Nations.[92]

In all of these incidents, the United States had employed the most negative instruments of its containment strategy; nothing had been done to entice the Yugoslavs away from the Soviet orbit or to drive a wedge between the two communist states. Although at least one U.S. diplomat attempted to implement such a strategy in 1947, the government as a whole had not yet committed itself to this policy. The United States sought only "to loosen the brutal, oppressive authoritarian grip of the Tito regime on all aspects of Yugoslav life."[93] The Yugoslav regime, committed as it was to Marxist orthodoxy and its own independence, did not react well to this approach and U.S.-Yugoslav relations remained strained.

In the years immediately following World War II, the U.S. Embassy, its staff, and anyone in contact with its representatives found daily life in Yugoslavia difficult. In early June 1946, Counselor Shantz complained to Secretary Byrnes that "harassment of our Embassy through official malice, stupidity or both continues daily." One example he cited concerned a Serb engineer who had built a cemetery for U.S. war dead, only to be arrested by Yugoslav police at the cemetery's dedication ceremony.[94] In a statement indirectly critical of Washington's policy, Shantz stated that the U.S. and British embassies had served their purpose, "namely, to show that they condone country's subjugation to status of slave province," and that the government was now determined to render both embassies ineffective.[95]

The situation grew worse after the aircraft attacks. On 17 September 1946 Ambassador Kosanović, in a meeting with Walworth Barbour of the State Department's Southeast European Division and Acting Secretary Clayton, claimed that U.S. planes had been smuggling arms into Yugoslavia to those opposed to the regime. He also stated that Yugoslav authorities had uncovered a "spy ring," which he claimed had been headed by Eric Pridonoff, a former member of the embassy staff and constant critic of the Tito regime. The ring supposedly

92. Sava Kosanović to Byrnes, 27 September 1947, Byrnes Papers; Byrnes to Kosanović, 28 September 1947, Byrnes Papers.
93. U.S. Department of State, *Policy and Information Statement on Yugoslavia*, 30 July 1946, Byrnes Papers.
94. Shantz to Byrnes, 1 June 1946, *FRUS, 1946*, 6:894–95.
95. Shantz to Byrnes, 6 June 1946, *FRUS, 1946*, 6:897–98.

still included a Yugoslav employee of the embassy named Miliutin Stefanovich. Several other Yugoslavs had already been arrested and soon all would be tried for espionage.[96]

Ambassador Patterson characterized these charges to Byrnes as a "dangerous mixture of fact and fiction." The embassy had to maintain contacts with various Yugoslavs to obtain statistics and other needed information, but the Tito regime considered the release of such information by Yugoslav citizens a criminal offense. Patterson insisted that no grounds existed for implicating embassy personnel in plots against the government; "confidential sources" had told him that the Yugoslav government was "out to get the Embassy." An official of the Yugoslav secret police had also said that it was of no importance whether the men charged were guilty of espionage "as long as we have caught one of them to make an affair of it—we must do things to 'quiet' some of the reactionary Embassies."[97]

The Yugoslav government tried the eight men for espionage from 31 December 1946 to 4 January 1947. The prosecution repeatedly named Harold Shantz, counselor at the embassy from 1945 to 1946; Eric Pridonoff, economic analyst at the embassy in 1945; and Lt. John D. Kosunich, assistant naval attaché in 1945, as the Americans to whom the accused Yugoslavs passed their information. Pridonoff had allegedly formed the ring in 1945, with Shantz assuming control after Pridonoff left the country.[98] The court found all of the defendants guilty of carrying on political warfare by giving state and military secrets to "foreign i.e. American spies." The court sentenced Miliutin Stefanovich, the translator considered most active in the ring; Zelko Sushin, a former Partisan officer; and Branko Jovanovich, a journalist, to death. The remaining five defendants received long prison terms. Embassy counselor Thomas Hickok, who had earlier advised that some inexperienced embassy personnel might have "gone beyond their competency" but had not intended to overthrow the regime, reported that the trial evidence "showed that Pridonoff was active in seeking secret information through Stefanovich group and paid 3,000 dinars ($60) to Sushin for what he received." Hickok admitted that "in this sense Pridonoff was shown to have acted in manner of spy" but that nothing similar had been proven against other embassy personnel.[99]

96. American Delegation at the Paris Peace Conference to the Acting Secretary of State (for Dunn), 5 September 1946, *FRUS, 1946*, 6:948; Walworth Barbour, memorandum of conversation, 17 September 1946, ibid., 951–53.

97. Patterson to Byrnes, 18 September 1946, *FRUS, 1946*, 6:954–55.

98. "Yugoslavs Accuse Two Ex-U.S. Aides," *New York Times*, 1 January 1947, 28.

99. Thomas A. Hickok to Byrnes, 16 November 1946, *FRUS, 1946*, 6:975–76; Hickok to Byrnes, 7 January 1947, *FRUS, 1947*, 4:744–46.

The United States government later offered, as "a gesture of good faith," to grant Yugoslavia's request that those named in the trial be withdrawn from the embassy staff. The Yugoslavs accepted.[100] However, the Yugoslav government refused to commute the death sentences of the condemned and executed them on 14 January 1947.

The espionage charges had more truth to them than Patterson acknowledged, since the United States gathered intelligence on the Yugoslav regime as it did on other regimes. The principal sources of information listed by the State Department for Yugoslavia consisted of the embassy in Belgrade; Special Service representatives throughout the Balkans and Europe; British intelligence reports; and Yugoslav newspapers and radio broadcasts. In mid-1946, topics of special interest to the United States included Yugoslavia's economic relations with the Soviet Union; the "potentialities" of those opposed to Tito's regime; and the future political plans of the government.[101] Pridonoff also admitted obtaining information from the Yugoslavs who were put on trial. John Cabot, a career Foreign Service officer who served as the chargé d'affaires in Belgrade in 1947, was convinced that some on the embassy payroll had engaged in small-scale espionage. In his memoirs, Cabot wrote of a "rather aggressive air attaché" who carried out "some ambitious intelligence activities with the help of two Yugoslavs," one of whom was a member of Tito's secret police. Cabot insisted, however, that the Yugoslavs had a much larger and more active spy network; the United States, he wrote in his diary, "was much more spied upon than spying."[102]

The Yugoslav motive in escalating such a small-scale U.S. operation into a sensational public trial is easily discerned. The Yugoslav government clearly took advantage of actions like Pridonoff's to harass the U.S. Embassy and its staff. The immediate postwar period was a time of intense socialist development in Yugoslavia and of profound commitment to Marxist orthodoxy; harsh repressive measures against dissident elements within the country were not uncommon.[103] The

100. American Embassy in Yugoslavia to Yugoslav Ministry of Foreign Affairs, 10 January 1947, *FRUS, 1947*, 4:748; Hickok to Byrnes, 5 January 1947, ibid., 749–50.

101. U.S. Department of State, *Policy and Information Statement on Yugoslavia*, 30 July 1946, Byrnes Papers.

102. Interview with John M. Cabot, Washington, D.C., March 1974; John Moors Cabot, *First Line of Defense: Forty Years' Experiences of a Career Diplomat* (Washington, D.C.: School of Foreign Service, Georgetown University, n.d.), 30; Cabot Diary (at that time in Cabot's possession), 18 July 1947.

103. George Zaninovich, *The Development of Socialist Yugoslavia* (Baltimore: Johns Hopkins University Press, 1968), 39–46.

attacks on the U.S. Embassy were part of this campaign. The Tito regime arrested and tried Yugoslavs connected with the U.S. Embassy through 1947, until there were no Yugoslav nationals employed by the Americans. What better way to demonstrate one's Stalinist credentials than by impeding the diplomatic activities of the United States, the very symbol of both capitalism and anticommunism. The alleged subversive activities of the embassy could also be used by Tito to justify government repression within Yugoslavia. Although in the end Cabot concluded, "Nothing really makes sense—but then, nothing ever does here,"[104] there was no doubt a Yugoslav method behind the seeming madness.

That the Yugoslav government did not really view the U.S. presence as an overwhelming threat may be seen in an exchange that took place between Undersecretary Acheson and Yugoslav ambassador Kosanović in February 1947. At this meeting, Acheson protested the treatment of an American named Ivan Pintar, who resided in Yugoslavia as a private citizen but who had been arrested, tried for espionage, and sentenced to death. Acheson requested that the sentence be reduced, and also expressed concern over the continued arrests of translators and other Yugoslavs employed by the embassy and requested that such activities cease. Although the Yugoslavs did eventually commute Pintar's sentence, in this meeting Kosanović merely repeated the espionage charges while also requesting that the U.S. government not carry through its proposed plan to forbid Americans to travel in Yugoslavia because of the incidents.[105] Tito's regime obviously needed foreign currency and trade more than it feared American spies.

The final stage of the espionage crisis ran its course without the presence of the U.S. ambassador. Patterson had returned to Yugoslavia at Truman's insistence; the aircraft attacks and spy trials only increased his wish to leave his post. On 7 September 1946, Patterson wrote to the White House to ask about his transfer, because "I am of no use in this distant land."[106] He was less despondent but just as eager to leave in a letter he wrote to a fellow businessman a few days later: "I am most receptive to a transfer. The past three weeks with the Tito regime have been a nightmare, but the job is intriguing just the same. Marshall Tito plays a hard game of chess and he is not easy

104. Cabot Diary, 18 July 1947.

105. Barbour, memorandum of conversation, 13 February 1947, *FRUS, 1947*, 4:757–61.

106. Patterson to Edwin Pauley, 7 September 1946, Patterson Papers, File: Belgrade Correspondence P.

to out-maneuver."[107] By the end of the month, Patterson confided to a friend that the administration may want him to stay on, but that he "cannot financially afford to remain."[108]

Patterson also corresponded with Eric Pridonoff, who had figured so prominently in the espionage cases and who was then writing for the Hearst papers.[109] In his letter, Patterson joked about the attacks leveled against him in the Communist press and expressed the hope of seeing Pridonoff while in the United States. Things had not improved in Yugoslavia and he was "still sitting on a keg of dynamite." In response to Pridonoff's inquiry about a book he planned to write on Yugoslavia, Patterson stated that "any book written on Yugoslavia and giving the truth will be helpful," since the American public had not been "enlightened on the true conditions in this Communist country."[110]

When Patterson wrote this letter, his tour of duty in Yugoslavia had almost run its course. In October 1946, the United States charged Yugoslavia with using American citizens, both naturalized and native born, as slave laborers and released several months of correspondence on the issue with Tito's government.[111] Yugoslavia denied the charges, calling them part of a "hostile campaign against Yugoslavia." The individuals concerned, according to the Yugoslavs, had collaborated with the Axis during the war but were being treated fairly. Patterson, in diplomatic correspondence and in the press, countered that "slave labor has existed in Yugoslavia and does exist today in its vilest form."[112] A short time later, Patterson returned to the United States on home leave.

President Truman reluctantly accepted Patterson's resignation as ambassador to Yugoslavia in late March 1947. In a subsequent editorial, the *New York Times* praised Patterson's tenure and expressed the hope that he would "speak plainly to the country about his experiences

107. Patterson to Cyrus S. Ching, 9 September 1946, Patterson Papers, File: Belgrade Correspondence C.

108. Patterson to Floyd Odlum, 25 September 1946, Patterson Papers, File: Belgrade Correspondence O.

109. Eric Pridonoff to Patterson, 6 October 1946, Patterson Papers, File: Belgrade Correspondence P.

110. Patterson to Pridonoff, 21 October 1946, Patterson Papers, File: Belgrade Correspondence P.

111. *FRUS, 1946*, 6:969, editorial note; Hickok to Byrnes, 30 October 1946, ibid., 971–74; "U.S. Charges Enslavement of Americans by Yugoslavia," *New York Times*, 19 October 1946, 1, 7; "U.S. Note to Tito Charging Slave Labor," ibid.

112. "Yugoslavs Dispute U.S. 'Slave' Charge," *New York Times*, 21 October 1946, 14.

in Yugoslavia" now that he was free of diplomatic constraints.[113] Patterson's diplomatic colleagues, both American and Yugoslav, had less complimentary but far more accurate assessments of his tenure. John Cabot, who spent much of 1947 attempting to repair U.S.-Yugoslav relations, believed that Patterson "had made a god-awful mess of things in Belgrade."[114] Balkan expert John C. Campbell also rated Patterson's performance as "very poor."[115] Leo Mates, who at the time was an official in the Yugoslav Foreign Ministry and later served as his country's ambassador to the United States, characterized Patterson as "very bad for both countries."[116]

If Patterson's account of his August 1945 meeting with Truman is accurate, he had carried out the president's suggestion to "use a two-fisted, tough policy with Tito" to the letter.[117] But he had punched for the sake of punching, with nothing tangible to show for his efforts. The Tito regime had not altered its policies in response to American criticism, and the ability of the United States to influence Tito had been reduced through the purges of the embassy staff.

Attempts to use economic aid to force changes in Tito's policies also had few positive results, because Yugoslavia refused to make any concessions in return for aid. As Ambassador Simić told Clayton, any linkage of economic and political questions constituted the use of pressure and this "would be difficult to tolerate. . . . Yugoslavia could get along without a loan. It could wait."[118] By July 1946 the Department of State considered it "doubtful" that in return for credits the Yugoslav government would "give and abide by any assurances representing a major departure from its present objectives and methods." Tito probably would subject his people to deprivation rather than tie himself in such a way to the West.[119] Yugoslavia also had other choices. Although much of the country's industrial capacity had been destroyed in the war, many of the plants that remained had been operated by the Germans or by collaborators. The government used

113. Harold B. Hinton, "Patterson Is Out as Belgrade Envoy," *New York Times*, 27 March 1947, 20; "Patterson to Stay as a Consultant," ibid., 28 March 1947, 7; editorial, "Two American Ambassadors," ibid., 27 March 1947, 26.

114. John M. Cabot, Oral History, Truman Library, 50.

115. John C. Campbell, Oral History, Truman Library, 129.

116. Interview with Leo Mates, Belgrade, Yugoslavia, September 1988.

117. Patterson, memorandum of meeting with the President, 31 August 1945, Patterson Papers, File: Belgrade Correspondence T.

118. Kingsley W. Hamilton, memorandum of conversation, 22 February 1946, *FRUS, 1946*, 6:869–70.

119. U.S. Department of State, *Policy and Information Statement on Yugoslavia*, 30 July 1946, Byrnes Papers.

this as justification for their nationalization and then ran them for the benefit of the nation's total recovery. Reparations taken from Germany, Italy, and Romania facilitated the reconstruction of the rest of Yugoslavia's industry, as did the aid provided by UNRRA.[120]

In the interval between Patterson's departure and the new ambassador's arrival, John M. Cabot, who served as the chargé d'affaires in Belgrade, attempted to improve U.S.-Yugoslav relations. Cabot even used the contentious issue of war criminals and quislings as his vehicle. The question of these peoples' repatriation not only pitted a communist state against its noncommunist former allies, but highlighted the emotional divide separating a country like Yugoslavia, which had fought a civil war on its soil as well as a war against the Axis, from countries such as Britain and the United States, with less divisive war experiences. The Yugoslavs made no distinction, as the British and U.S. governments did, between people "innocent of willful collaboration with enemy," such as Chetniks, and members of the Ustasha. The Yugoslavs simply demanded that all "collaborators" residing in Allied prisoner-of-war camps, most of whom were in Italy, be returned to Yugoslavia. The British and Americans believed political retribution rather than justice motivated the Yugoslav request and agreed "that it would be undesirable to hand over Yugoslav deserters who may be political refugees to Yugoslav authorities." Only proven members of the Ustasha would be surrendered.[121] After Italy and Yugoslavia resumed diplomatic relations in March 1947, the Allied military authorities thought themselves bound only to return those persons already identified and known to be in military custody.[122]

Throughout the spring and summer of 1947 the Yugoslav government claimed that even this policy was not being followed and that those already identified as quislings were not being returned to Yugoslavia. The U.S. ambassador in Italy, James Dunn, disputed this, charging that the demands and complaints of the Yugoslav government gave credence to the Allied suspicion that the real aim of the government was to capture all those opposed to the present regime.[123] Cabot disagreed with Dunn's assessment and supported the Yugoslav

120. David McClellan, *Dean Acheson: The State Department Years* (New York: Dodd, Mead, 1976), 125–28; Lampe, Prickett, and Adamović, *Economic Relations*, 17.

121. Combined Chiefs of Staff to State Department and British Embassy, dispatch, 7 August 1946, RG 59, no. 194, 740.00116EW/8-746; Acheson to Cabot, 11 March 1947, *FRUS, 1947*, 4:779–80.

122. Combined Chiefs of Staff to the Department of State and the British Embassy, memorandum, 29 May 1947, *FRUS, 1947*, 4:803–4.

123. Cabot to Marshall, 8 April 1947, *FRUS, 1947*, 4:784–85.

complaint that U.S. authorities had "not shown due intelligence in seeking out and handing over persons in Italy who are in fact guilty of serious war crimes."[124] He urged the State Department not to ignore "the deplorable picture which our record in this matter represents" and to take steps to correct "a shocking situation rather than to cover over its existence."[125] No genuine change occurred. In May, Cabot reported that three men the British and U.S. authorities had agreed to surrender to the Yugoslavs were recently discovered to be living in prisoner of war camps under their own names.[126]

Cabot believed that the Allies had to honor the Yugoslavs' requests, yet the Yugoslav government's treatment of the prisoners returned to them alarmed Allied authorities and caused State Department officials to further harden their attitude. In late May 1947, the U.S. government withdrew its pledge to surrender the Ustasha as a group and announced it would reserve the right to investigate the case of each individual requested by the Yugoslavs. The United States did so on the grounds that the Yugoslav government treated those already returned harshly and used charges of collaboration "as a weapon in an increasingly severe campaign of repression against opposing elements." In such a matter, which involved the responsibility of the United States to protect those people under its jurisdiction, the U.S. government could not be bound by its earlier pledges.[127]

In June 1947, the United States concluded an agreement with the International Refugee Organization to help Yugoslav refugees resettle in other countries. The Yugoslavs covered included those who had served with Mihailović or with the German army but who had not actually committed war crimes. The Yugoslav government included such people in the quisling category, but the United States did not.[128] Cabot objected strongly. He saw this policy shift as a clear violation of an earlier commitment that he maintained the government was obliged to honor. His files at the embassy showed that the United States not only protected those guilty of "terrible crimes in Yugoslavia" but actually helped them escape punishment. Cabot warned that if the Yugoslavs protested to the United Nations, the United States would not be able to defend its record.[129]

As these exchanges indicated, Cabot was constantly at odds with

124. Cabot to Marshall, 9 April 1947, *FRUS, 1947*, 4:786.
125. *FRUS, 1947*, 4:791 n. 3.
126. Cabot to Marshall, 15 May 1947, *FRUS, 1947*, 4:799–800.
127. Barbour to Peter Solly-Flood, 19 May 1947, *FRUS, 1947*, 4:800–802.
128. *FRUS, 1947*, 4:811 n. 3.
129. Cabot to Marshall, 11 June 1947, *FRUS, 1947*, 4:811–12.

the State Department during his time in Belgrade. Although Cabot's attitude toward the Tito regime reflected the mutual hostility that marked U.S.-Yugoslav relations in the immediate postwar years, he alone attempted to implement something akin to a wedge strategy in Yugoslavia. Cabot, whose experience and expertise was in Latin America, served in Yugoslavia on a temporary basis in 1947. Before assuming his post, he received only a general outline of U.S.-Yugoslav relations and instructions to act as a caretaker until the new ambassador arrived.[130] Yet Cabot chose to involve himself deeply in the complex problems in Belgrade. A thoughtful observer of international affairs, Cabot wondered, as he watched the hardening of relations between East and West, whether there was "any major responsibility on our part for the increasing hostility between the two blocs. Could there be mutual accommodation?"[131]

Cabot had no sympathy for communist ideology or practice, noting in his diary soon after his arrival in Belgrade that communism was "unethical; it teaches anything is fair to spread communism." He feared a "new dark ages . . . with communism triumphant over large parts of the world. . . . I hope US will hold torch of civilization."[132] At the same time, he believed the Yugoslavs had legitimate grievances against the United States and sought during his brief tenure in Belgrade to find some common ground on which to establish a better relationship between the two countries, however "hopeless" that might appear.[133]

The harassment of embassy personnel was at its height when Cabot arrived in Yugoslavia, but Cabot believed a change for the better was possible. As he wrote to another colleague in the Foreign Service:

> Belgrade is about as difficult and exasperating a post as I have ever had and I must confess it is a depressing experience to be here. However I see a few small projections in the monolithic mass which I may be able to grab hold of and I shall do my best to do so. At the moment the Jugs are conducting a charming campaign to harass, humiliate and intimidate the Embassy by pinching Jug employees, giving officers the runaround, etc. Give me, oh Lord, a long temper![134]

130. Interview with Cabot, March 1974.
131. Cabot, *First Line of Defense*, 29.
132. Cabot Diary, 17 February 1947.
133. Cabot, Oral History, Truman Library, 54.
134. Cabot to Sidney E. O'Donoghue, 20 February 1947, in *The Diplomatic Papers of John Moors Cabot*, part 2, *Europe*, reel 6 (Frederick, Md., 1984) (hereafter referred to as Cabot, *Papers*, with reel number).

In a long dispatch sent to Washington on his own initiative in mid-February 1947, Cabot commented on Yugoslav behavior and suggested a number of U.S. responses. Cabot surmised that the Tito government's harassment, arrests, and trials of embassy personnel represented a deliberate attempt by the Yugoslavs "to intimidate and humiliate Embassy and perhaps to put it out of business." The United States had several policy options to choose from in forming a response, including that of inaugurating a "positive policy of conciliation." "Observers" in Belgrade had informed him that the Yugoslav government had a "sincere sense of grievance" against the United States and that much of the difficulties with the Yugoslavs arose from "clumsy [U.S.] diplomacy." These observers had urged that the United States adopt a more conciliatory policy, but Cabot disagreed with such a philosophy of "unilateral concessions." He also realized that while the U.S. government must strive to eliminate genuine grievances such as the war criminals issue, that may have no effect because the "whole pattern of Communist diplomacy" suggested to him that "Yugoslavia would be actively hostile to whatever course" the United States adopted. Although the Yugoslavs felt sincerely aggrieved, their complaints were "but wolf's excuse for malevolent course they would have followed in any case." Cabot observed that nothing in his experience had convinced him that dictators could be appeased. Yet the United States should not "slam the door in Tito's face" and "should not needlessly . . . offend Yugoslav nationalist sentiment."

Cabot, previewing in a concise summary the carrot-and-stick approach that would come to characterize the wedge strategy, counseled that long-range U.S. policy should center on urging the Yugoslav government to respond to the wishes and needs of its people rather than to "Soviet directives." Factions existed within the regime that favored such a course and the United States should take care not to alienate them. Cabot therefore intended to explore the possibility of meeting some of the Yugoslavs' minor demands in return for the release of those embassy employees most recently arrested. He reminded the State Department that such a course would fail if the Yugoslavs did not believe that the United States was acting in good faith and again urged that the department "eliminate their just grievances." If his overtures achieved nothing, Cabot asked that the State Department not resort to the practice of reacting to Yugoslav actions with "protest and astonishment," for that would be "futile, counterproductive," and would "further embitter situation." Instead, the United States should block all Yugoslav assets remaining under U.S. control and forbid all financial transactions between Yugoslavia and the United States without special license. This, Cabot claimed as he neared the end of his message, would be effective because "their assets are our most important weapon."[135]

In his initial meetings with Deputy Foreign Minister Vladimir Velebit Cabot tried to arrive at some agreement on the points at issue between the two governments. Cabot explained that the United States would not release former Chetniks, whom they considered "mere obstructionists" rather than collaborators. However, Cabot pledged to do all he could to justify the Yugoslavs' legitimate requests for war criminals, such as members of the Ustasha and former followers of the German puppet Milan Nedić. Cabot also raised the issue of the harassment of the embassy staff by the Yugoslav government and secret police. Velebit replied that it was a constant source of surprise to his government that the Americans employed only people who were opposed to the Tito regime and in some cases closely linked with those who had collaborated during the war.[136] Cabot had clearly achieved nothing in this first attempt of "trading" grievances.

At a later meeting on 1 March Cabot mentioned some minor issues that he hoped might be more easily solved. Velebit, in a tone that Cabot noted was even "less affable" than that used previously, expressed little interest in the suggestion. He said that more major concerns, such as Trieste and the quisling issue had to be settled before minor concerns could be discussed.[137] After this meeting a pessimistic Cabot wondered if anything could be done to "bridge the gap" between the communist and capitalist worlds. Shouldn't the West simply see communism "with all its terrible acts, inherently immoral like Nazism?"[138]

Cabot remained convinced that "the cold unyielding hatred" of the Yugoslav government for the United States hampered his activities.[139] He characterized the Yugoslavs as basically untrustworthy (in his diary he refers repeatedly to the "Jugs" as "liars"), yet he clung to the hope that it was possible to improve operating conditions for the embassy and to create a credible record in Yugoslavia for the United States. But he was constantly discouraged because Acheson and others in the State Department either ignored each of his policy recommendations or misread his suggestions.[140]

135. Cabot to Marshall, 15 February 1947, *FRUS, 1947*, 4:761–64.
136. Cabot, memorandum of conversation, 25 February 1947, *FRUS, 1947*, 4:765–69.
137. Cabot, memorandum of conversation, 1 March 1947, *FRUS, 1947*, 4:771–75.
138. Cabot Diary, 2 March 1947.
139. Interview with Cabot, March 1974.
140. Cabot Diary, 20 March 1947.

In April, for example, Velebit informed Cabot that the Yugoslav government desired an early settlement of U.S. property claims and proposed that direct negotiations on the matter begin. The two countries had been at an impasse for many months regarding $47.8 million in claims made by U.S. companies and residents against Yugoslavia, and Yugoslavia's insistence that the United States release the $46.8 million it held in Yugoslav gold reserves, moved to the United States by the Royal Yugoslav Government-In-Exile during the war. Cabot told Velebit that his government would be pleased by his suggestion concerning negotiations. He then cabled Washington for instructions, while confiding to his diary that Velebit was so affable that he couldn't help but "wonder what is up?"[141] Cabot, adhering to his own quid pro quo philosophy, also suggested to the State Department that the United States request the release of those embassy employees still in Yugoslav custody in exchange for Yugoslav gold reserves.[142] To Cabot's anger, Washington minimized the importance of Velebit's statement and instructed Cabot that he must not be lulled into a false sense of security merely because Velebit had offered to open negotiations.[143]

Cabot's other recommendations all received only negative and "pretty discouraging" replies.[144] The late May instructions from State to do nothing other than protest the actions of the Tito government with notes and press releases finally caused Cabot to "go through roof." He despaired that the State Department, by allowing him "merely to pinprick" Yugoslav authorities, seemed interested only in stirring up a maximum of resentment, while achieving a minimum of results.[145]

Cabot's prescient reading of the Yugoslav-Soviet relationship fueled his desire to implement an early version of the wedge strategy. Cabot's observations and his talks with the representatives of other governments in Yugoslavia convinced him that despite propaganda to the contrary, the Yugoslav and Soviet governments were not on the best of terms. Cabot was sure that "Yugo national interests" were bound to conflict eventually with those of the Soviet Union and that "Yugos may not always blindly follow Russian instructions." The arrogance of the Yugoslavs was such that Cabot would find it "surprising if they were not at times irked at not being masters in their own

141. Cabot to Marshall, 1 April 1947, *FRUS, 1947*, 4:783–84; Lampe, Prickett, and Adamović, *Economic Relations*, 25; Cabot Diary, 1 April 1947.
142. *FRUS, 1947*, 4:784 n. 4.
143. Cabot Diary, 4 April 1947.
144. Ibid., 23 and 29 May 1947.
145. Ibid., 29 May 1947.

house." He also knew that some in Tito's government favored better relations with the West. Because of this, the best course for the United States to follow was one of "firmness in action but suavity in approach." The United States should retaliate when the Yugoslavs were guilty of specific offenses, but should also remedy their legitimate complaints. If the United States followed such a course, Cabot remained convinced that some in the Tito government would work to improve general U.S.-Yugoslav relations.[146]

In a letter to Representative Claude Pepper in mid-June, Cabot candidly reviewed his thoughts and experiences since arriving in Yugoslavia. His initial attempts to improve U.S.-Yugoslav relations had been hampered because in the recent past the "Embassy had been indiscreet, and had shown a natural but unwise hostility" to Yugoslavia. Since then he believed both sides had "made some progress in improving our respective attitudes and clearing up outstanding contentions, though fundamentals have not changed."[147] A few weeks later Cabot reported that Yugoslav Foreign Office officials were "troubled by the course of events in Hungary and Greece, realizing that Yugoslavia is caught in an increasingly embarrassing and dangerous position." He concluded, almost a full year before the Tito-Stalin split, that the Yugoslavs "may now be susceptible to the argument that they should not keep all eggs in Soviet basket."[148]

In early July, Cabot sent a long valedictory to Washington. His mood was bleak; his diary entry noted "my own work to little purpose, people at home fatuous in facing international crisis, world collapsing into communism." He feared he might regret writing his dispatch as "it doesn't exactly follow official thinking since it emphasizes suavity as well as firmness and selectivity in opposing the regime."[149] Yet the document is important because of Cabot's perceptions of the present and future situation in Yugoslavia and for the State Department's reaction to it.

Cabot began his assessment, which like his diary entry was dated 7 July, with some general statements on communist relations with the West, which were of a piece with most of the official thinking of his day. He believed that the communists aimed at world domination, but that the communist bloc would not be able to challenge the West directly for many years. In the interim, the United States must resist

146. Cabot to Marshall, 7 June 1947, *FRUS, 1947*, 4:806–8.

147. Cabot to Claude Pepper, 12 June 1947, Cabot, *Papers*, reel 6.

148. Summary, 23 June 1947, Truman Papers, Naval Aide Files/State Department Briefs, File: State Department Briefs, June–August 1947.

149. Cabot Diary, 7 July 1947.

the present thrust of communist policy, which would insure a clash if and when the communists have gathered sufficient strength to attack the West. He urged the government never to despair of reaching an understanding with the communists because "communism had shown itself before to be more flexible in deed than in dialectic, if more flexible in its scruples than in either." "Communism in Yugoslavia . . . is not a political creed," Cabot observed, "it is a faith" and its adherents are "passionately sincere." During the war, "Yugoslavia's internal hatreds proved stronger than hatred of the enemies," and this led to the collaboration of Mihailović and others with the Axis. The communists, to their "credit," have "softened [ethnic] hatreds," but this had been accomplished "in part by polarizing all hatreds on the Communist vs. anti-Communist issue." Cabot considered the masses of the people dissatisfied, but not "bitterly opposed" to the Tito regime. Tito had taken great pains to gain the support of the people, and the United States should not disregard his success. Yet the Partisans were a "very heterogenous group" and "opposition to Soviet domination is more likely to come from Partisan ranks than from the opposition." He believed that conflicts with the Soviets were "inevitable" and that the "intense nationalism of the country might play a decisive role if an acute situation arose."

Cabot then recommended that the United States keep alive the hope that the present government will adopt a position more independent of the Soviet Union or even be overthrown by elements friendlier to the West. The United States should "hammer constantly on the clashes of interest between Russia and Yugoslavia" and work to "drive a wedge" between the extremists and moderates in the government. If the United States worked earnestly to keep the peace, only to have it broken again by "totalitarian aggression," at least the U.S. government could "go to the people with clean hands" and could "present an impelling case at the bar of world opinion."

During his months in Yugoslavia, Cabot finally acknowledged, there had been no substantial change in U.S.-Yugoslav relations. Yet some progress had been made in claims negotiations, trading agreements, and the protection of Americans residing in the country. The "mess" of the jailed employees and the "incredibly clumsy cloak and dagger adventures" that had existed earlier had eased. Cabot credited this change to the policy of firmness coupled with cooperation that he had begun and to the excellent work done by others in the embassy staff. The Yugoslavs sought to deal with the West on their own terms, but Cabot believed that with "skill and patience" the United States could have its views accepted as the basis for relations.[150]

Cabot's superiors in Washington heavily annotated this dispatch, although most of its recommendations were not followed until after the Tito-Stalin split in 1948. One set of comments made by H. Freeman Matthews, director of the Office of European Affairs, took umbrage with Cabot's derogatory references to U.S. policy. For example, Cabot's characterization of the United States's attitude on the question of Austrian reparations to Yugoslavia as "intransigent" was labeled with the phrase "That's a hell of a thing to say!" A friend in Washington told Cabot that "one of the top officials" regarded his report as "stuff and nonsense." Yet when the break between Tito and Stalin finally occurred less than a year later, Cabot "felt a little pleased with myself, having been so wrongly condemned by the top echelon."[151]

Cabot held the same anticommunist convictions as his peers, but he was astute enough to see that Yugoslavia was not the Soviet Union and that the same policy should not be used for both nations. He was more practical than his superiors in Washington, who spoke of bringing democracy to Eastern Europe, but who had no way to accomplish this. Cabot doubted the ability of the United States to liberate Yugoslavia; his main concern centered on the reputation and image of his country. Yet he was also almost alone in perceiving that all was not well in the Soviet-Yugoslav relationship, and in reading the signs that other diplomats would consistently miss. In June 1947 for example, while he wrote in his diary that "there seems definite reason to suppose some opposition developing in government to Russian arrogance,"[152] other observers saw only a Moscow-oriented regime.

When Washington policymakers refused to accept Cabot's analyses, he blamed much of their rigidity on the force of public opinion. The general public had a very negative image of Tito; particular groups, such as the Catholic Church and veterans organizations, frequently appealed to the U.S. government to object to Tito's policies.[153] The sweeping rhetoric of U.S. initiatives such as Truman Doctrine also did little to educate the American public to the complexities of international relations. Washington was simply not prepared to deal with a communist state in a manner unrelated to the Soviet Union. In turn,

150. Cabot to Marshall, dispatch, 7 July 1947, RG 59, no. 1663, 680.H00/7-747.
151. Ibid.; Cabot, Oral History, Truman Library, 57; interview with Cabot, March 1974.
152. Cabot Diary, 8 June 1947.
153. Interview with Cabot, March 1974.

Yugoslavia's conduct toward the U.S. Embassy and its treatment of returned prisoners hardened America's attitude toward the Tito regime. The actions of each antagonized the other, and both governments continued to see each other as an adversaries with whom cooperation was impossible.

Fortunately, the new ambassador, Cavendish Cannon, shared many of Cabot's views. Cannon, a career Foreign Service officer with Balkan experience, arrived in Belgrade in July 1947. When Cabot first heard of Cannon's appointment in the spring he was "a bit sore" because Cannon was his junior in the Foreign Service. He regretted that he would be marking time, just when "I really feel I was making progress" and hoped that Cannon would "not return to a wholly negative policy."[154] After the ambassador arrived, Cabot gladly noted in his diary that Cannon shared his views "in most important respects."[155]

John C. Campbell, the Department of State's veteran Balkan expert, later recalled that Matthews and John D. Hickerson, director of the Office of European Affairs, had persuaded Secretary of State Marshall that "Cannon was the one man who ought to go to Yugoslavia." No one held much hope for an improvement in U.S.-Yugoslav relations. As Campbell noted: "our Embassy was under siege, more or less; all the local employees were being persecuted, and we weren't able to do anything in negotiations." Only an experienced diplomat could cope with such circumstances; Belgrade was clearly no place for another political appointee such as Patterson.[156]

After a few weeks of observing conditions in Yugoslavia, Cannon, in a report similar to but less optimistic than those filed by Cabot, concluded that Tito's "minority regime" had "entrenched its position and has been able to hold in check old conflicts between Croats and Serbs." While opposition existed "among peasantry at large and among Roman Catholic element," it lacked "cohesion, organization and program." No internal attempt to overthrow the regime therefore appeared likely or feasible. Although Yugoslavia was the "most important satellite in Russian orbit," Tito ran his own affairs and had taken positions on international issues that were "more advanced than Moscow seemed prepared to support." This led Cannon to label Yugoslavia "as Soviets' most faithful and conscientious collaborator rather than satellite and at the same time spearhead of dynamic expansionist Communism." Like Cabot, Cannon speculated that Yugoslav "nation-

154. Cabot Diary, 24 March 1947.
155. Ibid., 16 July 1947.
156. Campbell, Oral History, Truman Library, 128–29.

alism may some day conflict with Soviet purpose" but he doubted this would occur in the short term.[157]

In the short term, Yugoslavia's standing within the Soviet system appeared to increase. The offer of Marshall Plan aid, extended to all of the European states in June 1947 but subsequently rejected by the Soviets and Eastern Europeans, had confirmed the division of Europe into U.S. and Soviet spheres. In the fall of 1947, the Soviets created the Communist Information Bureau, or Cominform, consisting of the communist parties of France, Italy, the Soviet Union, and Eastern Europe (excluding Albania). The Soviets intended the organization to serve as a counter to the unifying effects of the Marshall Plan and as an instrument of control of other states' communist parties. The USSR used the first meeting in Warsaw to highlight the divisions between East and West, with Soviet theoretician A. A. Zhadavov declaring that the West had divided the world into two opposing camps and was planning a preemptive war against the Soviets. Deputy Prime Minister G. M. Malenkov, in a more positive address, offered the assistance of the Soviet Union to all states requesting aid.[158]

The Cominform meeting also featured attacks upon deviations within the communist movement, with the Yugoslavs instructed by Stalin to take the lead in criticizing the ideology of the Western communists. Stalin also insisted that the Cominform and its paper, *For a Lasting Peace, For a People's Democracy*, be headquartered in Belgrade. While this could have been interpreted as a Soviet recognition of Yugoslavia's primacy among the communist states outside the USSR, the Yugoslav delegates suspected Stalin's real intention was to control Yugoslavia and isolate it by turning the other parties against them. The Yugoslavs also resented their grouping in the Cominforn with states whose parties did not share their guerrilla history. An illustration of this occurred at the Cominform meeting when Yugoslav Foreign Minister Kardelj pointedly praised his party's wartime heroism while making no reference to the Soviet role in the liberation of the Balkans.[159]

The administration as a whole failed to note this or any other sign of friction between the Soviets and Yugoslavs. A Central Intelligence Agency (CIA) evaluation of the implications of the Cominform's forma-

157. Cannon to Marshall, 7 September 1947, *FRUS, 1947*, 4:840–42.

158. Peter Calvocoressi, *Survey of International Affairs, 1947–1948* (London: Oxford University Press, 1952), 49–51.

159. Adam B. Ulam, *Titoism and the Cominform* (Westport, Conn.: Greenwood Press, 1971), 53–54; George W. Hoffman and Fred Warner Neal, *Yugoslavia and the New Communism* (New York: Twentieth Century Fund, 1962), 126–27.

tion, completed in mid-October 1947, correctly surmised that the Soviets designed the organization to provide them with more control over both the satellite and West European communist parties. However, the CIA, reflecting the administration's primary concerns, believed the Cominform's focus to be on Western Europe, with the coordination of communist parties there designed to "prevent European economic recovery under US leadership." The Cominform offered further proof that the Soviets had abandoned the use of parliamentary tactics "to revert to subversive activities, such as strikes and sabotage, in order to undermine the stability of Western Europe governments." The delegates meeting in Warsaw were all "hardbitten Communists of long-standing," such as the Yugoslav Milovan Djilas, ready to serve the Soviet end of expelling socialists from the governments of Europe to create a "hard nucleus of ideologically sound Communists, capable of direct action and of reversion to underground methods if such procedure becomes necessary." The CIA pictured Yugoslavia as the "logical choice" for the Cominform's headquarters, because of the "success and stability" of its communist regime, "the character and experience of its ruling clique, and its proximity to high priority Communist targets such as Greece and Italy."[160] Yugoslav still appeared to be the most loyal of the Soviet satellites.

In the years immediately following World War II, the United States based its Yugoslavia policy on the imperative of resisting communist expansion. The U.S. government's doubts about the effectiveness of continued cooperation with communist states, coupled with Yugoslavia's determination to expand into the Julian Region and to assist in toppling the Greek government, brought the Truman administration and Tito into direct conflict. Yugoslavia's attacks on two U.S. aircraft made a bad situation dangerously worse. Even after tensions eased, Cabot's attempts to find common ground with the Yugoslavs proved fruitless. His criticism of U.S. policy and his suspicion of a rift between the Soviets and the Yugoslavs, correct though they were, provoked only derision among his superiors in Washington. The wedge strategy had not been developed fully and most policymakers believed one communist to be indistinguishable from another. The Yugoslavs themselves also gave little overt sign of a wish for improved relations. As Ambassador Cannon observed in November 1947, after a Yugoslav campaign against American journalists in Yugoslavia, the publication

160. CIA Special Evaluation No. 21, "Implications of the New Communist Information Bureau," 13 October 1947, Truman Papers, NSC-CIA File: Special Evaluations.

of anti-American articles in the Yugoslav press, and continued dead-lock in the negotiations on United States claims and Yugoslav gold, Yugoslavia's attitude toward relations with the United States "had never been so bad."[161] Little did he know that the most challenging phase of the Yugoslav-United States relationship was about to begin.

161. Naval Aide-State Department Brief, November 1947, Truman Papers, File: State Department Briefs, September–December 1947.

CHAPTER TWO

1948–1949
"A LOYAL AND COOPERATIVE ATTITUDE"

By 1948, Tito appeared to the United States to be the most loyal and belligerent of the Kremlin's European satellites. As John C. Campbell later recalled: "We regarded the Yugoslavs as being the toughest pro-Soviets of all the Eastern European governments."[1] The break between Tito and Stalin, marked by the Cominform's expulsion of Yugoslavia in June 1948, came as a surprise to the Truman administration. In time, the growing conviction that the split was genuine and that it marked the first substantial challenge to Soviet leadership within the international communist movement led to U.S. assistance for the Tito regime. For the remainder of its time in office, while both the Cold War abroad and the Red Scare at home were at their height, the Truman administration made the maintenance of Yugoslav independence a central aspect of U.S. foreign policy.

The new relationship established between the United States and Yugoslavia served the needs of both countries. For the United States, a Yugoslavia independent of Soviet control insured that the USSR would be denied that country's military resources, which equaled over thirty divisions in the critical area of central Europe. Tito's bid for autonomy also represented a destabilizing influence within the bloc,

1. Campbell, Oral History, Truman Library, 104.

one that the satellite states might attempt to emulate. By assisting Yugoslavia, the United States could demonstrate that autonomous communist regimes would receive a cordial welcome in the West. The wedge strategy, still more of a notion than a policy, would have a tangible exhibit. Yugoslavia, for its part, needed outside assistance to survive, but Tito was no more willing to compromise his country's independence to obtain American aid after 1948 than he had been in the years immediately following World War II. He had little choice other than to court the United States, but he did so with little warmth.

The United States was equally wary of establishing ties with communist Yugoslavia. George Kennan, who envisioned containment as a policy opposed to "the system of power organized, dominated and inspired by Joseph Stalin" always deplored the tendency, prevalent among both policymakers and the public to divide the world into communist and noncommunist halves and to blindly oppose one and assist the other.[2] In 1947, while Cabot attempted to improve U.S.-Yugoslav relations with his own version of the wedge strategy, Kennan tested the waters as well by imagining the advantages the United States would reap if a communist government outside the Soviet Union "turned on its masters, repudiated the Kremlin's authority, and bit the hand which had reared it."[3] But how much support could the United States extend to a communist state that remained communist without weakening its ties to its noncommunist allies? Could the American public and Congress, repeatedly urged to fight a cold war against communist aggression, differentiate between a Tito and a Stalin? Would the administration continue to celebrate Yugoslav independence if that independence involved a resistance to United States guidance as well as to Soviet demands? All of these questions complicated Truman's response to Yugoslavia after the Tito-Stalin split.

Melvyn Leffler has characterized the first few months of 1948 as a period when United States officials harbored some "uncertainty about Soviet intentions." Western initiatives such as the Truman Doctrine and the European Recovery Program (ERP) had thwarted but surely not erased Stalin's ambitions. Did Stalinist purges in Eastern Europe signify a possible move against Czechoslovakia, still a democracy with

2. George F. Kennan, *Memoirs: 1925–1950* (Boston: Little, Brown, 1967), 323, 365–66.

3. As quoted in Gaddis, *Long Peace*, 151; Beatrice Heuser's assertion that Kennan's views were "woolly" is superficial and takes little notice of the risks that policymakers had to consider in implementing the wedge strategy. Heuser, *Western "Containment" Policies*, 15.

ties to the West, or simply a desire to solidify the Soviet sphere in the face of temptations such as the Marshall Plan?[4] Nothing seemed predictable but the continued division of Europe.

During those same months, little in the U.S.-Yugoslav relationship appeared to change. There were a few signs that strains existed between Yugoslavia and the bloc, but the Truman administration did not grasp their significance. The two countries continued to bicker over Tito's requests for trade and credits, while a settlement on mutual claims left over from the war remained elusive. In matters of trade, the United States applied the same restrictions to Yugoslavia that it enforced with regard to the Soviet Union and its satellites in Eastern Europe. By late 1947 the State and Commerce Departments, along with the National Security Council (NSC), had decided that the U.S. commitment to the ERP and the Soviet bloc's resistance to it necessitated a reorientation of U.S. trade policy. The Truman administration therefore prohibited, through an export-licensing program announced in January 1948, the shipment to the Soviet Union and its satellites of critical commodities that were in short supply or had military potential.[5] By late March the government had added military goods themselves to the list of controlled commodities. The implementation of this policy caused a substantial drop in U.S. trade with Eastern Europe.[6]

The United States also continued to object to various aspects of Yugoslavia's internal and foreign policies, and this too served as a barrier to better relations. As Ambassador Cannon told Tito in early January 1948, he could not expect an improved economic relationship with the United States as long as the American public perceived Yugoslavia to be in opposition to all American efforts "for establishing peace and reconstruction." Cannon expressed particular concern about "Yugoslav provocation" in Trieste and the continuing strife in Greece. Tito countered that Yugoslavia desired only peace and an opportunity to develop its own economy. In his report to the State Department, Cannon characterized this exchange as "curious," with Tito appearing reluctant to discuss political issues, even though he claimed to be meeting with Cannon to continue a conversation begun at the end of the preceding year. Tito had not met with any other foreign diplomats

4. Leffler, *Preponderance of Power*, 204–5.

5. Willis C. Armstrong to Edwin McCammon Martin, 10 December 1947, *FRUS, 1948*, 4:509–11; ibid., 511 n. 1; Department of Commerce Press Release, 15 January 1948, ibid., 4:514.

6. Bennett Kovrig, *The Myth of Liberation: East Central Europe in U.S. Diplomacy and Politics since 1941* (Baltimore: Johns Hopkins University Press, 1973), 92.

for some weeks but for some reason "seemed to think it useful to have
contact with American representative."[7]

In subsequent cables, Cannon observed that Tito showed little
interest in routine trade agreements, and sought primarily to acquire
the machinery and electrical equipment he needed for his five-year
plan but was unable to obtain from the bloc. Tito also wanted the
United States to lift its ban on tourist travel to Yugoslavia because of
the country's need for foreign exchange and to release Yugoslav
gold reserves in the United States. Cannon reiterated the embassy's
impression that the Soviets were not giving adequate support to
Yugoslavia's five-year plan and generally opposed the development of
a self-sufficient industrial system in Yugoslavia. The ambassador
postulated that the Soviets sought a dependent Yugoslavia, with
industries oriented toward military production and the overall needs
of the bloc,[8] but did not suggest that these strains between the Soviets
and Yugoslavia benefited the West.

In any case, the administration's attention that spring remained
focused first on Czechoslovakia, where a February coup against the
coalition government brought the communists into full power, and
France and Italy, where communist electoral gains threatened a similar outcome. At the same time, messages from the U.S. commander in
Berlin, General Lucius Clay, indicated ominous changes in Soviet
behavior, which in a few months would lead to the Berlin blockade.
These events all contributed to the March Crisis of 1948, during
which the CIA predicted that war could well occur within sixty
days. Although George Kennan later dismissed this "dither" as a
misunderstanding of what were essentially Soviet defensive reactions,[9] the administration used the crisis to its advantage. In a speech
to the Congress in mid-March, Truman demanded full funding of the
ERP and denounced the "Soviet Union and its agents," who had
"destroyed the independence and democratic character of a whole
series of nations in Eastern and Central Europe."[10]

To the United States, Yugoslavia remained one of the Kremlin's
"satellite police states" assisting the Soviets in their "drive toward
world conquest."[11] The administration also held Tito himself in little

7. Cannon to Marshall, 3 January 1948, *FRUS, 1948*, 4:1054–56.
8. Cannon to Marshall, 4 January 1948, *FRUS, 1948*, 4:1056–58.
9. Kennan, *Memoirs*, 400–401.
10. *Public Papers of the Presidents of the United States*, Truman, 1948, 182–86.
11. Sidney Souers to the NSC, 30 March 1945, with enclosure, NSC 7, "Report by the
NSC on the Position of the United States with Respect to Soviet Directed World
Communism," *FRUS, 1948*, 1 (2):544–50.

regard. As President Truman told a group of business and trade paper editors in April of 1948: "I am told that Tito murdered more than four hundred thousand of the opposition in Yugoslavia before he got himself firmly established there as a dictator."[12]

Within this context, no one appreciated the signs of trouble that surfaced in Yugoslavia during the first months of 1948. In late February for example, U.S. intelligence analysts simply recorded that Ambassador Kosanović had been recalled hastily to Belgrade, and that Yugoslav ambassadors from the Eastern European satellites had been summoned home as well.[13] In April, the director of the Office of European Affairs, John Hickerson, sent a memo to Undersecretary of State Robert A. Lovett detailing a number of "suspicious activities" by the Yugoslav government, the significance of which was "not yet clear." These included restrictions on the use of automobiles, the establishment of a "ten-mile closed frontier zone," the posting of guards near the homes of Tito and other high officials, and shortages of certain foodstuffs and suspected food stockpiling by the military. The memo, however, was not forwarded to Lovett, because as Robert G. Barnes, chief of the Policy Registry Branch explained, its lack of interpretation rendered it "meaningless."[14]

Throughout the spring, foreign diplomats reported that Tito appeared less sure of himself in public.[15] Cannon himself advised the State Department in early June that the "confidence" of the Tito regime "in its ability to move forward boldly in new Stalinist world seems faltering"; however, the ambassador attributed this to the strength of U.S. policy, the recovery of Western Europe, and Yugoslavia's own economic problems. Several Yugoslavs, including high-ranking officials Sreten Žujović and Andrije Hebrang had been arrested and/or tried for treason, but Cannon believed this due to an internal party conflict caused by "sense domestic economic ill-being." He also characterized recent increases in military spending as doctrinaire ideological responses to the country's economic problems. To Cannon, the focus of the regime seemed to be on the "consolidation party ranks" with the secret police "influential and omnipresent"; he saw no need for any change in U.S. policy.[16]

12. *Papers of the Presidents*, Truman, 1948, 232.

13. Commander Grantham to Fleet Admiral Leahy (from Roscoe H. Hillenkoetter), 25 February 1948, Dennison Papers, File: White House Message Traffic 1948.

14. John D. Hickerson to Robert A. Lovett, 23 April 1948, *FRUS, 1948*, 4:1067 and n. 3.

15. Robert M. Blum, "Surprised by Tito: The Anatomy of an Intelligence Failure," *Diplomatic History* 12 (Winter 1988): 44–45.

16. Cannon to Marshall, 8 June 1948, *FRUS, 1948*, 4:1070–72.

As Cannon drew these conclusions, the Yugoslavs suddenly agreed to settle their claims disputes with the United States. The two parties reached a final understanding in mid-June 1948, providing for settlements of U.S. property and other claims against Yugoslavia and for lend-lease and other pre-UNRRA aid furnished to the Yugoslav government. The United States also released the Yugoslav assets frozen since the war.[17]

While the claims settlement aroused little comment, U.S. diplomats took note of what appeared to be a quarrel between Yugoslavia and the Soviet Union concerning a conference, called by the Council of Foreign Ministers in 1946, to settle a controversy between the United States and the Soviets concerning international control and free navigation of the Danube.[18] The conference was scheduled to be held in Belgrade in late July, but in June the Soviets announced that Yugoslavia would have difficulty providing facilities on the specified date and suggested the meeting be moved to the capital of another Danubian state. Two days later, Yugoslav foreign minister Simić informally told the U.S. chargé d'affaires R. Borden Reams that all was in readiness for the meeting and that an air-conditioned school would be provided for the delegates' comfort. In a formal meeting with Reams on 16 June, Simić stated that the earlier Soviet view concerning Belgrade's lack of readiness had been based on his personal opinion, which had not been cleared with his government. The error had now been rectified, and the conference would proceed as scheduled in Belgrade. The Soviets subsequently announced that Simić had indeed misled them and that the conference would be held in Belgrade on the thirtieth of July.[19]

In the midst of this confusion, Moša Pijade, the leading theoretician of the Yugoslav Communist Party, published a defense of his party's policies in *Borba*. Reams, who kept the State Department informed in Cannon's absence, viewed this as a response to an editorial critical of non-Soviet parties that had appeared a few weeks earlier in the Cominform journal *For a Lasting Peace, For a People's Democracy*. A Cominform editorial published on 15 June attacking those communist parties that rejected criticism and failed to acknowledge their errors

17. *FRUS, 1948*, 4:1093, editorial note.

18. For a discussion of the background to this issue see Thomas G. Paterson, "Eastern Europe and the Early Cold War: The Danube Controversy," *Historian* 33 (February 1971): 237–47.

19. Embassy of Soviet Union to Secretary of State, 12 June 1948, *FRUS, 1948*, 4:614–15; R. Borden Reams to Marshall, 16 June 1948, ibid., 615–16; Secretary of State to Ambassador of Soviet Union, 18 June 1948, ibid., 616.

also aroused Reams's interest. In a dispatch sent to Marshall on 18 June, the astute chargé correctly guessed that these exchanges and the Danubian Conference episode masked a more profound rift between Tito and Stalin. He characterized Yugoslavia's determination to hold the conference despite Soviet objections as the "first direct and irrevocable challenge any satellite to supreme authority Communist overlords in Kremlin." Tito's "apparent decision to challenge Stalin" represented the "most significant political event here since US recognition" and foreshadowed a possible "split in Soviet bloc if breach allowed to widen." While certain that all of this had been spearheaded by Tito, Reams judged that the Yugoslav leader could not have acted alone. Reams also alluded to past events that had been difficult to interpret in light of the Western belief that "harmony" reigned between Yugoslavia and the Soviet Union, but which now seemed less mysterious. Rumors reported by the British of a personal letter of rebuke from Stalin to Tito, coupled with the recent press exchanges, all pointed to Soviet "displeasure" with Yugoslav policies and Yugoslavia's refusal to admit error.

Yet Reams doubted that any theoretical conflict had caused the seeming quarrel between the USSR and Yugoslavia. He instead credited the Soviets' refusal to support Tito in his five-year plan and their irritation with his "personal ambitions to lead own sphere in southeast Europe" with causing the rupture. Yugoslavia's "precipitate settlement" of its claims dispute with the United States and continuing interest in expanding trade could reflect Tito's resolve to "seek greater independence from Soviet economic bloc." From the evidence reviewed in this dispatch, Reams concluded that a "definite split" existed between Yugoslavia and the Soviet Union. Because of Tito's record as a resistance leader during the war, Reams believed he occupied an "exceptional position" from which to pursue and maintain a policy independent of the Soviet Union, but it was too early "to appraise extent of opportunity schism affords us to penetrate and disunite Soviet bloc."[20]

Charles G. Stefan, who served in the U.S. embassy's political section in 1947 and 1948, detailed the time-consuming care with which the embassy staff composed the above cable in a *Diplomatic History* article published in 1982. The significance of the rift between the Soviets and one of their "first and most devoted allies" demanded that the embassy "sift carefully all the evidence at our disposal" and "avoid drawing

20. Reams to Marshall, 18 June 1948, *FRUS, 1948*, 4:1073–75.

unsubstantiated conclusions." Yet Stefan recalled that Washington made no significant reply to their effort.[21]

The analysis so finely drawn by Reams, Stefan, and their colleagues that summer was of course correct; the conflict between Stalin's resolve to create a Yugoslavia dependent on the Soviet Union and Tito's equal determination to resist had reached its climax. In addition to their disagreements with Tito over Yugoslavia's domestic policies, the Soviets had not adequately supported the Yugoslav position on Trieste or Tito's call for the formation of a Balkan Federation of Yugoslavia, Bulgaria, and Albania under his leadership. When Stalin spoke of such a federation, he assigned a major role in it to Bulgaria rather than to Yugoslavia. Indeed, the strained relations between Yugoslavia and the Soviet Union actually dated from the war and had simply accelerated in the postwar period. As Djilas later theorized, Stalin feared "that the creation of revolutionary centers outside of Moscow could endanger its supremacy in world Communism," and so he supported revolutions "only up to a certain point—up to where he could control them—but he was always ready to leave them in the lurch whenever they slipped out of his grasp."[22] By 1948, Stalin had decided, in the words of Stephen Clissold, that Tito "must be taught a lesson or, if necessary, be replaced."[23]

In January 1948, a Yugoslav delegation, which included Milovan Djilas, journeyed to the USSR for discussions on military and political assistance, but little had come of the talks. In February, while the Yugoslavs languished in Moscow, Stalin suddenly summoned the leadership of both Bulgaria and Yugoslavia to the Kremlin to discuss the Balkan federation. Tito, claiming ill health, refused to attend; Kardelj and Vladimir Bakarić joined Djilas to represent Yugoslavia in his stead. Before their meeting with Stalin, Djilas warned his fellows that Stalin would attempt "to force Yugoslavia down to the level of the occupied East European countries." When he met with the Yugoslavs and the Bulgarians, Stalin criticized the independent behavior of both countries and called for the formation of a Yugoslav-Bulgarian federation. Although he had previously promised Yugoslavia that it could absorb Albania, he now declared that could occur only after the creation of the federation. Stalin also demanded that the civil war in Greece end, on the grounds that Great Britain and the United States,

---

21. Charles G. Stefan, "The Emergence of the Soviet-Yugoslav Break: A Personal View from the Belgrade Embassy," *Diplomatic History* 6 (Fall 1982): 400–402.

22. Djilas, *Conversations with Stalin*, 132.

23. Clissold, *Yugoslavia and the Soviet Union*, 50.

the latter pictured by him as the most powerful state in the world, would never permit the communists "to break their line of communication in the Mediterranean." In addition, the Soviet leader later insisted that the Yugoslavs sign an agreement with the USSR calling for consultation on foreign policy issues. Kardelj, whose "blood boiled" at this insult, signed the document in the middle of the night and only at Molotov's insistence.[24]

By the first of March, the Yugoslavs had decided to resist Stalin's demands. Within a few weeks, the Soviets notified Tito that they intended to withdraw all military and civilian advisers and technicians from his country in response to their unfriendly treatment. The two countries' communist party central committees then exchanged letters in which the Soviets charged the Yugoslavs with various ideological errors and anti-Soviet actions and the Yugoslavs proclaimed their innocence. This exchange culminated in the Cominform's expulsion of Yugoslavia on 28 June 1948 and Stalin's call on the people of Yugoslavia to overthrow Tito.[25] The Cominform also gradually imposed a blockade on trade with Yugoslavia to deprive it of the goods vital to its reconstruction and economic development.

The Yugoslavs had refused the Soviet suggestion that the argument between them be settled by the Cominform and did not attend the June meeting, which denounced them for their "departure from Marxism-Leninism" at home and abroad. The Yugoslav party rejected the Cominform's action and called on its members to "close their ranks" with the masses and "work even more persistently on the building of our socialist homeland." Only such actions would demonstrate the falsity of the Cominform's charge.[26]

Dedijer later wrote that until the spring of 1948 "conflict between the new Yugoslavia and the Soviet Union had seemed impossible to me."[27] Veteran Yugoslav diplomat Leo Mates also recalled the "shock" felt by the Yugoslavs, as well as "the suspicion that the old fox has some designs" on his country.[28] The letters exchanged in secret by the

---

24. Vladimir Dedijer, *The Battle Stalin Lost, 1948–1953* (New York: Viking Press, 1970), 32–33; Djilas, *Conversations with Stalin*, 172, 177, 183; Robert Conquest, *Stalin: Breaker of Nations* (New York: Viking, 1991), 286–287; Clissold, *Yugoslavia and the Soviet Union*, 51; Kardelj, *Reminiscences*, 110–11.

25. For texts of the correspondence see Robert H. Bass and Elizabeth Marbury, eds., *The Soviet-Yugoslav Controversy, 1948–1958: A Documentary Record* (New York: Prospect Books, 1959).

26. Ibid., 62, 79.

27. Dedijer, *Battle*, 36.

28. Interview with Mates, Belgrade, 1988.

two countries' communist organs and leaders throughout the spring reflected this Yugoslav sense of unease as Tito and the party stressed their conviction that the Soviets had been misinformed and that a meeting between the two parties would clear the air. The Yugoslavs continually asserted their loyalty to Marxism, the Soviet Union, and their own country, noting their wish to be the Soviets' "most faithful friend and ally."[29] Mates believed that Tito knew from the beginning that the Soviet complaints about their advisers' treatment was simply a "pretext" and that the Yugoslavs therefore sought through their letters to elicit Stalin's true designs upon them, which they assumed involved subjugation or attack. As the correspondence proceeded, the Soviets charged the Yugoslavs with reverting to capitalism; the Yugoslavs labeled such ideas "insulting." Tito also leveled charges of his own, asserting that the Soviets had wronged Yugoslavia by providing only meager aid and recruiting spies from within the party and government.[30]

The Cominform's expulsion of Yugoslavia, coming after "the longest" ten days Charles Stefan ever remembered, proved the U.S. embassy's earlier analysis to have been "on target."[31] Reams immediately cabled the department to ask what position he should take "in this brilliantly fluid situation" if, as he expected, the Yugoslavs requested U.S. assistance. He also urged the United States to issue a general statement reaffirming its determination to protect the territorial integrity of small nations.[32] The U.S. military and naval attachés in Belgrade shared Reams's opinion that the West's strong support for Tito as a member of the United Nations would influence the policy of the Soviet Union. Tito's "claim to independent leadership" raised "a basic issue" for the Kremlin; he was "master in his own Communist house and Stalin cannot oust him quickly without war." In short, all three advised the State Department that "no event could be more momentous for the attainment of our foreign policy objectives than the permanent alienation from Moscow of this key regime."[33]

The initial estimates of the Central Intelligence Agency sent to the president by Director Admiral Roscoe H. Hillenkoetter on 29 and 30 June, confirmed the importance of Tito's action. Hillenkoetter speculated that the Cominform denunciation of Tito represented a

29. Bass and Marbury, *Soviet-Yugoslav Controversy*, 19, 29–30.

30. Interview with Mates, September 1988; Bass and Marbury, *Soviet-Yugoslav Controversy*, 28.

31. Stefan, "Emergence," 403.

32. Reams to Marshall, 29 June 1948, RG 59, no. 789, 860H.00/6-2948.

33. Reams to Marshall, 30 June 1948, RG 59, no. 799, 860H.00/6-3048.

"desperate attempt" by the Soviets to "restore strict international Communist control over the more nationalist Yugoslav Communist Party," and that only the failure of other means of subjugation had forced Moscow "to the distasteful necessity of airing publicly a Soviet-Satellite dispute." The CIA agreed that Tito had control of Yugoslavia; his policy would be to strengthen his internal position and to "extend cautious feelers to determine Western reaction if Yugoslavia should withdraw from Soviet bloc."[34] The other satellites could not readily follow Tito's example, but if Tito survived it would be harder for the Kremlin to discipline other "nationalist" factions within the bloc.[35]

It fell to Kennan and the Policy Planning Staff (PPS) he headed to formulate the administrations's response to the rift between Tito and Stalin. Despite Kennan's earlier musings, his response was a cautious one. The split between Tito and Stalin had occurred without any actions by the West and even without its knowledge. But its existence, in Kennan's words, posed an "entirely new problem": how to fashion a policy toward "a communist state resting on the basis of Soviet organization principles and for the most part on Soviet ideology, and yet independent of Moscow." Any action taken by the administration "may constitute an important precedent" for future policy, since Tito's example could cause further dislocations within the bloc. The position taken by the United States could also help determine whether any of the satellites followed Tito's example and Tito himself remained in power. If the West "is too cold toward Tito," the Soviets would use this to demonstrate that communist states had no choice but to remain within the bloc; however, a Western move to embrace Tito could undermine his position among his followers in Yugoslavia as well as arouse "strong and justifiable criticism in this country." The State Department and its personnel must therefore "observe extreme circumspection" with regard to Yugoslavia. The administration's policy would be that it "would welcome a genuine emergence of Yugoslavia as a political personality in its own right" and not allow the internal communist nature of the regime to impede the "normal development of economic relations" between Yugoslavia and the West, provided the former was "willing to adopt a loyal and cooperative attitude in its international relationships."[36]

Although this represented more of a "wait and see" response than

---

34. Hillenkoetter to Truman, 29 June 1948, ER086, Truman Papers, PSF.
35. Hillenkoetter to Truman, 30 June 1948, ER0108, Truman Papers, PSF.
36. Policy Planning Staff (PPS) 35, "The Attitude of this Government Toward Events in Yugoslavia," 30 June 1948, Truman Papers, PSF.

an explicit statement of the wedge strategy, Kennan based his policy report (PPS 35) on the assumption that a "new factor of fundamental and profound significance has been introduced into the world communist movement by the demonstration that the Kremlin can be successfully defied by one of its own minions." He was certain that the "possibility of defection" would now be on the minds of other communist leaders.[37] Kennan's paper, which by July had become National Security Council report no. 18 (NSC 18),[38] established the policy followed by the United States in the immediate aftermath of the Tito-Stalin split. With occasional modifications and increasingly explicit definitions of the disruptive value of "Titoism" and its place in the wedge strategy, the NSC 18 series also guided U.S.-Yugoslav relations for the next several years. The Truman and Eisenhower administrations proved more than willing to extend assistance to Yugoslavia and for the most part demanded no specific concessions in return. However, the need for Yugoslavia to exhibit "a loyal and cooperative attitude" remained an essential component of that aid policy. The failure of Yugoslavia to meet this expectation, coupled with U.S. resolve to cling to it often placed the wedge strategy in jeopardy.

Since Yugoslavia's defection posed such a threat to Soviet power, the United States surmised that Stalin's determination to crush Tito could involve military action. The administration therefore had, in Acheson's words, to "thwart" Stalin "without provoking him in the process." At the same time, the United States could harbor no illusions about Tito's regime; he remained "the dictator of a police state" and to portray him as ally of the West was both "bad politics and bad morals."[39] Indeed, Washington saw no ideological point of contention between Tito and Stalin. As Kennan told the National War College in October 1948, the Kremlin had not been content with Tito as a "normally loyal and . . . reasonably cooperative servant of the Politburo" but had attempted to infiltrate and more directly control the power apparatus in Yugoslavia. Tito had refused to allow that and the split had occurred.[40] That split could now be exploited to benefit the West, but the methods used had to be careful and discreet.

Other diplomats, especially those in the field like Reams, appreci-

37. Ibid.

38. NSC Meeting No. 19, 2 September 1948, Truman Papers, PSF, NSC Meetings 14–27 (1 July–23 November 1948), File: NSC Meeting No. 19, 2 September 1948.

39. Acheson, *Present at the Creation*, 332.

40. George F. Kennan, "The Soviet Internal Political System," National War College, 14 October 1948, George F. Kennan Papers, Seeley G. Mudd Manuscript Library, Princeton University, Princeton, New Jersey.

ated this need for caution but advocated a policy more aggressively supportive of Yugoslavia, one that would "make the gulf unbridgeable" between that nation and the Soviet Union. A source close to the Yugoslav leadership had warned Reams that the United States must not make the situation within Yugoslavia more difficult by public statements either in support of or opposition to the Tito regime. Yet that same individual had inquired about the prospects for increased U.S. assistance and had assured Reams of Yugoslavia's willingness to settle such divisive issues as Greece as quickly as possible.[41]

Walter Bedell Smith, the United States ambassador to the Soviet Union, also advised Washington to encourage Tito. His wartime assessment of the Yugoslavs' "arrogance, truculence and independent attitude" convinced him that the breach with the Soviets would "widen rather than narrow." Yet he expressed some doubt about how long "the rebellious child" could withstand Soviet pressure without outside assistance.[42] Others in the government shared Smith's concern. Secretary of the Army Kenneth Royall, Undersecretary of the Army William Draper, Lieutenant General Albert C. Wedemyer, and Frank G. Wisner, deputy to the assistant secretary of state for occupied areas all suggested to the State Department that Tito be assured secretly and informally that the United States was willing to assist him. W. Averell Harriman, then serving as a special representative in Europe, agreed with this course of action, fearing that if the United States did not demonstrate more interest in assisting Tito, his resolve to resist the Soviets would suffer.[43]

The Department of State, conscious of the twin perils of doing too much and too little, considered the situation in Yugoslavia "too fluid" to allow anything but continued observation.[44] The British also saw no need for a change in policy. Britain had instructed its representatives in Belgrade to be willing to listen to whatever the Yugoslavs had to say, but viewed approaches by Yugoslavia to the West with "suspicion" until Tito matched his words with deeds.[45]

Reams rejected British concerns about the validity of the breach between Yugoslavia and the Cominform. In a prescient analysis sent

41. Reams to Marshall, 2 July 1948, RG 59, no. 816, 860.00/7-248, and no. 825, 860H.00/7-248.

42. Walter Bedell Smith to Marshall, 1 and 2 July 1948, *FRUS, 1948*, 4:1082–84.

43. William H. Draper to Kenneth C. Royall, 6 July 1948, *FRUS, 1948*, 4:1085–87; Harriman to Marshall, 7 July 1948, ibid., 1088.

44. Marshall to Royall, 7 July 1948, *FRUS, 1948*, 4:1087.

45. Frederick T. Merrill, memorandum of telephone conversation, 3 July 1948, *FRUS, 1948*, 4:1084.

to the State Department on 7 July, Reams detailed the Kremlin's efforts "to impose on Tito program of self destruction." Conflict between the two states was "irrepressible" and would propel Tito toward the West. For the short term, and while the quarrel remained on the party level, Reams speculated that the Yugoslavs would reaffirm their loyalty to Marxist-Leninist principles in such settings as the forthcoming Yugoslav party congress and the Danubian Conference. The Soviets would not resort to overt action against Yugoslavia, but would rely on a "cold war" of threats and economic sanctions to force the Yugoslavs to back down. If the Soviet Union did move against Yugoslavia, the United States should respond with "quick and decisive action." Otherwise, Reams endorsed the Department's "waiting line" with one exception, urging that quiet encouragement be given to developing trade in goods without war potential.[46]

Secretary Marshall discussed the proposals made by Reams and company with the president and cabinet, but all agreed that the more cautious policy set forth by the State Department in PPS 35 should still be followed.[47] This did not imply that the United States would "repulse" Tito's suggestions for a "closer association with the West." The administration would instead handle each request "on merits" and in light of the circumstances surrounding each case. Harriman agreed with this policy, but continued to urge that a "secret approach" be made to Tito to convince him of the West's interest. Small shipments of a needed commodity such as fuel could serve as a gesture of the West's intent.[48]

As these deliberations occurred, other events again intruded on the amount of time the United States could give to an analysis of Yugoslavia; however, this time the distractions added to the importance of Tito's defection. Only a few days before the Cominform expelled Yugoslavia from its ranks, the Soviets had initiated their blockade of Berlin. Secretary Marshall, in discussing the administration's policy options with the president, characterized the Soviets as generally defensive and particularly "shaken by the Tito incident."[49] This assessment doubtless contributed to the decision by the United States and Great Britain to move a step beyond simple observation of the Tito-Stalin split, as Harriman and others recommended. By the end of July, the Truman administration had responded to Yugoslavia's "indirect"

---

46. Reams to Marshall, 7 July 1948, RG 59, no. 825, 860.00/7-248.
47. *FRUS, 1948,* 4:1087 n. 4.
48. Marshall to Smith, 21 July 1948, *FRUS, 1948,* 4:1093–94.
49. Millis, *Forrestal Diaries,* 459.

request for crude oil, and both the United States and Great Britain had provided several thousand tons, on the grounds that such "favorable responses" would indicate to Tito the West's willingness to meet additional requests. However, a "more aggressive policy" still carried too great a risk of "jeopardizing Tito's position with the Yugoslav Communist party" and compromising the United States's own past denunciations of repressive regimes such as that in Yugoslavia.[50] Truman, having just been nominated in his own right for the presidency, also would have found it difficult to justify assistance to Yugoslavia while resisting the Soviets' pressure in Berlin.

The Danubian Conference provided the first genuine test of Yugoslavia's attitude toward the Soviet Union since the split had become known. The United States, United Kingdom, Soviet Union, and France sponsored the meeting; the Ukraine, Romania, Bulgaria, Hungary, Czechoslovakia, Yugoslavia, and Austria attended, although the Soviet bloc refused to grant Austria the right to vote. The Western powers, determined to counter the Soviets' insistence on riparian control of the river with a proposal for international control and free navigation, had little hope of success with or without the Austrian vote. Before the conference opened Reams speculated that the Soviets would force Yugoslavia to take the initiative in opposing the plans of the United States and the United Kingdom, thus preventing any future understanding between Yugoslavia and the West. Yugoslavia might unwittingly assist the Soviets, since Tito, as Reams had suggested earlier, would be anxious to demonstrate his communist orthodoxy and his willingness to stand up to the West.[51]

The Soviets acted as Reams had predicted, and the Yugoslav delegation supported the Soviet Union on every vote. With its satellites and the assistance of Yugoslavia, the Soviet Union controlled seven of the conference's ten votes and used this advantage to secure an agreement calling for the control commission for the Danube to be limited to riparian states.[52] Campbell, who attended at the special request of Ambassador Cannon because of his expertise in the Balkans, consid-

50. Frank W. Wisner to Harriman, 22 July 1948, *FRUS, 1948*, 4:1095–96. Then deputy to the assistant secretary of state for occupied areas, Wisner was soon to head a new covert operations unit within the CIA—a unit that by 1949 "was fairly brimming with ideas for exploiting the Tito-Stalin split." Michael Warner, ed., *CIA Cold War Records: The CIA under Harry Truman* (Washington, D.C.: Center for the Study of Intelligence, Central Intelligence Agency, 1994), xxi–xxiii.

51. Reams to Marshall, 7 July 1948, *FRUS, 1948*, 4:623–24; Paterson, "Danube Controversy," 244–45.

52. Campbell, *United States in World Affairs, 1948–1949*, 128–32.

ered the meeting a "travesty of an international conference, in which nothing we said had any effect." Cannon, to ascertain if the disunity reflected in the Tito-Stalin split could be exploited, "tried to put the Yugoslavs on the spot, to see if there would be any way in which they would assert themselves against the Soviets."[53] His strategy produced mixed results. Although they supported the Soviet position, the Yugoslavs informed Western representatives that they regretted some of the more offensive remarks made by their delegation, and both the United States and Yugoslav delegates kept their lines of communication open.[54]

On balance though, as Ambassador Cannon told Marshall, Yugoslavia's public conduct offered only "renewed proof that they are the Soviet Union's most energetic associate." Yet Cannon judged the rift between Tito and Stalin to be genuine. The Soviets, despite Yugoslavia's support at the conference, had stated that a rapprochement depended on the "liquidation" of the present Yugoslav leadership. Cannon therefore agreed with the State Department's continuation of a "waiting line" while quietly developing trade in items without war potential, but also advised that the time would soon be "ripe" for "active and open intervention economically" by the West.[55]

In September 1948, when Yugoslavia asked to purchase oil-drilling equipment in exchange for ores and minerals, the State Department, still awaiting a "loyal and cooperative attitude," deemed the request "unattractive." The administration reasoned that Yugoslavia had not manifested any deviation from the Soviets' foreign policy line; the danger remained that equipment sent to Yugoslavia could be diverted for Soviet use. However, since the acquisition of such material might be so vital that Yugoslavia would "provide more significant concessions" of "sufficient political magnitude" to justify the exports, the United States would "leave the door open" for future requests.[56]

Reams, who considered Yugoslavia's support of Soviet policy "hardly pertinent" to the issue at hand, disagreed. It remained too early for the West to expect or demand political concessions. He argued that the Yugoslavs needed the equipment to replace that withdrawn by the Soviets; the U.S. economy would benefit from the Yugoslav ores and

53. Campbell, Oral History, Truman Library, 114–25.

54. Cannon to Marshall, 3 August 1948, *FRUS, 1948*, 4:649–50; Cannon to Marshall, 8 August 1948, ibid., 672–74.

55. Cannon to Marshall, 12 August 1948, RG 59, no. 1078, 860H.00/8-1248.

56. Marshall to Certain Diplomatic Missions, 3 September 1948, *FRUS, 1948*, 4:1105–6.

minerals. The transaction itself also would enable the United States to assist Yugoslavia in an area in which the Soviets had defaulted.[57]

Despite U.S. hesitancy, Yugoslavia continued its overtures. In an October meeting with Eric Johnson, an American motion picture industry official visiting in Yugoslavia, Tito declared that the breach with the Cominform could be healed only if the Kremlin admitted it had erred. Tito reiterated Yugoslavia's desire for Western trade, coupled with his long-standing refusal to make political concessions to obtain it. But Tito also assured Johnson that Yugoslavia would not re-export any goods it received from the United States.[58] Later that month, Cannon had a cordial session with recently appointed Foreign Minister Edvard Kardelj, a man who, as Cannon explained to the State Department, was not known for his willingness to deal with foreigners. Kardelj spoke to Cannon of Yugoslavia's desire for trade with the United States, either directly or through the ERP. The foreign minister doubted the Soviets would resort to a full blockade of Yugoslavia, but expressed his confidence in his country's ability to survive if that occurred.[59]

The lengths to which the Soviets would go to subdue Yugoslavia occupied the minds of both Yugoslav and U.S. policymakers during the summer and fall of 1948. By September, Reams advised that a Soviet attack appeared unlikely, since Yugoslavia's ability to mount a guerrilla campaign made an invasion too costly. Tito retained control inside Yugoslavia despite great economic difficulties, and Reams speculated that may have already become a source of inspiration in the bloc. Complaints by the Poles and Czechs against various aspects of Soviet policy in their respective countries and "signs of schism in principle western CPs" seemed to be caused by "contagiousness of Yugoslav experiment in independence." Reams urged the administration to discard its policy of "watchful waiting" and take more "affirmative action," such as the "quiet progressive relaxation" of export controls.[60] To Reams, the "importance of maintaining independent defiant Yugoslavia cannot be overestimated." Tito's influence on the other satellites could "well become irresistible" if he remained in power.[61]

Although Washington did not go as far as Reams intended, the administration did make an incremental but important change in its

---

57. Reams to Marshall, 14 September 1948, *FRUS, 1948,* 4:1106.
58. Reams to Lovett, 5 October 1948, *FRUS, 1948,* 4:1113.
59. Cannon to Marshall, 28 October 1948, *FRUS, 1948,* 4:1113–14.
60. Reams to Marshall, 15 September 1948, *FRUS, 1948,* 4:1106–10.
61. Reams to Marshall, 4 October 1948, *FRUS, 1948,* 4:1112–13.

policy. Lovett, in response to Reams's September request for a loosening of trade restrictions and Kardelj's October discussion with Cannon, agreed to expedite trade items, other than the oil-drilling equipment, for which export license applications had been made. The United States would also continue to consider any suggestions made by the Yugoslavs for the improvement of trade relations. Kennan concurred with these conclusions and added them to PPS 35.[62]

In December 1948, Tito publicly announced that he would divert strategic raw materials to the West in return for increased trade, and support grew among members of the U.S. press for aid to Tito.[63] Joseph Alsop, in a blistering article printed in February 1949, criticized the failure of the United States to take advantage of Tito's overtures. He chided U.S. diplomats for being "indecisive to the point of neurotic incompetence." Ambassador Cannon had done a great deal to prepare for an improved relationship by assuring the Yugoslavs that the United States did not wish to interfere in their internal affairs, but Alsop concluded, the United States must assist Tito and give him the opportunity to adopt a friendlier attitude toward the West.[64] As the Cominform blockade of Yugoslavia tightened throughout 1949, editorial writers continually emphasized that expanded trade would benefit general European recovery and might encourage the Soviets' other satellites to follow Tito's example.[65]

The American public did not support aid to Yugoslavia to the same degree as did the press. In a public opinion survey conducted in February 1949, only 47 percent of those responding were aware of the Tito-Stalin split; 51 percent of that group favored increased trade with Yugoslavia, whereas 30 percent opposed it.[66] In another survey taken in mid-1949, only 52 percent of those responding knew who Tito was; of those polled, 21 percent favored cooperation and trade, 20 percent did not favor it, and 11 percent had no opinion.[67]

Congress also held mixed views, with the suppression of religious freedom in Yugoslavia causing representatives from heavily Catholic areas to be particularly critical of the regime. In February 1949 Congressman John McCormack of Massachusetts, referring to recent discussions of Tito's quarrel with Stalin, said that the United States must view the break with "considerable suspicion." If Tito were sincere

62. Hickerson to Kennan, 26 November 1948, *FRUS, 1948*, 4:1117–18.
63. AOR, December 1948.
64. Joseph Alsop, "Tito and the West," *Washington Post*, 9 February 1949, 11.
65. AOR, 31 August 1949.
66. AOR, February 1949.
67. *Public Opinion Quarterly* 13 (Winter-Spring 1949–50): 726.

in seeking independence from Moscow, he could prove it by releasing his religious prisoners and by refusing to support the communist guerrillas in Greece.[68]

As these opinions circulated, the Truman administration gradually adopted a more explicit formulation of the wedge strategy and its applicability in Yugoslavia. In August 1948, the administration had began deliberations on NSC 20/1, "U.S. Objectives with Respect to Russia." The final document, NSC 20/4, signed by President Truman on 24 November 1948, guided United States containment policy until the adoption of NSC 68 in April of 1950. The NSC 20 series identified the threat posed by the Soviet Union as the greatest danger to U.S. security and posited ways to meet and reduce the power and influence of the Soviets. These included not only an increase in Western strength but pressures designed to effect the dissolution of Soviet control over its Eastern European satellites. As NSC 20/1 stated, the "disaffection of Tito . . . has clearly demonstrated that it is possible for stresses in the Soviet-satellites relations to lead to a real weakening and disruption of the Russian domination." Tito's defiance of the Kremlin and the Soviets' attempts to crush him had revealed the true nature of Soviet-satellite ties and "raised a great question mark as to how this system will work in the future." Methods used by the Soviets in the past to condemn "heresy," such as "police repression," "character assassination," and "excommunication," had proved ineffective against Tito, a man in control of his own instruments of power. His example could "split the whole communist movement, as nothing else was ever able to do, and cause the most grievous damage to the myth of Stalin's omniscience and omnipotence."[69]

The NSC concluded that these recent events were a significant opportunity for the United States and its allies to undermine the Soviets' control of the international communist movement. The "disaffection of Tito" and the pressures caused in the bloc by the ERP had "clearly demonstrated that it *is* possible for stresses in the Soviet-satellite relations to lead to a real weakening and disruption of Soviet

68. *Congressional Record*, 81st Cong., 1st sess., 21 February 1949, 95(1):1439.

69. Report by the NSC to the Department of State: Summary of Conclusions NSC 20/1, "U.S. Objectives with Respect to Russia," 18 August 1948, *FRUS, 1948*, 1(2):609–11; Report to the President by the NSC, 23 November 1948, with enclosure, NSC 20/4, "Report by the National Security Council on U.S. Objectives with Respect to the USSR to Counter Soviet Threats to U.S. Security," ibid., 662–69; NSC 20/1, "United States Objectives with Respect to Russia," in Thomas H. Etzold and John Lewis Gaddis, eds., *Containment: Documents on American Policy and Strategy, 1945–1950* (New York: Columbia University Press, 1978), 173–203.

domination." It was imperative that the West do all it could to increase these strains to enable the satellites "to extricate themselves from Russian control and to find, if they so wish, acceptable forms of collaboration with the governments of the West."[70]

In a November analysis of Soviet-Yugoslav relations, the CIA reinforced the idea of the damage done to "the advancement of world communism" and to Soviet control of the satellites by Tito's revolt. In an attempt to recoup, the Soviets had already begun a purge of "unreliable" elements in Eastern Europe; actions to repress the anti-Soviet feelings of the satellite peoples would probably follow. The CIA doubted, however, that the Soviets would take any immediate aggressive action against Tito because of their current preoccupation with the West. Tito's "best chance for survival" lay in avoiding clashes with the Soviets, in the hope that a compromise to the quarrel could be found. For this reason, and since Tito was a communist as well, Yugoslavia would probably continue to support Soviet foreign policy. Yet the CIA thought any accommodation between Yugoslavia and the Soviets unlikely; as the Soviets purged nationalists from Eastern Europe, the differences between Yugoslavia and the bloc would only increase. As that occurred, Tito, for his own survival, would probably modify his internal policies and seek more trade and assistance from the West. In the future, then, the breach would widen, and as it did the Kremlin's desperation and willingness to resort to military action against Tito could increase.[71] The wedge strategy had taken its place in the administration's arsenal, but at this early stage the United States had a clearer appreciation of its perils than its benefits.

As the effects of the Cominform blockade worsened, Tito did turn more and more to the West. By the spring of 1949, Yugoslavia's trade with Romania, Hungary, and Albania had all but disappeared and that with Poland had been reduced by one-half. Only trade with Czechoslovakia continued at its 1948 levels.[72] In early January 1949, Cannon reported that Yugoslavia had offered to sell copper and lead to the United States in return for export licenses for capital equipment, particularly a steel blooming mill. What had seemed "illogical and unreasonable" just a few months ago had now occurred: Soviet and bloc pressure had caused Tito to divert his trade from East to West, a development that could only aid the recovery of Western Europe.

70. Etzold and Gaddis, *Containment*, 182–83.

71. CIA, ORE 49–48, "The Trend of Soviet-Yugoslav Relations," 18 November 1948, Truman Papers, PSF, Intelligence File, CIA Reports 48-57, File: CIA Reports, ORE 1948, Nos. 48–57.

72. Calvocoressi, *Survey of International Affairs, 1949–1950*, 260.

Cannon reminded Washington, however, that Yugoslavia would make no political concessions to obtain aid; its goal was to build its own self-sufficient industrial system, dependent on neither East nor West. If the West met this need, Yugoslavia would reciprocate with ores and minerals. Nonetheless, he advised that export controls be liberalized, since trade with Yugoslavia would serve "our national interest." The State Department responded that it favored granting a license for the blooming mill, but was discussing the matter with other relevant government agencies.[73]

That discussion, which involved both commerce and defense, proved to be long and contentious. The mill, while it would not increase "the basic steel-making capacity" of the Yugoslavs, would enable them to process more steel and would thus strengthen their "steel industry as a whole." Since this enhancement could increase a country's military ability, the technology in question had the "highest security classification" in the export control program applied to Eastern Europe.[74] Could the administration take the risk of giving this technology to a country so lately viewed as one of the Soviets' most aggressive followers? Did the wedge strategy demand the risk be taken?

At the end of January, Cannon invoked that strategy on Yugoslavia's behalf once again in a forceful and well-argued cable to Acheson. The embassy's reading of the Yugoslav and Cominform press had disclosed, as Cabot and Reams had long surmised, that the Tito-Stalin dispute was not an ideological battle between parties, but a conflict involving the more profound questions of equality between states and the place of nationalism within the international communist movement. Cannon believed the "public manifestations" of this development were "momentous for the attainment of our strategic political objectives." Tito's "tight Communist dictatorship" remained firmly in control inside Yugoslavia, but could not match Soviet strength without Western assistance. The United States could lay the foundation for its long-range policy of disrupting the Soviet system by securing that aid for Yugoslavia. The Yugoslavs had begun to make public charges of Soviet "colonization" and "subordination" of Yugoslav interests to the "dictates of Soviet military planning." This served as the "best illustration" the West could have that the "primary target of US policy is not any particular economic system per se but Soviet imperialism."

But to take advantage of this, Cannon advised, the State Department would have to discard some "stultifying misconceptions." These

73. Cannon to Marshall, 10 January 1949, *FRUS, 1949*, 5:854–56.
74. Willard L. Thorp to James E. Webb, 9 June 1949, *FRUS, 1949*, 5:898–99.

included the notion that the split was a hoax "employed for some devious purpose by inscrutable Soviets"; that the policy of watchful waiting would widen the breach between the Yugoslavs and Soviets; that the West had no interest in the fate of Tito and his fellow "bloody Communists"; and that a Western-oriented replacement for Tito could be found. The last two assumptions seemed particularly foolish to Cannon. The United States had to remember that Tito represented the sole instrument available to the West "for undermining Soviet influence in East Europe." Tito's fall from power would not produce a better, but a worse regime in Yugoslavia; there was no anticommunist opposition strong enough "to supplant Tito." While the Cominform would "exploit by force any weakening in Tito's security apparatus," the West was not ready to do so "and not likely to be." There were, Cannon concluded, only two choices in Yugoslavia: "Tito or a Moscow tool."[75]

Although the other Western embassies in Belgrade believed Tito must make concessions in return for aid, Cannon did not. The Yugoslavs occupied too precarious a position to drastically change their policies; a loosening of domestic control now would simply give Stalinist agents more freedom to undermine Tito's rule. Cannon cautioned that even a settlement of the Trieste issue would weaken Yugoslavia's security by removing Allied troops from a vulnerable area. Tito also would probably make no genuine concessions regarding Greece. In general, it better served U.S. policy in Eastern Europe for Tito to remain an "orthodox but prosperous Communist," since Cominform propaganda had predicted that a ruined and bourgeois country would result from Tito's heresy. U.S. policy, in short, should strike a balance between aid to sustain Tito and restraints to illustrate the long-term dangers he faced without the West.[76]

In language that closely echoed Cannon's, the PPS recommended in February 1949 that the United States relax its export controls even though Tito's attitude toward the West "has softened only slightly." Tito had successfully defied the Kremlin, and "it is in the obvious interests of the United States that 'Titoism' continue to exist as an erosive and disintegrating force operating within the Kremlin's power sphere." Tito was "performing brilliantly in our interests" by attack-

75. Cannon to Acheson, 31 January 1949, FRUS, 1949, 5:856–59. According to Tito biographer Jasper Ridley, Cannon wrote this dispatch in angry reaction to an unsuccessful CIA attempt earlier in January to encourage an anti-Tito coup by parachuting a number of former Chetniks into Yugoslavia. Jasper Ridley, Tito: A Biography (London: Constable, 1994), 296.
76. Cannon to Acheson, 31 January 1949, FRUS, 1949, 5:859–61.

ing "Soviet imperialism" from within the system and "is perhaps our most precious asset in the struggle to contain and weaken Russian expansion." It remained essential that Tito demonstrate "on his own Communist terms that an Eastern European country can secede from Moscow control and still succeed." In the future his actions could give hope to the other satellites and could draw Yugoslavia closer to the West.[77] Or as the CIA more candidly put it, as Yugoslavia's economic situation deteriorated and Tito's dependence on the West grew, "he may be forced to modify his hitherto vigorous anti-Western foreign policy."[78]

To accomplish these goals, the PPS recommended that the United States ship Tito material that did not endanger U.S. security. The departments of State or Commerce would license the actual shipments of previously prohibited munitions and other war-related goods, with Commerce being "guided by the foreign policy considerations which will be set forth by the Secretary of State." This would all be done in a "quiet and routine" manner, lest the public perceive a "radical" policy change. If comment did occur, the government should indicate that it was receiving strategic raw materials in return for the goods sent to Yugoslavia, and that relaxation of trade restrictions did not signify approval of Tito's regime.[79]

The NSC approved these recommendations and adopted them as NSC 18/2, although not without some dissent. At the NSC meeting, Secretary of Defense James Forrestal raised the military's concerns about the degree of consultation that would occur before the licensing of specific munitions-related items for shipment. Acheson assured the secretary that consultation would be adequate, but insisted that it would not include "a review of the overall policy with respect to each item that came up." The Department of State would give the greatest discretion on these matters to Ambassador Cannon. Finally, the Council agreed to amend the document to provide for "appropriate consultation with the military on the licensing of munitions or munitions producing goods." But some doubts still remained. General Dwight D. Eisenhower, serving as a consultant to the administration, pronounced the overall report sound, but wanted it reviewed frequently, claiming Yugoslavia's defection might not turn out to be genuine, but "merely

77. PPS 49, "Economic Relations Between the United States and Yugoslavia," 10 February 1949, RG 59, Records of the Policy Planning Staff, 1947–1953.

78. CIA, ORE 16-49, "The Yugoslav Dilemma," 10 February 1949, Truman Papers, PSF, Intelligence File, CIA reports, File: ORE 16-49.

79. PPS 49, "Economic Relations Between the United States and Yugoslavia," 10 February 1949, RG 59, Records of the Policy Planning Staff, 1947–1953.

an extremely subtle trick." Acheson again assured the group that Cannon would be "continuously consulted," and the discussion closed with Forrestal expressing his great confidence in the ambassador.[80] President Truman approved NSC 18/2 on 18 February 1949.[81]

In relaying NSC 18/2 to Ambassador Cannon in Belgrade, Acheson emphasized that the United States still intended to pressure Tito to abandon his aid of the Greek guerrillas. Indeed, aid would continue only on that basis.[82] However, other demands relative to Tito's internal policies would not be pressed. When Cannon was informed, for example, of inquiries from members of Congress concerning the linkage of aid to the release of Archbishop Alojzije Stepinac,[83] he countered that both the "cause of religious freedom" in Yugoslavia and the chances of "widening Tito-Stalin break" demanded a minimizing of the Stepinac issue. If Tito agreed to this or any other concession, his own position would weaken and Catholic persecution, which had lessened, would only increase.[84] The Congress nonetheless passed a resolution condemning the imprisonment of both Stepinac and the Hungarian cleric Cardinal Mindszenty as religious persecution and a violation of the UN Charter.[85]

The actions of Congress reflected the tension in relations between the Soviets and the West. Throughout 1949, as the West constructed the North Atlantic Treaty and prepared to support the creation of a federal republic in West Germany, the Soviets waged a "peace offensive," characterized by appeals to President Truman for bilateral negotiations designed to end the Cold War. These statements, issued by the Soviets, by Western communist parties, and by communist-affiliated labor and youth groups, all cited the aggression of the United States and its allies as the basic cause of East-West tension. U.S. officials perceived this campaign, not as a genuine initiative to settle outstanding disputes, but as "a propaganda maneuver designed to confuse and disrupt western thinking."[86]

As the Soviets vilified the Marshall Plan and the NATO treaty, they

80. NSC Meeting No. 34, 17 February 1949, Truman Papers, PSF, NSC Meetings 28–37 (2 December 1948–7 April 1949), File: Memos for the President, 1949.

81. *FRUS, 1949*, 5:868–69, editorial note.

82. Acheson to Cannon, 25 February 1949, *FRUS, 1949*, 5:873–75.

83. Acheson, memorandum of conversation, 9 February 1949, Dean Acheson Papers, File: Memoranda of Conversations, January–February 1949, Truman Library.

84. Cannon to Acheson, 17 February 1949, RG 59, no. 165, 860H.00/2-1749.

85. *DSB*, 20 February 1949, 20:231.

86. Foy D. Kohler to Marshall, 15 January 1949, *FRUS, 1949*, 5:556–58; Bohlen, memorandum, 17 January 1949, ibid., 558–59.

also conducted purges of the communist leadership of the Eastern Europe satellites to root out any vestiges of Titoism. In March, border incidents between the satellites and Yugoslavia had reached a level serious enough to cause Cannon to raise the possibility of providing military assistance to Yugoslavia. By early May, the State Department concluded that the Soviets would probably not resort to military aggression against the West in 1949, but did not rule out local acts of force against Yugoslavia.[87]

Yet one bright spot existed. Cannon, in reviewing the effects of initiatives like the Marshall Plan, NATO, and the Berlin airlift, concluded that the U.S. policy of "firmness and constancy" had been "dead right" and had produced local dividends. The Yugoslavs, because of the "constant but informal pressure" of the United States, had ceased their aid to the Greek rebels. But despite such actions, he warned that Yugoslav leaders remained "unhappy about idea of permanent alienation from Soviet Union." Many, including Tito, nursed the hope that "Stalin will perceive justice" of their position and "somehow fit it into Soviet system."[88]

The United States did all it could to make an affiliation with the West more attractive by approving over $17 million dollars worth of export licenses for Yugoslavia, including those for oil-drilling rigs, lard, and gasoline. However, the administration questioned the Yugoslavs' request for over $200 million dollars in loans from the International Bank for Reconstruction and Development (IBRD), the Export-Import Bank, and various private banking institutions, because of concerns about Yugoslavia's ability to handle such a large indebtedness.[89] In a two-hour talk with Cannon in early June, Kardelj and Vice Foreign Minister Alês Bebler argued their case for the loans by detailing the strains caused in the Yugoslav economy by the split and the Cominform blockade and the resulting reorientation of their five-year plan. Kardelj also confirmed that his government was not sending matériel to the guerrillas in Greece, but refused to elaborate beyond that statement.[90] About a month later, Tito formally announced the closing of the Greek-Yugoslav frontier.[91] By the time Tito took this

87. Cannon to Acheson, 8 March 1949, *FRUS, 1949*, 5:877–79; G. Frederick Reinhardt to Kennan, 4 May 1949, ibid., 1:293.

88. Cannon to Acheson, 26 May 1949, *FRUS, 1949*, 5:894–96.

89. Current Economic Developments, No. 207, 20 June 1949, *FRUS, 1949*, 5:900–902; NSC Progress Report NSC 18/2, 27 May 1949, Truman Papers, PSF, NSC Meetings 28–37, File: NSC Meeting 34, 17 February 1949.

90. Cannon to Acheson, 9 June 1949, *FRUS, 1949*, 5:896–98.

91. Campbell, memorandum of conversation, 16 August 1949, Acheson Papers, File: Memoranda of Conversations, August 1949.

action, the rebellion in Greece was a lost cause;[92] however, Dedijer later wrote that his government closed the frontier, as Tito had publicly stated, not because of pressure from the West but because of the Greek communists' support for the Cominform sanctions against Yugoslavia.[93] Reams had advanced that theory some weeks before Tito's announcement: the Greek rebels supported the Cominform and the Yugoslavs had too many needs of their own to send goods to a group "whose success would only mean completion of Moscow curtain around them."[94]

As if on cue, Tito's decision concerning Greece coincided with the administration's verdict on his request for a license to purchase a steel blooming mill. Because the mill fell under the highest security classification relating to goods linked to Yugoslavia's war-making potential, Tito's government viewed it as the most important test of the administration's new policy. By June, the State Department recommended approval of the license as consistent with the policy adopted in February in NSC 18/2, and as the kind of aid that might encourage the satellites to assert their independence. The Commerce Department, under Charles Sawyer, also favored approval of the request, but the National Military Establishment (NME) strongly objected on the grounds that the mill would increase Yugoslavia's economic potential and create a military hazard.[95] After reviewing the objections of the NME, the Commerce Department informed State on 22 June that the license would be granted. The State Department then informed Yugoslavia that its application had been accepted. Despite these actions, both the NME and Secretary of Defense Louis Johnson continued to insist that the government's decision be reversed.[96]

The resulting conflict, which revealed a great deal of the philosophy behind the administration's decision to assist Yugoslavia, was one of several between Acheson and Johnson during Johnson's brief tenure. Johnson, a former national officer of the American Legion, had served as assistant secretary of war from 1937 to 1940. He had been widely praised for his efforts on behalf of preparedness but Roosevelt had not appointed him to the department's top position when the vacancy arose in 1940. Johnson returned to private life until 1948, when he directed Harry Truman's presidential fundraising campaign. Truman, who "despised" Johnson, appointed him to head the Department of

92. Pavlowitch, *Yugoslavia*, 221.
93. Dedijer, *Battle*, 270; Pavlowitch, *Yugoslavia*, 219.
94. Reams to Acheson, 24 June 1949, *FRUS*, *1949*, 5:903–4.
95. Thorp to Webb, 9 June 1949, *FRUS*, *1949*, 5:898–99.
96. Thorp memorandum, 8 July 1949, *FRUS*, *1949*, 5:905–7.

Defense in 1949 only after one of his advisers had promised Johnson the post. Within a few months Johnson instituted a controversial austerity program, marked by efforts to impose a budget ceiling of $13.5 billion on Defense. Press speculation that he hoped to be the Democratic Party's presidential nominee in 1952 further complicated his public image.[97] Johnson's opposition to Acheson's Yugoslav policy put him in rare agreement with his critics in the military and may have been geared toward improving his deteriorating relationship with his former supporters in the American Legion, who had consistently opposed aid to Yugoslavia.

Johnson argued his case in a meeting with Acheson on 21 July. In disagreeing with Acheson, Johnson challenged not only the steel mill decision but the rationale behind the policy adopted in the NSC 18 series on the grounds that the military risks involved in assisting Yugoslavia far outweighed any foreign policy considerations. Johnson protested that the Commerce Department had decided to grant the license despite NME objections and his own misgivings. He also insisted that the JCS opposed the shipment to Iron Curtain countries of goods that would increase their military and economic strength. The secretary hoped that this matter could be resolved without involving the president, but if the issue did go to Truman, Johnson told Acheson and Sawyer that he would be compelled to inform the president that approval of Yugoslavia's request "would set loose such a wave of public indignation as to seriously threaten the ability of the present administration to win the 1950 elections."

Acheson countered that the question of assistance to Yugoslavia must be analyzed on a "factual and unemotional" basis and stressed the gains the United States would accrue from the steel mill deal. Tito's five-year plan had to succeed if he were to win his struggle with Stalin, and the United States had to assist Tito in the fight. The Yugoslavs themselves considered the steel mill agreement to be symbolic of the West's willingness to help them. Moreover, Acheson noted that two satellites regimes had been denied licenses for similar mills and that the approval of Yugoslavia's request would indicate the benefits that a state "not under Kremlin orders" could receive from the West. Acheson also challenged Johnson's assertion that the mill increased Yugoslavia's and the Soviet Union's war-making potential.

97. Warner R. Snilling, Paul Y. Hammond, and Glenn H. Snyder, *Strategy, Politics, and Defense Budgets* (New York: Columbia University Press, 1962), 293; "Johnson or Truman in 52," *U.S. News and World Report*, October 1949, 27; James A. Bell, "Defense Secretary Louis Johnson," *American Mercury*, June 1950, 643–53; Warner, *The CIA under Harry Truman*, xxiii.

Johnson stuck to his position, however, and both he and Acheson
agreed to state their views in writing and to bring the matter to the
president if it could not be resolved.[98]

In his written statement, Johnson questioned the meaning of the
NSC's February recommendation. He interpreted the document to
require that when licensing disputes arose, the secretary of commerce
would be guided by the foreign policy considerations outlined by the
State Department and by other national interests outlined by Defense.
In this case, it was the opinion of the NME that national security
prohibited the shipment of goods of "high war potential" to a nation
still in the Soviet "shadow." Johnson therefore recommended that the
NSC decision be reevaluated and that the secretaries of defense,
commerce, and state confer before licenses were granted.[99]

Ambassador Cannon, informed of this dispute by Acheson, repudiated Johnson's objections by declaring that doubt about Tito's break
with Stalin "cannot seriously be held." The blooming mill was not
designed for arms production but for peacetime steel requirements.
Yugoslavia's entire steel industry was "far below modern standards";
data indicating this had already been furnished to Washington. The
Yugoslavs viewed the license application as a "test of our intentions";
the administration simply could not back out at this stage.[100]

Acheson also rebutted Johnson's claims by reiterating the argument
that aid to Tito served the national interests of the United States.
Failure to aid him and to achieve the anticipated policy objectives
would seriously affect Western security. The West had already profited
from Tito's announced closing of the Greek-Yugoslav frontier. Acheson
had no illusions about Tito's regime, but he believed "the maintenance
of the Tito-Kremlin split to be an important objective" of current U.S.
policy. He agreed to Johnson's request that the NSC decision be
reevaluated, but he doubted any change in policy would occur.[101]

On 8 August Sawyer, Acheson, and Johnson met to resolve their
differences on the steel mill issue. Johnson finally acquiesced in the
decision to grant the licenses, provided the government reviewed the
matter in a year, before the material was actually shipped. Johnson
claimed at the meeting that he had not realized such a review was
possible, even though Acheson pointed out that he had made that clear
in their earlier correspondence. Johnson, however, continued to take

98. E. M. Martin, memorandum of conversation, 21 July 1949, Acheson Papers,
File: Memoranda of Conversations, July 1949.
99. Louis Johnson to Acheson, 28 July 1949, FRUS, 1949, 5:911–14.
100. Cannon to Acheson, 29 July 1949, FRUS, 1949, 5:914–15.
101. Acheson to Johnson, 4 August 1949, FRUS, 1949, 5:915–20.

issue with the belief of Acheson and Sawyer that the NSC's recommendations mandated that foreign policy considerations were to prevail in any licensing questions, offering, in Sawyer's words, "to fight to the death, privately or publicly" on that issue. Sawyer replied that such a conflict was not necessary; an NSC meeting on the interpretation of NSC 18/2 could decide the issue. The three finally agreed to consult on "important cases before any action by Commerce," thus sidestepping the issue of the letter of the NSC document. They then decided that the licensing decision should stand, but that "knowledge about the blooming mill should be held as closely as possible." The breach between Tito and Stalin would be reviewed before the mill was shipped to Yugoslavia.[102]

By the end of August, the CIA had intercepted a report from Kardelj to Tito that confirmed U.S. speculation that Yugoslavia was serious in its negotiations with the United States and anxious to improve U.S.-Yugoslav relations.[103] Although the decision regarding the mill had already been made, such information probably made the administration more comfortable with its decision. In September, the United States and Yugoslavia formally announced the licensing of the steel mill; that same month the Export-Import Bank granted Yugoslavia's request, first made in May and renewed in August, for a $20 million credit. The International Monetary Fund also approved a $3 million drawing for Tito's government. Although the United States agreed to the acquisition of loans, credits, and markets without strings attached, the issue of political concessions and the direction of the Yugoslav economy remained close to the surface of any aid discussion. In a meeting with Bebler in mid-September for example, Cannon pointed out that loans and credits would require congressional and public support, coupled with more scrutiny of Yugoslavia's internal and foreign policies.[104] Yugoslavia would, in Kennan's words, have to demonstrate a "loyal and cooperative attitude" to secure continued assistance.

102. Acheson to Webb, 8 August 1949, FRUS, 1949, 5:920–21; Charles S. Sawyer, "Account of Meeting with Acheson/Johnson in Acheson's Office," 8 August 1949, Charles S. Sawyer Papers, File: Yugoslavia—Proposed Blooming Mill for, Truman Library.

103. Trevor Barnes, "The Secret Cold War: The C.I.A. and American Foreign Policy in Europe, 1946–1956, Part II," Historical Journal 25.3 (1982): 651.

104. Yugoslavia was not unaware of its need to alter its internal economic policies. When the Yugoslavs renewed their request for credits in August, they coupled the request with the final dissolution of the joint transport companies created with the USSR in 1946. Lampe, Prickett, and Adamović, Economic Relations, 31; Cannon to Acheson, 14 September 1949, FRUS, 1949, 5:954–55.

The Truman administration gave little publicity to its new relationship with Yugoslavia. Discretion, the hallmark of the policy first proposed in PPS 35, remained the better part of valor for an administration less and less able to count on congressional support for its foreign policy. Although the Democrats had a majority in both houses of Congress after the president's election victory in 1948, Republican isolationists, who objected to increasing expenditures for initiatives like NATO, and conservatives who decried Truman's lack of support for the Nationalists in China, made life difficult for the administration.[105] In August, when Acheson was arguing the case for Yugoslav aid with Louis Johnson, he was also releasing the "China White Paper," in a vain attempt to convince Congress of the merits of the administration's China policy. As James Riddleberger, U.S. ambassador to Yugoslavia under Eisenhower later recalled, in the Cold War atmosphere then prevailing, the decision to assist Tito was "one of the most courageous decisions that Truman had taken."[106]

Fortunately, the aid package encountered little serious opposition. Indications that the government intended to assist Tito had been appearing in American newspapers and magazines since March 1949. Most comment on the steel mill deal itself was favorable, with many columnists congratulating the State Department for its success in convincing opponents of the policy that the risk was well worth taking.[107] The *Saturday Evening Post* and *Commonweal* criticized the government's decision, but most other periodicals and daily newspapers approved it.[108]

In any case, the United States based its decision to assist Tito on foreign policy considerations; domestic events had little influence. The government acted because several members of the administration, most notably Kennan, Acheson, and their colleagues in the State Department, understood that Tito's defection from the communist bloc had political and military significance for the West. The U.S. objective in Eastern Europe continued to be the reduction and eventual elimination of Soviet influence, and this could be achieved in part through the

105. Robert A. Divine, *Since 1945: Politics and Diplomacy in Recent American History* (New York: John Wiley & Sons, 1975), 25–27.

106. James R. Riddleberger, Oral History, Oral History Collection, Seeley G. Mudd Manuscript Library, Princeton University, Princeton, New Jersey, 105 (hereafter cited as Riddleberger, Oral History, Princeton, with page number).

107. AOR, August 1949.

108. Editorial, "Yugoslavia Is a Good Place to Let the Dust Settle," *Saturday Evening Post*, 10 September 1949, 12; editorial, "Loan to Yugoslavia," *Commonweal*, 23 September 1949, 573.

encouragement of non-Stalinist regimes, such as Tito's Yugoslavia.[109] The Soviets would do all they could to prevent other Titos from emerging, but Titoism bespoke a "profound weakness" in the Soviet system of empire that the West could and must exploit.[110]

The NSC reviewed and further codified its wedge strategy in NSC 58/2, which Truman approved in December. In this study the Council acknowledged that Soviet control, to date, had been challenged only in Yugoslavia, as the result of a dispute between Tito and Stalin rather than as the outcome of U.S. policy. Tito had been able to withstand Soviet pressure because of his complete control of Yugoslavia's party and government apparatus and because of public support. He had turned to the West not as a true ally but out of "crafty self-interest." While such a situation was not "congenial" to the United States, it was at least "far less inimical" than a Yugoslavia tied to the Kremlin.

The satellite states of Eastern Europe were not in a position to duplicate Tito's action; nor could the United States reasonably expect those countries to create democratic governments. Yet the NSC believed the United States could design policies to promote "schismatic Communist regimes" that would displace the present Stalinist governments. The administration should therefore attempt "to foster a heretical drifting-away process on the part of the satellite states." Two communist groups might then emerge—one Stalinist, the other "a non-conformist faction, either loosely allied or federated under Tito's leadership." While pursuing this policy of division, the United States always had to consider what effect such actions would have on the Soviet Union and act accordingly, but the strategy must be implemented.[111]

Unanswered was the question of what lengths the United States and its allies would go to in order to protect Yugoslavia. Cannon had raised the possibility of Western military assistance for Yugoslavia in the spring; in June, the CIA had speculated that the United States might have to furnish enough military assistance to Yugoslavia to insure its "self-protection." Two months later, Alan G. Kirk, who had replaced Walter Bedell Smith as U.S. ambassador to the Soviet Union,

109. PPS 59, "U.S. Policy Toward the Soviet Satellite States in Eastern Europe," 25 August 1949, *FRUS, 1949*, 5:21–26.
110. Cannon to Acheson, 25 April 1949, *FRUS, 1949*, 5:886–89; William Leonhardt, "Origins of Titoism and Prerequisites for its Recurrence," 25 April 1949, RG 59, no. 162, FW860H.00/4-2549; Kohler to Acheson, 20 May 1949, RG 59, A-517, 860H.00/5-2049.
111. NSC 58/2, "United States Policy Toward the Soviet Satellites in Eastern Europe," 8 December 1949, RG 319, Records of the Army Staff, National Archives.

advised that the time may have come for the United States and Britain to consider the military "aspect of keeping Tito afloat."[112]

Additional satellite troop movements on the Yugoslav border that same month renewed discussion in the West of a possible Soviet or satellite attack on Yugoslavia. The U.S. Embassy in Belgrade speculated that the Soviets might only be seeking to cause turmoil within Yugoslavia, in order to undermine that country's potential for gaining loans in the West.[113] At his news conference on 31 August, Acheson, in response to a reporter's question, characterized the troop movements on the border as another act in the war of nerves being waged by the Soviets, but stated that Yugoslavia had not forwarded any arms requests to the United States.[114]

By the end of August the CIA ruled a Soviet attack on Yugoslavia "doubtful" unless the Kremlin was prepared to risk a general war and a protracted struggle within Yugoslavia.[115] The British, however, thought an attack on Yugoslavia more likely and for the next several weeks discussed with the United States the possibility of bringing the Soviet-Yugoslav dispute before the United Nations, both to deter the Soviets and to discredit their peace offensive.[116] Acheson thought it unwise for anyone but Yugoslavia to invoke the United Nations, although recourse to that body in case of Soviet aggression would be "logical and necessary." Both the British and the Yugoslavs, whom the two powers had consulted, agreed with this assessment.[117]

Kennan and the PPS weighed in as well, but on different sides. Kennan believed that a Soviet attack on Yugoslavia would discredit the Soviets around the world by disclosing the true nature of their system. Others would then attempt to defect from the Kremlin orbit. Kennan's colleagues on the PPS dissented, claiming a Soviet move against Yugoslavia would simply show the "hopelessness" of challenging Soviet power. In any case, the PPS as a whole agreed that if a

112. CIA, ORE 44-49, "Estimate of the Yugoslav Regime's Ability to Resist Soviet Pressure During 1949," 20 June 1949, Truman Papers, PSF, Intelligence File; Kirk to Acheson, 13 August 1949, *FRUS, 1949*, 5:922–24.

113. Summary, 25 August 1949, Truman Papers, Naval Aide Files/State Department File: State Department Briefs, May–August 1949.

114. Memorandum of the Secretary of State's Press and Radio News Conferences, 24 August 1949, *FRUS, 1949*, 5:932.

115. CIA, Intelligence Memorandum no. 216, 29 August 1949, Truman Papers, NSC Records–CIA File, File: NSC/CIA (5-11) Intelligence Memoranda, December 1948–December 1949.

116. Lewis F. Douglas to Acheson, 26 August 1949, *FRUS, 1949*, 5:933–34.

117. Acheson to Embassy in United Kingdom (Holmes), 29 August 1949, *FRUS, 1949*, 5:937–40.

Soviet and/or satellite attack on Yugoslavia occurred, the United States would consider it an "open violation" of the United Nations charter and support "appropriate" Security Council action. If the conflict lasted for some time, the United States would "permit Yugoslavia to purchase arms in the U.S. and be prepared to furnish arms directly to Tito if political and military conditions seem to warrant." If no attack occurred, but the present Cominform pressure against Yugoslavia increased, coupled with attempts to assassinate Tito or incite an internal rebellion against him, the United States would allow Tito to secure arms if he requested them, while keeping the situation under constant review.[118]

In late September, the Soviets formally canceled the treaty of cooperation and mutual assistance they had signed with Yugoslavia in April of 1945. The satellites then abrogated their various friendship treaties with Tito. A more ominous development involved the growth in Soviet forces stationed near Yugoslavia; an increase the CIA believed to be from five to as many as nine divisions. Although the agency calculated that the Soviets would need at least fifteen divisions to "subdue" Tito, his liquidation clearly remained "a primary objective" of Soviet policy.[119]

Yugoslavia took steps on its own to surmount its vulnerability by seeking a seat on the United Nations Security Council in October. The election for the Eastern European seat involved a conflict with the Soviets, who claimed the right to it for a member of the bloc.[120] With its wedge strategy in mind, the United States supported Yugoslavia, a state certain to take a more independent line in the world body than Czechoslovakia, the Soviet candidate. A choice for Yugoslavia also signaled U.S. support for a small nation in the face of great-power intimidation.[121] Nevertheless, the United States and its allies avoided a campaign on Yugoslavia's behalf lest the Soviets use that to their own propaganda advantage.[122]

United Nations Secretary General Trgyve Lie opposed Yugoslavia's

118. Record of the Under Secretary's Staff Meeting, 16 September 1949, *FRUS, 1949*, 5:959–61; PPS 60, "Yugoslav-Moscow Controversy as Related to U.S. Foreign Policy Objectives," 12 September 1949, ibid., 947–54.

119. CIA Intelligence Memorandum no. 232, 5 October 1949, Truman Papers, NSC Records–CIA File, File: CIA Intelligence Memo 232.

120. Webb to Austin, 6 October 1949, *FRUS, 1949*, 2:260–61; Austin to Acheson, 19 October 1949, ibid., 275–78.

121. John C. Ross, memorandum of conversation, 3 October 1949, *FRUS, 1949*, 2:259–60.

122. Webb to Austin, 21 September 1949, *FRUS, 1949*, 2:245–46.

election, since, as he told U.S. delegate Eleanor Roosevelt, it represented a "direct affront to Stalin." When Mrs. Roosevelt related this
information to Secretary Acheson, he agreed that Yugoslavia's candidacy presented problems. He wished that the Yugoslavs had not put
themselves forward, but since they had, they were preferable to the
Soviets' choice.[123] The Yugoslavs won election to the Security Council
seat in early October, and the Soviets did not withdraw from the
United Nations in retaliation as Lie had feared.[124] When Soviet Deputy Foreign Minister Andrey Vyshinsky had insisted on speaking
against Yugoslavia's candidacy, United Nations General Assembly
President Carlos P. Romulo had ordered the sound system turned off,
and Vyshinsky had simply taken his seat.[125] The CIA saw great
benefits in all of this: Yugoslavia's election had taken the Tito-Stalin
split "into the international arena" and given "worldwide significance"
to Yugoslavia's role as a communist state independent of the Soviet
Union. Yugoslavia's new position was bound to enhance prospects for
the growth of Titoism, while reducing Moscow's ability to control
the international communist movement and to engage in acts of
aggression.[126]

The question of Yugoslavia's place in U.S. foreign policy occupied
the minds of diplomats in the field as well as those in Washington. The
chiefs of U.S. missions in Eastern Europe, meeting in London in
October 1949, agreed that Tito should be assisted, but that economic
pressure be maintained elsewhere in the bloc. U.S. economic restrictions had reduced the industrial expansion and output of Eastern
Europe, forcing the satellites to turn to the Soviet Union, which
remained unable to meet their industrial demands. Such refusals
served the wedge strategy by increasing the strains already extant
between the Soviet Union and the bloc.[127] The U.S. ambassadors to
the Western capitals, meeting at the same time in Paris, also believed
that the West should keep Tito "afloat." James C. Dunn, the ambassa-

123. Minutes of the Eleventh Meeting of the United States Delegation, 30 September
1949, *FRUS, 1949,* 2:256–57.
124. Thomas F. Power Jr., memorandum of conversation, 20 October 1949, *FRUS,
1949,* 2:280–81.
125. Cabinet Meeting, 21 October 1949, Matthew J. Connelly Papers, File: Notes on
Cabinet, 3 January–30 December 1949, Truman Library.
126. CIA, Intelligence Memorandum no. 242, 17 October 1949, Truman Papers,
NSC Records–CIA File, File: NSC/CIA (5–11), Intelligence Memoranda, December
1948–December 1949.
127. Conclusions and Recommendations of the London Conference of October 24–26
of the United States Chiefs of Mission to the Satellite States, undated, *FRUS, 1949,*
5:28–31.

dor to Italy, cautioned, however, that the Italians were skeptical and anxious, fearing the policy would have an adverse effect on Italian interests.[128]

In a new installment of the NSC 18 series, dated 17 November and numbered NSC 18/4, the Council claimed that Tito's break with Stalin in and of itself had improved the security of the West. The failure of Tito to maintain Yugoslavia's independence would cause "a renewal and intensification of threats to the security of Greece and Italy and a serious political reverse for the United States and the Western European nations." The inhibitions that Yugoslavia's defection had placed on Soviet aggression would cease; Greece would probably fall to communist pressure; and the expansionism of the Soviet Union would experience "increased momentum." A defeated Yugoslavia would thus represent not merely a return to Europe's pre-1948 status quo but a reversal of two years of Western gains.

The NSC was certain that Tito could withstand Soviet pressure, even pressure that involved guerrilla attacks from neighboring states, but needed economic and military aid from the West to do so effectively. The Yugoslavs' "determination to resist such aggression" would be strengthened by "assurances from the United States that military supplies would be obtainable." In addition, Yugoslavia's "increasing dependence" on the West would enhance chances for a Trieste settlement and a general accommodation with Greece and Turkey. In case of a long struggle "the United States and the West would have greater opportunities, by helping him maintain Yugoslavia's independence, of drawing Yugoslavia closer to the West."[129] The CIA was certain that political considerations would not deter Tito from requesting U.S. arms; after accepting economic assistance, Tito would see the move to military aid as "minor." Indeed, the CIA noted, the Yugoslav government had already approached the United States informally for military assistance.[130]

Ironically, the continued presence of U.S. and British forces in Trieste, perceived as a burden before June 1948, became an asset as the Soviet threat to Yugoslavia increased. Because of Cold War ten-

128. Summary Record of a Meeting of United States Ambassadors, Paris, 21–22 October 1949, *FRUS, 1949*, 4:473–94.

129. Report by the NSC to the President, 17 November 1949, NSC 18/4, "United States Policy Toward the Conflict Between the USSR and Yugoslavia," *FRUS, 1950*, 4:1341–48.

130. CIA, Intelligence Memorandum no. 255, 9 December 1949, Truman Papers, NSC Records–CIA File, File: NSC/CIA (5-11) Intelligence Memoranda, December 1948–December 1949.

sions, the United States, Britain, and the Soviet Union had not been able to agree on a governor for the Free Territory of Trieste. As a consequence, the settlement outlined in the Italian peace treaty of 1947 had never been implemented and British and U.S. military forces remained in Zone A. By early 1948, both the United States and Great Britain had rejected the FTT concept, fearing that it would simply open the door for Yugoslav penetration of the area. In addition, concerns about the political situation in Italy, centering on fears that the Italian left would gain strength in the elections scheduled for April 1948, prompted the Western allies to seek some other solution to the Julian Region dispute. To bolster the chances of the Western-oriented factions in Italy, the United States, Britain, and France announced in March 1948 that they were abandoning the earlier agreement and now favored returning the whole FTT, rather than just Zone A, to the Italians. Yugoslavia immediately protested the decision; the Soviets did as well, but on milder terms than the Yugoslavs. After the Christian Democrats won a majority in the Italian elections, the Western powers invited the Soviets to a conference to revise the FTT proposal. The USSR refused, and there the matter rested.[131]

By the end of 1949, with Yugoslavia at odds with the Soviets, the Western powers quietly moved away from their Tripartite Declaration to suggest that the Italians and Yugoslavs directly negotiate a settlement, based on a simple division of the region along the current Zone A and Zone B lines. All parties but Italy agreed; the Italian refusal caused Yugoslavia to demand territory in Zone A, and the dispute dragged on.[132] But a Western military presence near a Yugoslavia now threatened by the Soviets continued as well.

The constant specter of Soviet aggression against Yugoslavia also caused the Truman administration to finally take one of the actions that Reams had urged since the summer of 1948. In December, the new U.S. ambassador to Yugoslavia, George V. Allen, told the press that in his pre-departure talk with the president, Truman had reaffirmed U.S. opposition to aggression and support of the principle of sovereignty of nations. "As regards Yugoslavia," Allen said, "we are just as opposed to aggression against that country as against any other, and just as favorable to the retention of Yugoslav sovereignty."[133] Although John Campbell recalled that Allen's comment had not been "carefully drafted" in the State Department, Truman

131. Rabel, *Between East and West*, 102–18.
132. Ibid., 125–31.
133. "Truman Reaffirms Aim on Aggression," *New York Times*, 23 December 1949, 6.

confirmed the intent of his ambassador's remarks in a press conference that same day. When asked about Allen's statement, Truman replied that the United States was opposed to aggression against any country, "no matter where situated." In response to a question about whether this represented a change in policy toward Yugoslavia, Truman responded: "Not at all, not at all. That has always been our policy."[134]

In the 1990s, Stalin biographer Robert Conquest wrote that Stalin's quarrel with Tito "shows Stalin at his most incompetent."[135] While that word would not have been applied to the Soviet dictator by many in the Truman administration, U.S. policymakers did see the quarrel as ripe with possibilities. The break between Tito and Stalin, neither anticipated nor caused by the United States, gave the Truman administration its first opportunity to penetrate the Soviet bloc. By 1949, the United States had extended economic aid to Tito and had even discussed the possibility of dispatching military assistance to this still communist but now outcast regime. The administration acted because Tito's defection represented a decrease in Soviet power and a corresponding gain for the West. Events in Yugoslavia also gave substance to the hope that communist states would eventually resist domination by the Soviets and could be pried away from the bloc by Western aid. It remained to be seen, however, whether Yugoslavia shared and would assist in the achievement of that goal.

134. Campbell, *Tito's Separate Road,* 17; *Papers of the Presidents,* Truman, 1949, 585.
135. Conquest, *Breaker of Nations,* 288.

CHAPTER THREE

1950–1952
A QUESTION OF MILITARY TIES

By 1950, the United States and Yugoslavia had embarked on a new but uncertain relationship. The United States, presented with the gift of a Tito-Stalin split, had formulated an explicit wedge strategy, with Yugoslavia at its European center. Yugoslavia, because of Tito's willingness to resist Stalin and to adopt a less belligerent posture toward the West, had secured the economic aid and international support it needed to withstand the pressure exerted by the Cominform. The possibility of Soviet retaliation also had prompted the United States and its allies to discuss providing military assistance to Yugoslavia if the Soviets or their satellites should attack; however, the United States did not know how much of a role Tito would be willing to play in a wider European war or in the Western defense system. These issues, aggravated by the outbreak of war in Korea, brought the military implications of the wedge strategy to center stage during the last years of the Truman administration.

As Ambassador Allen assumed his post in Belgrade, the United States continued to view Tito's heresy as a "major problem" for the USSR and an advantage for the West. In reviewing the relative positions of free and communist states after the turbulent events of 1949, which included the "loss" of China, State Department Counselor Kennan concluded that Tito's defiance "has roughly offset communist successes in China." Efforts by the communist bloc to unseat Tito had so far been unsuccessful, but the Truman administration estimated that by the spring of 1950, the Soviets would have to decide whether to move against Tito militarily or continue to allow him "to disrupt unity and discipline of communist world."[1]

U.S. observers also perceived a "mounting militancy" and a new "boldness" in Soviet actions, making an attack on Yugoslavia appear even more likely. Paul Nitze and the PPS he now headed believed that this behavior originated from the Soviets' eagerness to exploit the opportunities afforded by their success in China and apprehension that the Chinese might copy Tito's example. Tito's deviation had been "a severe reverse" for the Kremlin; similar behavior by the Chinese "would threaten the structure of the Soviet imperialist system." In general though the Kremlin appeared confident; it had, after all, acquired the bomb and did control Eastern Europe. The USSR's own progress in reconstruction and constant hope that the West would face a debilitating economic crisis increased their optimism. The PPS predicted that the Soviets, carefully weighing opportunities and deterrents, would seek to consolidate and protect their gains, while looking for "soft spots" to exploit.[2]

The Yugoslavs, hoping to have company in their quarrel with Stalin but aware of the consequences, held a more alarmist view of Soviet intentions. They feared that the USSR, to counter the certain growth of Titoism in China, would seek a "compensating victory" in Western Europe or the Balkans. The U.S. Embassy in Belgrade advised Washington that the Yugoslavs based this prediction partly on their belief that "Sino-Soviet difficulties are increasing and partly on wishful thinking."[3]

U.S. policymakers, willing to use Tito but conscious of the contradictions inherent in such a match, resolved to exploit fully "the advantages presented to them by Tito's quarrel with the Kremlin in encouraging all signs of Titoism in the Soviet satellites," while keeping in mind "that the majority of the people in those countries oppose all varieties of Communism."[4] Yet the administration did not plan to

1. Kennan to Acheson, 6 January 1950, *FRUS, 1950*, 1:127–38.

2. Study Prepared by the Director of the PPS (Paul Nitze), 8 February 1950, *FRUS, 1950*, 1:145–47.

3. Summary, 13 February 1950, Truman Papers, Naval Aide Files/State Department Briefs, File: State Department—Summary of Telegrams, January–April 1940.

4. Paper Prepared in the Office of Eastern European Affairs, undated, *FRUS, 1950*, 4:14–17.

demand political concessions from Yugoslavia in return for aid. This was not, as Acheson said, for "sentimental reasons but simply because it is in the interests of US, as of Yugoslavia, that the latter continue to maintain its independence."[5]

The United States had "legitimate interests," however, in certain aspects of Yugoslav foreign policy,[6] which were often indistinguishable from demands. In February 1950, for example, Acheson informed the Yugoslav government that its possible recognition of Ho Chi Minh and the government of North Vietnam, which was engaged in guerrilla warfare with France, would have a "provocative and disruptive effect" in the United States and might negate the "extraordinary steps" the administration was taking "to find funds with which to support Yugoslav independence."[7]

Tito reacted angrily to what he perceived as a U.S. attempt to control him. He not only recognized Ho's regime, but publicly reaffirmed his country's determination to join no bloc and to tolerate no interference in its internal affairs. Yugoslavia's foreign policy was inseparable from its "socialist principles," Tito declared. His people "should prefer to go naked" rather than make concessions in return for aid. During the Cominform dispute, Tito reminded his listeners, Yugoslavia "did not bow to the Soviets; . . . how could we then, bow to the West."[8] Ambassador Allen, demonstrating a clear grasp of the wedge strategy's most essential tenet, saw no reason to quarrel with Tito's attitude, since Yugoslavia's value to the West was "as a Communist state independent of both East and West."[9] The continuation of this independence remained "essential to our immediate purpose of promoting disharmony in the ranks of world communism and thus weakening Kremlin's aggressive power."[10]

Despite these tensions, the United States supported Yugoslavia's continued request for loans and credits. When the Export-Import Bank required a letter confirming that aid for Yugoslavia constituted part of the United States's national security policy, Acheson quickly complied, optimistically adding that with such a grant Yugoslavia would

5. Acheson, memorandum of conversation, 19 June 1950, *FRUS, 1950,* 4:1421–23.

6. Webb to Embassy in Yugoslavia, 15 May 1950, *FRUS, 1950,* 4:1416–17.

7. Acheson to Allen, 7 February 1950, *FRUS, 1950,* 4:1365–66.

8. Allen to Acheson, 19 February 1950, *FRUS, 1950,* 4:1370–71; M. S. Handler, "Tito Warns West Against Pressure," *New York Times,* 19 February 1950, 1.

9. Allen to Acheson, 19 February 1950, RG 84, no. 215, and 20 February 1950, RG 84, no. 216, 350 Yugoslavia, Post Files, Washington National Records Center, Suitland, Md.

10. Allen to Acheson, 20 April 1950, *FRUS, 1950,* 4:1404–7.

be able to "pay its own way during 1951 and after."[11] The bank acted just as rapidly, approving a $20 million credit for cotton and other raw materials within two weeks. Acheson briefly delayed the announcement of the bank's move, however, to ensure that it would not follow on the heels of Tito's recognition of North Vietnam. As he explained to the U.S. Embassy in France, Tito "is a Communist and must be expected to act like a Communist and periodically to demonstrate in some objectionable fashion his independence of the West." Such actions, the secretary declared, should not deter the United States from its basic policy of assisting the regime in its defiance of Moscow.[12]

Outside assistance became even more crucial for Yugoslavia by the summer and fall of 1950, as the results of a devastating food shortage became apparent. The food crisis, precipitated by a severe drought, was exacerbated by Tito's collectivization and forced delivery policies, imposed on the Yugoslav people to demonstrate the regime's communist orthodoxy despite its clash with Stalin.[13] Because of the political instability the food crisis could cause, the administration's fears of Soviet aggression against Yugoslavia deepened. Tito had not formally requested military assistance from the United States but by May the Truman administration, acting in accordance with NSC 18/4, had completed an assessment of Yugoslavia's military needs and the United States's ability to meet those needs. The administration discussed military aid for Yugoslavia with the British and French, but all agreed that the extension of assistance had to await "specific Yugoslav requests."[14]

In June, Acheson authorized the service attachés in Belgrade to increase their contacts with Yugoslav military authorities, while cautioning them not to engage in any "advance planning for material assistance" to Yugoslavia. Acheson also advised Allen that the State Department did not intend to inform the Yugoslavs of any deliberations taking place on their behalf; nor would the United States provide

11. Acheson to Herbert E. Gaston, 21 February 1950, *FRUS, 1950,* 4:1372–73.

12. Gustavus Tuckerman, memorandum of conversation, 7 March 1950, RG 59, 768.5/3-750. According to John Lampe, the State Department favored cotton credits because cotton was part of the U.S. agricultural surplus and because the commodity was both cheap and of minor strategic significance. Lampe, Prickett, and Adamović, *Economic Relations*, 31; Acheson to David K. E. Bruce, 22 February 1950, *FRUS, 1950,* 4:1373–74.

13. Lampe, Prickett, and Adamović, *Economic Relations*, 29; Robert M. Hathaway, "Truman, Tito, and the Politics of Hunger," in William F. Levantrosser, ed., *Harry S. Truman: The Man from Independence* (New York: Greenwood Press, 1986), 134.

14. Webb to James S. Lay, 16 May 1950, Second Progress Report on the Impact of NSC 18/4, "United States Policy Toward the Conflict between the USSR and Yugoslavia," *FRUS, 1950,* 4:1418–20.

any assurances to Yugoslavia that military supplies could be furnished by the West. Acheson claimed that opposition in Congress to any military assistance for Yugoslavia dictated such discretion.[15]

While the Yugoslavs kept their silence on the question of military assistance, their discussions with the IBRD continued. The United States, although sympathetic, remained concerned that Tito's government, already millions of dollars in debt to American and European bondholders and without a plan to attract export earnings, could not repay the additional indebtedness it sought to incur. Assistant Secretary of State for Economic Affairs Willard L. Thorp carefully explained this to Yugoslavia's new ambassador Vladimir Popović,[16] only to have Tito declare in late May that his was the only "neutral and independent country that has no obligations toward either East or West" and that his people would never "sell ourselves for loans."[17]

The Yugoslavs were not being subjected to a different standard in their economic negotiations with the West. The IBRD had less than $3 billion at its disposal and committed its limited funds only to projects that would produce enough profit to attract other lenders. The Yugoslavs took a more ideological approach to economic growth. Popović, like many in the Yugoslav hierarchy who had risen through the ranks of the party, reflected this by supporting the development of heavy industry over export earnings. He simply expected the United States to accede to his country's demands, and this expectation made negotiations even more difficult.[18]

As the Yugoslavs haggled with Thorp over aid, the concerns expressed by the PPS earlier in 1950 about Soviet "militancy" did not dissipate. In a statement of security policy known as NSC 68, the NSC concluded in April that the Soviets still sought world domination. Although the Kremlin did not wish to engage in a general war, Soviet leaders would in the short term pursue policies designed to secure

15. Acheson to Allen, 28 June 1950, RG 59, no. 516, 768.5/6-1220.

16. Lampe, Prickett, and Adamović, *Economic Relations*, 36; memoranda of conversations, 2 June 1950, RG 59, 611.6831/6-250. Sava Kosanović left his post in March and was replaced by Deputy Foreign Minister Vladimir Popović. Reams advised the State Department at that time that Prica had told him that since Kosanović was not a Communist, the Yugoslavs feared that he "carried insufficient weight" in Washington because the Department was "not always sure that Kosanović was speaking with full authority." Reams to Acheson, 20 March 1950, RG 84, no. 368, 301-Yugoslavia. Allen noted that Popović, who had also served as the Yugoslav ambassador to the Soviet Union from 1945 to 1948, was very influential. His appointment indicated the importance Tito attached to relations with the United States. *FRUS, 1950*, 4:1421 n. 1.

17. "Tito Terms Yugoslavia 'Only Neutral Country,'" *New York Times*, 1 June 1950, 7.

18. Lampe, Prickett, and Adamović, *Economic Relations*, 35–37.

control of the Eurasian land mass. Their preferred technique was
"to subvert by infiltration and intimidation," while increasing their
military strength to make that intimidation more effective. To thwart
these designs, the framers of this analysis recommended that the
United States rapidly increase "the political, economic, and military
strength of the free world" in order to "wrest the initiative from the
Soviet Union."[19]

At the end of May, Kennan speculated that the Soviets, *if* in search
of an area where they could initiate an act of limited aggression,
might well be planning an attack on Yugoslavia.[20] When war erupted
in late June in Korea, rather than in the Balkans, administration
fears of additional Soviet aggression against Yugoslavia increased;
however, after initial discussions in which Kennan now voiced his
doubts, the NSC concluded on 1 July that a Soviet attack on Yugoslavia involved too many risks for the Kremlin. Although the possibility
existed that the analysts had erred or that the USSR might underesti-
mate the risks, the Council reaffirmed the conclusions reached in NSC
68 a few months before: "The Kremlin does not now intend to engage
in a major war" but would pursue policies designed "to frighten us and
our friends, to divert our attention, to waste our resources, and to test
our firmness." Recent Soviet and satellite troop movements near
Yugoslavia were designed to intimidate or neutralize Tito if a world
war should erupt "by inadvertence." If an attack against Yugoslavia
did occur, the United States, in accordance with NSC 18/4, would not
intervene directly but would support Tito by providing arms and
other "indirect assistance as well as participating in appropriate
UN action."[21]

Later in July, Acheson suggested that U.S., British, and French
officials coordinate their planning in anticipation of a Yugoslav request for military assistance.[22] By August, the CIA estimated that the
strength of the satellite armies on the Yugoslav border had increased
dramatically to a total force of 363,500, outnumbering the Yugoslav

19. Report by Lay to the NSC, NSC 68, "United States Objectives and Programs for
National Security," 14 April 1950, with enclosure 1, Truman to Lay, 12 April 1950, and
enclosure 2, "A Report to the President Pursuant to the President's Directive of January
31, 1950," *FRUS, 1950*, 1:234–92.

20. Fisher Howe to Evans, memorandum, 31 May 1950, RG 59, 661.68/5-5150.

21. Memorandum of NSC Consultants Meeting, 29 June 1950, *FRUS, 1950*, 1:327–30;
Report to the NSC by the Executive Secretary, 1 July 1950, with enclosure, NSC 73,
"The Position and Actions of the United States with Respect to Possible Further Soviet
Moves in Light of the Korean Situation." ibid., 331–38.

22. Acheson to Embassy in United Kingdom, 12 July 1950, *FRUS, 1950*, 4:1432–33.

army of 250,000. The Soviets also had at least six of their divisions with a thousand tanks in the satellites bordering Yugoslavia. While no hard evidence of a plan to attack existed, the buildup of forces, coupled with the "demonstration in Korea of Soviet capabilities for directing and supporting Satellite forces," would not allow the dismissal of such a notion. If the Soviets decided to engage in further aggression, the CIA believed it a "strong possibility" that such aggression would occur in the Balkans against Yugoslavia. Tito's ability to launch a viable defense would depend "on the degree and promptness of Western assistance."[23]

Much of this thinking rested on the premise that the attack in Korea represented a Soviet prelude to a wider war. By late summer, both Kennan and Alan Kirk disputed but did not completely dismiss that assumption. Kennan advised that the Soviets did not intend the attack in Korea to lead to a wider conflict or even to tie down the United States in a peripheral area; they simply wanted to control Korea and had not anticipated the United States would mount an effective response. The Soviets still wanted to avoid a general war, but would attempt by other means to sow disunity in the West. Ambassador Kirk agreed, predicting the Soviets would use the war scare to wage a war of nerves and seek to separate the United States from its allies.[24]

To prevent that, the Truman administration undertook a number of measures to increase NATO's strength and the U.S. presence in Europe. Although the North Atlantic Alliance had been in existence for several months, its military strength was inferior to that of the Soviets. In September of 1950, Acheson, who had previously decided that rearming West Germany within a unified NATO army was crucial to the defense of Europe, formally suggested both measures to the British and French. President Truman also increased U.S. troop strength in Europe, despite criticism from conservative Republicans that the real menace to U.S. security lay in Asia. By the end of the year, Truman had appointed General Dwight D. Eisenhower NATO commander, agreed to accept Greece and Turkey into that organization, and begun the task of improving relations with Spain, which was geographically important but like Yugoslavia, distastefully governed.[25]

23. CIA, Special Evaluation no. 40, "Possibility of Direct Military Action in the Balkans by Soviet Satellites," 29 July 1950, Truman Papers, Records–CIA File, File: Special Evaluation no. 40.
24. Kennan to Acheson, 8 August 1950, *FRUS, 1950*, 1:361–67.
25. Leffler, *Preponderance of Power*, 384–90, 408–9, 521–22.

Attempts to buttress the Tito regime continued as well, despite Tito's stance on the conflict in Korea. When the war began, Ambassador Allen advised the State Department that Yugoslavia's position would be that of a neutral, but he believed the United States had the right to "press their hand on this issue."[26] On 27 June 1950, Alês Bebler, Yugoslavia's permanent representative at the United Nations, voted against the UN resolution calling for the use of armed force to repel the North Korean attack; he then abstained on subsequent votes, except India's proposals for mediation.[27] Acheson, with a gift for understatement, found Yugoslavia's position of opposition "to UN measures against Sov inspired aggression to be particularly contrary to Yugo interest."[28]

Nonetheless, in mid-August the NSC concluded that the president could authorize the emergency provision of military equipment to Yugoslavia under the Mutual Defense Assistance Act of 1949. The act, passed as a companion to the North Atlantic Treaty, allowed military assistance for "any other European nation whose strategic location makes it of direct importance to the defense of the North Atlantic area and is vital to the security of the United States."[29] A few days later the JCS recommended that lists of Yugoslavia's military needs and U.S. capacities be correlated; that the necessary material be stockpiled near Yugoslavia for prompt delivery; and that planning meetings be held with the British and French. All of this should occur "without delay."[30] Although Tito's government was not privy to these discussions, Kardelj told Allen in August that Yugoslavia soon would make known its opposition to North Korean aggression; however, this would be coupled with an expression of distaste for the "new imperialism," which Kardelj described as Western support for "reactionary elements" in the Far East and a failure to promote reform.[31]

In early September, before leaving for New York to attend the United Nations General Assembly, Foreign Minister Kardelj issued a statement that condemned North Korean aggression. In his address to the United Nations, Kardelj fulfilled the second part of his statement to Allen by criticizing both the Soviet Union and the United States.

26. Allen to Acheson, 26 June 1950, RG 84, no. 820, 312.UN—Security Council.

27. Hamilton Fish Armstrong, *Tito and Goliath* (New York: Macmillan, 1951), 285.

28. Acheson to Allen, 28 June 1950, RG 84, no. 513, 312.UN—Security Council.

29. Lay to the NSC, 17 August 1950, *FRUS, 1950*, 4:1439–40; Acheson to Certain Diplomatic Offices, 3 November 1950, ibid., 1494–96.

30. JCS to Johnson, 23 August 1950, *FRUS, 1950*, 4:1441–44.

31. Summary, 29 August 1950, Truman Papers, Naval Aide Files/State Department Briefs, File: State Department Briefs—Daily Briefs, August–October 1950.

He cited the Soviets for their pressure on his country, which belied the USSR's talk in the United Nations of promoting peace and cooperation around the world. But Kardelj also chastised the United States for turning the war in Korea into a crusade against communism. In words that foreshadowed Yugoslavia's later nonaligned philosophy, Kardelj appealed for the separation of ideology from military threats and said the world body should fight only the latter. He called for cooperation among nations with different political and social systems, and for an increased international role for small states in opposition to Great Power hegemony. In the following months, Yugoslavia supported United Nations actions in Korea up to the Thirty-eighth Parallel.[32]

These actions demonstrated that Yugoslavia had, according to a CIA analysis, clearly reassessed "its previous estimate that the USSR would not seek its elimination through overt military action." The country's armed forces were in readiness, and its delegation at the United Nations had "apparently been instructed to emphasize whenever possible the dangers to world peace resulting from any Soviet-inspired aggression." The CIA did not think that Yugoslavia would identify itself with the West, but if the current crop failure proved as serious as it appeared, the regime's attitude toward the West would improve "as the question of Yugoslav survival becomes more critical and Western support becomes more tangible."[33] If the economy continued to deteriorate and Tito thus failed to sustain Yugoslavia's viability "outside the Soviet orbit," his own leadership would suffer, as would the appeal of national communism to other countries.[34]

On 10 August the Export-Import Bank, without publicity, extended a $15 million credit to Yugoslavia to finance purchases in the United States of raw materials and machinery.[35] The following month, IBRD president Eugene Black visited Belgrade at Tito's invitation to discuss Yugoslavia's request for a $25 million loan for the purchase of mining equipment, a transaction the IBRD did not favor. Although neither party changed its position, the meetings between Black and Tito were

32. Alvin Z. Rubinstein, *Yugoslavia and the Non-aligned World* (Princeton: Princeton University Press, 1970), 28–29; David Anderson, "Yugoslav Berates Russia in U.N. Body," *New York Times*, 26 September 1950, 1, 13, 14; Armstrong, *Tito and Goliath*, 285; Duncan Wilson, *Tito's Yugoslavia* (Cambridge: Cambridge University Press, 1979), 66.

33. CIA, Intelligence Memorandum no. 325, "Current Assessment of the Tito-Stalin Break," 13 September 1950, Truman Papers, NSC Records–CIA File, File: NSC/CIA 5-11, Intelligence Memoranda, January 1950–January 1951.

34. CIA, Intelligence Memorandum No. 333, 29 September 1950, Truman Papers, NSC Records–CIA File, File: NSC/CIA 5-11 Intelligence Memoranda, January 1950–January 1951.

35. *FRUS, 1950*, 4:1438, editorial note.

cordial. After the talks both Black and Allen speculated that a serious rift existed within the Yugoslav leadership, with "doctrinaire" communists like Ambassador Popović opposing concessions to the bank and more "practical" men like Vladimir Velebit favoring the continuation of discussions. Nonetheless, Allen viewed Black's visit as "highly useful." Black left convinced of Yugoslavia's genuine need for Western assistance (although he was still not certain the IBRD should provide it), while the Yugoslavs had had their notion that the bank was under U.S. control dispelled.[36]

While the loan negotiations remained stalled, the drought and resulting crop failure in Yugoslavia proved critical, with estimated shortfalls of one million tons of corn and five hundred thousand tons of wheat.[37] The country had no resources of its own left: as the *New York Times* reported, "people's belts already have been tightened to the last notch."[38] By early October, Tito's government informed Allen that it needed $100 million in emergency food assistance from the United States, emphasizing that a country so weakened by food shortages and unable to purchase raw materials was a country vulnerable to Soviet or satellite military action.[39]

Ambassador Popović and Foreign Minister Kardelj presented Yugoslavia's formal request for food assistance ($60 million for food purchases, $45 million to obtain the raw materials that would have been acquired through food exports) in meetings with Acheson in mid-October. The policies set forth in the NSC 18 series demanded the United States do what it could to meet Yugoslavia's food needs, but Acheson cautioned that acquiring congressional approval for any part of the aid package might prove difficult and that Yugoslavia would help its case "by putting relations with the US and with Yugoslavia's Western neighbors on the best possible basis." When the secretary also discussed Western concerns about Yugoslavia's economic program and its ability to handle the loans requested, Kardelj insisted that the political need to proceed with the five-year plan outweighed any economic considerations. He also claimed that Yugoslavia, in defending its own independence, had advanced the cause of world peace. His country had decided not to seek arms from the United States, lest that

36. Lampe, Prickett, and Adamović, *Economic Relations*, 36–38; Allen to Acheson, 25 September 1950, *FRUS, 1950*, 4:1454–55.

37. John H. Ohly to Lyman L. Lemnitzer, 9 October 1950, *FRUS, 1950*, 4:1462–63.

38. M. S. Handler, "World Bank Chief in Belgrade Talks," *New York Times*, 19 September 1950, 28; M. S. Handler, "Yugoslavs' Envoy to Seek U.S. Loan," ibid., 27 September 1950, 17.

39. Allen to Acheson, 5 October 1950, *FRUS, 1950*, 4:1459–60.

prove Soviet propaganda correct. But such a defense burden made the acquisition of outside economic aid even more critical; Yugoslavia's request therefore involved defense as much as economic needs. Acheson expressed his sympathy but also delivered a short lecture on the rules of capitalist banking. The meeting ended with both sides expressing their appreciation for the frank and sincere manner in which views had been exchanged.[40]

In subsequent weeks, Tito entertained visiting congressional delegations, assuring them of his intention to remain independent of Moscow and pledging that Yugoslavia would "loyally and fully" live up to its responsibilities as a member of the United Nations in the event of Soviet aggression in Europe.[41] Ambassador Popović, who previously had bristled at the mention of concessions in return for aid, inquired of Allen in November how Yugoslavia could improve its chances with U.S. lawmakers. Acheson, while affirming the U.S. resolve to "scrupulously avoid interference internal affairs" of other nations, advised Allen to press for more internal liberties for the people of Yugoslavia, such as greater press and religious freedoms. The ambassador should make no specific proposals regarding the imprisoned cleric Stepinac, but only suggest that his continued incarceration made it difficult "for many in the US, Catholics and non-Catholics, to support aid to Yugo." In addition, any support given to the Chinese communist actions in Korea would "only adversely affect attitude American public." The same "unfavorable reaction" would result if Yugoslavia supported the admission of Communist China to the UN Security Council.[42]

By the time Acheson had made these suggestions, Tito had already initiated a number of internal reforms that separated Yugoslavia from other communist regimes. Since January 1950, the Yugoslav government had released thousands of political prisoners and recently announced plans to free more, relaxed travel restrictions for its citizens wishing to visit the West, freed two Roman Catholic priests from jail, and allowed more churches of all denominations to reopen, promised to extend state social benefits to the clergy and their families and in general eased obstacles in the way of church attendance and religious instruction in the schools. It had also issued a decree removing the special food and housing privileges enjoyed by state, party, and

---

40. Acheson, memorandum of conversation, 19 October 1950, *FRUS, 1950*, 4:1474–78; Acheson to Lay, 16 October 1950, ibid., 1471–73.
41. Allen to Acheson, 23 October 1950, *FRUS, 1950*, 4:1478–80.
42. Acheson to Allen, 14 November 1950, *FRUS, 1950*, 4:1499–1501.

military officials; virtually abandoned the drive for collectivization in agriculture; and decentralized industry through the creation of worker-management councils.[43] The last three changes were especially significant and represented a genuine departure from the policies of both the USSR and the satellites.

The Yugoslavs also took additional steps in the United Nations to increase their security and enhance their ties with the West. In October, Yugoslavia supported the Uniting for Peace Resolution, which allowed the General Assembly to act in a given situation if the Security Council was prevented from doing so by a veto by one its permanent members.[44] Yugoslavia also supported the United States in its resolve to bring the Chinese intervention in Korea before the United Nations, and Tito told the *New York Times* in November that he would abide by any decision the UN took on the matter.[45] That same month Kardelj introduced a resolution to the United Nations titled "The Duties of States in the Event of the Outbreak of Hostilities," a move designed by the Yugoslavs to forestall a Soviet attack against them. The resolution, adopted by the General Assembly on 17 November 1950, called on states engaging in military action to mutually declare within twenty-four hours their willingness to cease hostilities and withdraw to their own territory. Any state failing to comply would be branded the aggressor and held responsible for breaking the peace.[46]

Yugoslavia's actions eased the administration's task as it continued to use its influence to obtain the emergency economic assistance Tito had requested. The United States not only secured funds for Tito's government from the Export-Import Bank, the Economic Cooperative Administration (ECA), and the Mutual Defense Assistance Program (MDAP) but also obtained $38 million for famine relief in December from Congress. In each case, the administration stressed the humanitarian aspect of assistance, but also claimed that the agricultural crisis in Yugoslavia weakened the ability of the Yugoslavs to defend themselves against outside aggression and thus threatened the security of NATO.[47]

An appeal to Congress for emergency legislation was not without risk, but as Acheson told the Cabinet, failure to assist Yugoslavia

43. CIA, NIE 7, 21 November 1950, "The Current Situation in Yugoslavia," Truman Papers, PSF, CIA–NIE Reports 1–52, File: CIA Reports–NIE 7–20.

44. Rubinstein, *Yugoslavia and the Non-aligned World*, 29.

45. CIA, NIE 7, 21 November 1950 (cited in full at note 43).

46. Rubinstein, *Yugoslavia and the Non-aligned World*, 29.

47. *FRUS, 1950*, 4:1507–9, editorial note.

could well result "in losing the friendship of that country."[48] John C. Campbell later recalled the "tremendous lift" the president's request for congressional relief gave those who had been working on the Yugoslav issue for some time and who believed it essential that the United States's Yugoslavia policy be "in a position in which it had general acceptance in the government and could not be labeled a conspiracy on the part of a few officers from the State Department to get aid to Yugoslavia."[49] Of course, the administration did not act solely to please either the Yugoslavs or its own Balkan experts. It acted because Yugoslavia's conflict with the USSR decreased the Soviets' power and because this particular crisis afforded the opportunity to draw Yugoslavia into Western defense efforts.

In August, the NSC had decided that emergency military assistance could be provided to Yugoslavia under the MDAP. In late October, the administration informed Allen that funds derived from the same program could be used to send emergency food assistance to the Yugoslav armed forces, with the goods being dispatched while Congress debated the relief bill. However, inclusion in the MDAP required "certain undertakings" by the Yugoslavs, such as the conclusion of a bilateral agreement accepting the principle of common defense and reciprocity. Allen, in presenting the proposal for such an agreement to Tito stressed that it included no political demands, but had the advantage of enabling "the President and Congress to demonstrate to the American people that we were getting something in return for our money." Tito, concerned that the Yugoslavs "show that they were reciprocating . . . and were therefore not merely accepting handouts," reacted favorably to Allen's suggestion that an agreement be made enabling MDAP funds to be used to feed the Yugoslav military.[50]

In the interim, Acheson prepared the ground for the passage of the relief bill by dispatching identical letters to relevant congressional committee chairs and members, recalling the U.S. policy of aiding Yugoslavia and the importance of sustaining Tito's government in its current crisis.[51] Ambassador Allen personally toured and took home movies of the areas hardest hit by the food shortages and showed the films to key members of Congress on a quick trip to the States.[52] He

---

48. Cabinet Minutes, 20 October 1950, Connelly Papers, File: Notes on Cabinet, 6 January–29 December 1950.

49. Campbell, Oral History, Truman Library, 143.

50. Memorandum Prepared by the Department of State, 25 October 1950, *FRUS, 1950,* 4:1480–82; Allen to Acheson, 31 October 1950, ibid., 1488–89.

51. Acheson to Tom Connally, 31 October 1950, *FRUS, 1950,* 4:1491–92.

52. Lampe, Prickett, and Adamović, *Economic Relations,* 32.

also made a number of public speeches in support of the legislation, stressing that Tito, although a communist, had broken with the Soviets and had his military positioned between the Soviets and the vital Mediterranean. As Campbell remembered: "George Allen . . . used to take those twenty Yugoslav divisions and parade them up and down all over the United States in order to persuade people there was a reason for our policy."[53]

To avoid a repetition of the complaints that had accompanied the UNRRA program, Allen and Yugoslav deputy foreign minister Leo Mates agreed that U.S. representatives would observe the distribution of foodstuffs in Yugoslavia. The Yugoslav government also would provide periodic reports on the use made of U.S. assistance.[54] Another set of agreements relating to the MDAP food assistance for the Yugoslav military stipulated that this assistance be used exclusively to prevent the weakening of Yugoslavia's defenses, that it not be transferred to any other country, and that Yugoslavia provide "reciprocal assistance" to the United States in the form of "raw and semi-processed materials required by the United States as a result of deficiencies or potential deficiencies in its own resources, and which may be available in Yugoslavia." The latter exchange would occur on a commercial basis.[55]

With these agreements concluded, the president announced his intention, as Congress assembled for a special session in late November, to use his statutory authority to shift a small percentage of MDAP funds to provide for the food needs of the Yugoslav military, citing the importance of Yugoslavia to the security of the North Atlantic Treaty area. Such an assurance was necessary; Congress had amended the MDA statute in 1950 to require an explicit "presidential finding" before aid was sent to a non-NATO country, specifying that aid was essential to the security of NATO and the United States. On 29 November, Truman formally asked the Congress to authorize additional economic aid in the amount of $38 million for Yugoslavia. In December, both houses approved Public Law 897, the Yugoslav Emergency Relief Act of 1950, which provided emergency assistance but also called on Yugoslavia to "take all appropriate economic measures to reduce its relief needs . . . and to lessen the danger of similar emergencies." The president signed the bill on 29 December 1950.[56]

---

53. Campbell, Oral History, Truman Library, 145–46.
54. Allen to Mates, 17 November 1950, *FRUS, 1950*, 4:1503.
55. Allen to Mates, 20 November 1950, *FRUS, 1950*, 4:1504–5.
56. Initial supplies from the ECA reached Yugoslavia by the end of November. "Truman Promotes Aid to Yugoslavia," *New York Times*, 28 November 1950, 20;

The arguments used by the administration to secure the relief bill's passage and the concerns raised by members of Congress during hearings on the bill illustrated many of the problems inherent in the U.S.-Yugoslav relationship, and by implication, in the wedge strategy itself. In his statement to the House Committee on Foreign Affairs on 29 November, Assistant Secretary of State for European Affairs George Perkins made the administration's by then familiar case for aid on both humanitarian and national security grounds, with the latter receiving more emphasis. He reviewed the history of the Tito-Stalin break and the West's response to it, claiming that Tito's defiance had "pushed back the iron curtain" and exposed "Moscow's methods of dominating and exploiting those weaker nations which are nominally its allies." Perkins admitted that Yugoslavia remained "a Communist state" and "a dictatorship," but the issue before the world was Yugoslavia's right to "national independence" and to freedom from "outside pressures and aggression." He assured the committee of the regime's commitment to distribute the aid fairly and give "full publicity" to the United States's role in providing relief.[57]

The committee responded with pointed questions about Yugoslavia's internal policies, with James P. Richards of South Carolina contrasting the United States's refusal to aid Spain, which limited American business operations, with the planned aid for Yugoslavia, whose practices were even more restrictive. Abraham A. Ribicoff of Connecticut followed this with the claim that Tito's collectivization and too-rapid industrialization policies had helped cause Yugoslavia's food problems. Perkins countered that the Yugoslavs had virtually stopped their collectivization drive, but agreed that the adoption of an industrialization program "which was far beyond their capacity" had aggravated the food crisis. Yet he assured Ribicoff that Yugoslavia had seen the need despite its "Communist theories" to "talk sense" in its investment program. Other members, recalling what they believed were Tito's abuses of the UNRRA aid program, pressed Perkins for additional assurances that the stopgap deliveries diverted from the MDAP were being properly distributed.[58]

On the whole Perkins handled his questioners well, but in his effort to convince the committee not to demand political concessions from Tito in return for aid, he oversold the extent to which Tito had relaxed

---

Campbell, *Separate Road*, 25 n. 11; *FRUS, 1950*, 4:1507–8, editorial note; *DSB*, 12 February 1951, 24:277.

57. U.S. House of Representatives, *Hearings Before the Committee on Foreign Affairs: Hearings on H.R. 9853*, 81st Cong., 1st sess., 29 and 30 November 1950, 1–5.

58. Ibid., 5–17.

his internal controls in response to criticism from the West. Perkins's claim that Yugoslavia was more "liberal" in its attitude toward religion than other communist states, for example, provoked James G. Fulton of Pennsylvania to remind Perkins of the fate of Stepinac and to wonder if the United States in rendering assistance to such regimes was not simply "gardening a group of pet dictators." When pressed to explain what advantage the United States accrued from its relationship with Yugoslavia, Perkins gave a clear definition of the wedge strategy by saying:

> What we are concerned with is containing, or driving a wedge, if you will, into Communist totalitarianism, and in containing in particular the Stalin breed of Communism, doctrine, or whatever you want to call it. We feel very strongly that it is essential that Tito, having made the break with Stalin, will succeed in that break because we can only break it down by driving wedges into it, and that is one of the most important wedges that has appeared. If we let that effort fail, whether we like Mr. Tito or not, it will be a very devastating thing from the point of view of anybody else who is going to think about trying to break away from the Stalinist doctrine.[59]

When General Omar N. Bradley, chairman of the Joint Chiefs of Staff, appeared before the same committee, the question of concessions by Tito at first dominated the session. Bradley easily deflected most of this by simply claiming that such matters were political in nature and therefore outside his purview. The rest of the questions then centered on Yugoslavia's military capacity and ability to defend itself if attacked, with Bradley speaking positively of Yugoslavia's strengths but avoiding any public speculation of a future relationship between Yugoslavia and NATO.[60]

At first glance, the context in which the debate over aid to Yugoslavia took place—U.S. forces engaged in combat with not one but two communist armies and a Congress dominated by conservatives critical of the foreign policies of the administration and who believed, in Acheson's words, that "Communists belonged to a genus without subordinate species"[61]—makes the outcome surprising. Even John Campbell thought it remarkable that "aid to a Communist country at

59. Ibid., 16–20.
60. Ibid., 35–42.
61. Acheson, *Present at the Creation*, 332.

the height of the Cold War" secured the support of Congress with "a minimum of public debate."[62] However, a closer look illuminates the reasoning of both Congress and the administration. Truman had responded to the attack in Korea not only by deploying troops there under the auspices of the UN, but by the already detailed changes in NATO. Whether the attack in Korea was the prelude to a wider war or only a test of the West's commitment to collective security, the continued existence of an independent Yugoslavia, "an uncommitted, unpredictable and possible hostile force on the flanks" of the Soviet satellites, enhanced the security of the United States and its allies.[63] Those security needs overshadowed the administration's misgivings about Tito's ideology or domestic policies; humanitarian issues supplied whatever additional justification Congress required.

The relief program proved a great success, in that it both alleviated hunger within Yugoslavia and improved U.S.-Yugoslav relations. Most of the stopgap supplies were distributed by February of 1951, when the aid financed by Congress began to arrive. Yugoslavia fulfilled its promise of equitable distribution, a process the Yugoslavs controlled and that only a small number of observers monitored.[64] None of the tension that had surrounded the UNRRA program reappeared, as each side seemed determined to demonstrate the workability of their new relationship.

Nonetheless, food aid alone could not render Yugoslavia secure. At the end of October 1950, the Tripartite Committee on Military Assistance to Yugoslavia, consisting of the United States, Britain, and France, completed a report detailing the requirements to be used for planning both peacetime and emergency military aid for Tito's regime. Each of the three governments then began individual deliberations on the document.[65] However, as Tito told the retiring British military attaché in December, he could not request Western arms even if he wished to, since his country's position was that of a neutral. "I cannot have people saying, 'That is an American tank, those are British guns. Yugoslavia is an Anglo-American base.' " He would request Western assistance only if attacked by the Soviets.[66]

The intelligence community in the United States had already concluded that while the Soviets possessed the capability to take military

62. Campbell, Oral History, Truman Library, 146–47.

63. Kennan to Secretary of State, 8 August, 1950, *FRUS, 1950*, 1:364.

64. Hathaway, "Politics of Hunger," 129–49; Lampe, Prickett, and Adamović, *Economic Relations*, 134.

65. *FRUS, 1950*, 4:1482–83, editorial note.

66. Allen to Acheson, 29 December 1950, *FRUS, 1950*, 4:1514–15.

action against Tito, no indications existed of an imminent attack.[67] To other observers, the possibility of a satellite or Soviet attack on Yugoslavia appeared increasingly likely. In late 1950 and early 1951, as negotiations on Yugoslavia's IBRD request and other economic and food needs continued, the communist bloc's military buildup near Yugoslavia proceeded as well. According to the recollections of Vladimir Velebit, it was at this juncture that Yugoslavia finally made a confidential, informal request for U.S. military assistance, a request that resulted in clandestine shipments of United States surplus military goods to Yugoslavia. Although previous authors have made reference to U.S. military shipments to Yugoslavia, only the recent release of classified material, coupled with the oral histories obtained by this author, make a more detailed history of these occurrences and their significance possible.[68]

Velebit, sent by Tito in the fall of 1950 to the United States for loan and aid discussions, recalled in a 1988 interview that IBRD president Black had advised him that Yugoslavia's food needs complicated its already objectionable balance of payments deficit. Additional assistance from the U.S. Congress for those needs was a prerequisite for IBRD loans. As a result, "lower level" people in the Yugoslav delegation continued negotiations with the IBRD, while Velebit and others concentrated on "lobbying Congress and the State Department." These activities consumed little of Velebit's time; he felt "idle" and so decided to try his hand at obtaining military assistance from the United States. "I didn't have any instructions from my government," Velebit claimed; "I knew it was very risky but I am a man who rather likes to take a risk."[69]

Velebit had a number of friends in the U.S. government, most notably former OSS officer and current PPS member Robert Joyce, who included the Yugoslav in gatherings at his home with "Chip Bohlen, Averell Harriman, Joe Alsop, and also an OSS, later CIA man Frank Wisner." Velebit talked to them of the grave situation confronting Yugoslavia and, after some weeks, was called to the State Department to present his views. The official with whom he met told him the United States would furnish the Yugoslavs with military assistance. Velebit then cabled Tito and informed him of the "unauthorized" talks that had resulted in an offer of aid from the United States.

67. NIE-15, "Probable Soviet Moves to Exploit Present Situation," 11 December 1950, *FRUS, 1951*, 1:4–7.
68. See for example, Brands, *Specter of Neutralism*, and Heuser, *Western "Containment" Policies*.
69. Interview with Vladimir Velebit, September 1988, Belgrade, Yugoslavia.

Tito summoned him to Yugoslavia for meetings with Kardelj, Vice-President Aleksander Ranković, and chief of staff General Koča Popović, where lists of Yugoslavia's military needs were compiled. No one but the highest members of the Party knew of these discussions. Velebit translated the lists into English himself to guard their secrecy. When he returned to the United States with these requests, deliberations on military aid began in earnest.[70]

Tito's previous comments regarding U.S. military assistance and the control he exercised over Yugoslavia's affairs make it doubtful that Velebit acted without Tito's support in his approach to State Department and other officials. As John Campbell has recorded, by the fall of 1950 the United States had received a message through the CIA, sent to the State Department via Robert Joyce, that Yugoslavia had dispatched someone to discuss military assistance. A number of official and unofficial discussions on aid subsequently ensued. The CIA then arranged for a secret shipment of arms to be sent to Yugoslavia, arms Campbell said had little military value (he described them as "one freighter full of some old guns") but which served to show the Yugoslavs that aid would be forthcoming if they were victims of aggression. To Campbell "the psychological effect of our being willing to supply military equipment to Yugoslavia at that stage was tremendously important."[71]

Such assurances were indeed crucial. According to Yugoslav diplomat Leo Mates, by 1951 Yugoslavia had begun to prepare in earnest for "the worst scenario—war." In addition to military steps, the government microfilmed archival and other documents and secreted them in "certain caves in the center of the country." This occurred without panic or publicity, but in Yugoslavia "all preparations for war were taken."[72]

Bela K. Kiraly, a former general in the Hungarian People's Army and commander of the infantry, has also testified to the threat of war in 1951. In an essay published in 1982, Kiraly recounted the "constant anti-Titoist indoctrination" that took place in the Hungarian military in the years after 1948. The military buildup in the satellites also accelerated after 1948, causing Romania, Hungary, and Bulgaria to exceed the force limits imposed in the Paris Peace Treaty by "between two and three-and-a-half times." The object of all of this, according to Kiraly, was a satellite war against Yugoslavia for which "preparations

70. Ibid.
71. Campbell, Oral History, Truman Library, 152–54.
72. Interview with Mates, September 1988.

had been completed as early as the summer of 1950." War games conducted with the Hungarian military in January 1951 centered on a full-scale Soviet and satellite campaign against Yugoslavia, with the Hungarians detailed south of the Danube and the honor of occupying Belgrade left to the Soviets. The games assumed the presence of U.S. troops in Yugoslavia, but a clash with the United States "was a risk Stalin was never seriously willing to take." The games of January were simply that; the forceful response of the United States and the United Nations to the attack on Korea had "nipped Stalin's pet project in the bud." Yet the Soviets did not fully discard the plan until after Stalin's death.[73]

Available U.S. government documents confirm Campbell's recollections and indicate that Robert Joyce and other U.S. officials discussed the issue of military assistance with Velebit on 22 November.[74] Frank Wisner, who had urged that assistance be given to Yugoslavia in the summer of 1948, now headed the CIA's Office of Policy Coordination (OPC), which carried out various covert operations in cooperation with the PPS and the Defense Department.[75] After Velebit's approach, Wisner discussed Yugoslavia's needs with Deputy Defense Secretary Robert Lovett, who assured Wisner of his personal support "in view of the large dividends which could presumably be had for a relatively small investment." Lovett suggested that Wisner and officials at the State Department transmit Velebit's requests to the defense establishment.[76] Franklin Lindsay, another former OSS operative who joined OPC, has written in a recent memoir that his organization had worked on "ways to strengthen Yugoslav capabilities to remain independent of Moscow" since the break in 1948. He too described Velebit's meetings with Joyce and the concern all present had about a Soviet

73. Bela K. Kiraly, "The Aborted Soviet Military Plans Against Tito's Yugoslavia," in Wayne S. Vucinich, ed., *At The Brink of War and Peace: The Tito-Stalin Split in Historic Perspective*, vol. 10 of *War and Society in East Central Europe* (New York: Columbia University Press, 1982), 273–88.

74. *FRUS, 1951*, 4(2):1721, editorial note.

75. Although the OPC was part of the CIA, the head of the OPC was appointed by the secretary of state and worked most closely with the PPS, implementing "unpublicized aspects of State Department policy" as well as those of Defense. Burton Hersh, *The Old Boys: The American Elite and the Origins of the CIA* (New York: Charles Scribner's Sons, 1992), 227–28; see also Arthur B. Darling, *The Central Intelligence Agency: An Instrument of Government, to 1950* (University Park: Pennsylvania State University Press, 1990).

76. Wisner, memorandum for the record, 7 December 1950, RG 59, 768.5/12-750.

invasion.[77] By the end of December, Velebit had submitted military equipment lists for study by the JCS.[78]

After additional discussions between Velebit and the State Department, Deputy Undersecretary of State H. Freeman Matthews informed Lovett in mid-January 1951 of Velebit's claim that the Yugoslavs had to increase their military strength from 400,000 to 600,000 men by the spring to meet a possible Soviet/satellite attack. While other demands on U.S. supplies and the confidential nature of the request made it almost impossible for the United States to meet Yugoslavia's full needs, Matthews believed some of the items on Velebit's list "may be regarded by the American military authorities as outdated and . . . in surplus in this country or may be available from stocks of captured World War II materiel." Matthews requested an immediate reply on this from Lovett, so that the Yugoslavs might know if "confidential channels" could provide them with the goods they needed.[79]

Yet Tito would still have to make a decision regarding long-term military aid. Token clandestine shipments of military surplus goods might serve to raise Yugoslavia's morale, but the United States could not, under existing mutual defense assistance legislation, meet that country's full military needs without a formal, public Yugoslav request for Western assistance. The law required that a bilateral agreement between the United States and the recipient nation be negotiated to ensure that the goods provided were used for the ends specified. A United States military mission also had to be stationed in the recipient nation.[80] The Yugoslavs, however, believed themselves menaced by the Cominform armies on their borders, armies that perhaps needed only the slightest premise to attack. An embrace of the West could either doom Tito's government or save it; an open request for Western military support might well be a fatal blow. Yugoslavia therefore remained hesitant, but Ambassador Allen advised Washington that this was caused as much by a continuing debate within the Yugoslav Politburo on the merits of a direct appeal to the West as by the fear of provoking Soviet aggression. Allen believed that "stern necessity will force Yugoslavs" to take that step, even though many officials found

77. Franklin Lindsay, *Beacons in the Night: With the OSS and Tito's Partisans in Wartime Yugoslavia* (Stanford: Stanford University Press, 1993), 335–36.

78. *FRUS, 1951*, 4(2):1721, editorial note.

79. Robert Joyce to H. Freeman Matthews, 12 January 1951, RG 59, 768.5/1-1251; Matthews to Lovett, 17 January 1951, *FRUS, 1951*, 4(2):1684–86.

80. Campbell, *United States in World Affairs, 1949*, 142–43.

it distasteful and Tito himself genuinely worried about provoking the Kremlin.[81]

While Tito's government considered its options, concerns about Soviet aggression in general and against Yugoslavia in particular continued to intensify. Observers ranging from *Foreign Affairs* editor Hamilton Fish Armstrong to members of the PPS advised Acheson that a Soviet and/or satellite attack on Yugoslavia could well occur by the spring. If the West did not respond, the collapse of the Western position in Europe and the Middle East could follow.[82] By early February, the JCS recommended that the tripartite report completed in October be approved and that MDAP requests for the 1952 fiscal year include $160 million for Yugoslavia. They also urged that the stockpiling of supplies near Yugoslavia begin as soon as possible with goods obtained on "a priority equal to that of NATO countries" with "immediate deliveries to Yugoslavia . . . once stocks are created."[83]

The record shows that after still more discussions between Velebit, Joyce, and G. Frederick Reinhardt, director of the Office of Eastern European Affairs, and other consultations between the JCS and the State and Defense Departments, the United States acceded to Yugoslavia's still "confidential approach" and agreed to use surplus military goods to supply items on Velebit's list. As Reinhardt noted in a contemporary echo of Campbell's recollection of "one freighter filled with some old guns," the amount of material being sent "does not amount to very much." However, deliveries of "more considerable stocks" of surplus material would require British and French participation, which Yugoslavia had not yet sanctioned. In addition, the administration believed the "far wider collaboration" that Velebit envisioned between his country and the West still depended on Yugoslavia's public request for inclusion under the MDAP.[84]

In March, President Truman approved NSC 18/6, which envisioned a more active role for the United States and NATO in sustaining Yugoslavia's independence. In addition to supporting the February

81. Allen to Acheson, 24 January 1951, *FRUS, 1951*, 4(2):1697–98.

82. Howe to Matthews, 19 January 1951, RG 59, 661.681/1-1951, with enclosure, memorandum of conversation, 19 January 1951, RG 59, 661.681/1-1951; John Paton Davis Jr., member of PPS, memorandum, 23 January 1951, *FRUS, 1951*, 1:19–20; John H. Ferguson and Robert W. Tufts of PPS, memorandum, ibid., 37–40.

83. J. H. Burns to Harriman, 26 January 1951, *FRUS, 1951*, 4(2):1706–8; Omar Bradley to Marshall, 2 February 1951, ibid., 1719–21.

84. *FRUS, 1951*, 4:(2)1721, editorial note; Matthews to Lovett, 8 February 1951, with enclosure, memorandum of conversation, 7 February 1951, ibid., 1725–27; Reinhardt, memorandum of conversation, 3 March 1951, ibid., 1742–43; Reinhardt to George W. Perkins, 5 February 1951, RG 59, 768.5/2-551.

recommendations of the JCS, the NSC concluded that if Soviet or satellite forces launched an attack, the United States should support action in the United Nations, consult with its allies, furnish equipment in accordance with Yugoslav requests, and prepare "to meet the increased threat of global war." However, this information would be kept on a "need to know" basis because of the sensitivity of the Yugoslav government to the issue of military assistance.[85]

Ironically, meeting Yugoslavia's constant economic demands proved more troublesome than providing military assistance. In the spring of 1951, the United States, Great Britain, and France, after discussions in London, reached an agreement on the level of aid necessary to sustain the Yugoslav economy and enable it to obtain IBRD and other assistance. The three nations ultimately devised a formula to provide not more than $265 million in assistance to Yugoslavia, according to the following percentages: United States, 65 percent; United Kingdom, 23 percent; France 12 percent.[86]

John Campbell, who participated in these talks, remembered that the three powers did not "want to be stuck with Yugoslavia forever" and sought to work out a long-term economic plan for the country. However, the allies' inability to agree on the extent of their respective obligations hindered the negotiations. The United States was willing to be apportioned "the biggest share" of the aid burden, but insisted that the British and French provide more than "a token contribution." Their participation would carry "conviction" only if they were "using resources which otherwise they would use for themselves." The British negotiator, "a very tough guy named Sir Francis Mudie," represented the British Treasury, which had precedence over the Foreign Office in economic matters, and Campbell believed that "the foreign policy objectives" of the aid program were not clear to him. In general, the French and the British questioned how much they, who were themselves still the recipients of Marshall Plan assistance, "should dig into their own pockets" for Yugoslavia. The resulting disputes were "not very edifying" and dragged on for several weeks before the three arrived at the above percentages.[87]

As these agreements were being negotiated, the Truman administration secured the approval of the necessary congressional committees and its NATO allies to use up to $29 million in MDAP funds

85. Memorandum for the President, by Lay, with enclosure NSC 18/6, "The Position of the United States with Respect to Yugoslavia," 7 March 1951, Truman Papers, PSF, NSC 80–85, File: NSC Meeting No. 85, 7 March 1951.

86. *FRUS, 1951*, 4(2):1743–45, editorial note.

87. Campbell, Oral History, Truman Library, 172–80.

to pay for Yugoslavia's raw material deficiencies.[88] However, some members of Congress again raised the kinds of questions and objections that became common whenever the Truman and later Eisenhower administrations sought aid for Tito's government.

When Assistant Secretary Perkins and other State, Defense Department, and ECA officials met with members of the House Foreign Relations Committee in late March, Perkins explained that the raw materials acquired with the MDAP funds would be those needed by the Yugoslav military, thus freeing the Yugoslavs to use other funds to fulfill the requirements of the civilian population. He admitted that the administration would make a request for additional funds for Yugoslavia for the next fiscal year, but also looked to other countries to assist Yugoslavia and to the IBRD to finance long-range development. Although none of the Congress members present seemed to reject the use of MDAP funds in this instance, Mike Mansfield noted that "as a Catholic, it was difficult for me to go down there and fight for the bill when we have men like Stepinac in prison." He cautioned that aid would not be forthcoming for Yugoslavia unless the government enacted some reforms.[89] In discussions with the Senate, Foreign Relations Committee Chairman Thomas Connally also voiced his disapproval of the aid decision, but did not indicate he would publicly oppose the administration.[90]

In the past, Allen had occasionally raised Stepinac's release with Tito but had made little progress, with Tito declaring that he would not act under pressure from the outside. By early March, the Yugoslav government appeared willing to free the archbishop on the condition he retire to a monastery or go into exile, but Campbell doubted that would satisfy Catholic opinion in the United States, "which has of course been the most vocal element in opposing our Yugoslav policy."[91] In a conversation with Perkins, Ambassador Popović offered life in a monastery as the only solution, claiming Stepinac's wartime role as a collaborator prevented reinstatement to his bishopric.[92] Nonetheless,

---

88. Foreign Aid Committee to International Security Affairs Committee, memorandum, 14 March 1951, *FRUS, 1951*, 4(2):1750–52; Perkins to Acheson, 20 March 1951, ibid., 1759–61.

89. George E. Truesdell, memorandum, 23 March 1951, *FRUS, 1951*, 4(2):1765–68: U.S. House of Representatives, Committee on Foreign Affairs, *Selected Executive Session Hearings of the Committee, 1951–56, European Problems* (Washington, D.C.: U.S. Government Printing Office, 1980), 15:24–25.

90. Jack K. McFall to Webb, 2 April 1951, *FRUS, 1951*, 4(2):1771–72.

91. Campbell to H. Randolph Higgs, 16 March 1951, RG 59, 611.68./3-1651.

92. Memorandum of Conversation, 29 March 1951, RG 59, no file number.

on 16 April, Truman issued his finding approving $29 million in aid to Yugoslavia under the Mutual Defense Assistance Act of 1949 (as amended) for "consumptive needs for supporting its armed forces." The United States and Yugoslavia concluded the agreement through an exchange of notes on 17 April 1951.[93]

Despite all of this assistance, the Yugoslavs remained insecure in their relationship with the United States and its allies. Vladimir Velebit met with Joyce and Reinhardt in early April after consultations in Belgrade to express his government's concern about the uncertainty existing in the West regarding Yugoslavia's intentions in case of aggression in Europe. Velebit, in response to an earlier U.S. suggestion for joint U.S.-Yugoslav staff talks, recommended that such discussions take place now but at "a much higher level." He suggested that General Koča Popović, chief of the general staff of the Yugoslav army, come to Washington for bilateral consultations, with a minimum of publicity.[94] All of the relevant departments agreed, provided, as the Department of Defense requested, that the talks were "exploratory in nature" and would "in no way involve any commitment on the part of the United States." Content would center on military problems of "mutual interest . . . which would arise in the event of an overt attack against Yugoslavia . . ." and military aid issues that would be of importance in the same circumstances.[95]

The bilateral consultations took place in Washington in May and June 1951 and included "long-range strategic discussions." They ended with an agreement providing for the rapid shipment of military goods to Yugoslavia and for additional talks between the militaries of both countries.[96] Discussions on a formal bilateral assistance agreement could begin as soon as Yugoslavia officially requested aid under the MDAP.[97]

Some U.S. military goods had of course already been dispatched to Yugoslavia, with the decision to do so made after Velebit's end-of-year approach and before the general's visit. The Department of Defense reluctantly and tersely admitted the fact of the shipments, without

93. *FRUS, 1951*, 4(2):1783, editorial note; "U.S. to Send Yugoslav Army $29,000,000 Worth of Aid," *New York Times*, 17 April 1951, 1, 12.
94. Joyce to Matthews, 9 April 1951, *FRUS, 1951*, 4(2):1776–78.
95. Burns to Matthews, 30 April 1951, *FRUS, 1951*, 4(2):1786–87.
96. Joyce to Matthews, 24 May 1951, RG 59, 768.5/5-2451; Acheson, memorandum of conversation, 18 June 1951, *FRUS, 1951*, 4(2):1815–16.
97. Acheson to American Embassy Paris, 11 June 1951, RG 59, no. 7000, 768.5/6-1151.

providing any details, to the *New York Times* in late June.[98] As a handwritten notation on a memo from Joyce to Matthews on the talks indicated, the shipments discussed in the spring by the United States and Yugoslavia included items in "the second installment of the OPC stuff."[99] Walworth Barbour, of the State Department's Office of Eastern European Affairs, later told Congress that "two token shipments of military material," mostly surplus in nature, were sent to Yugoslavia in the spring and summer of 1951. In that same set of hearings, General George H. Olmstead indicated that one shipment was sent before the staff talks and one after.[100]

On his way back to Yugoslavia, General Popović met with General Eisenhower in Paris. Popović explained to Eisenhower that one shipment of military goods had already been sent to Yugoslavia and that a second was being readied. The two men then discussed the Yugoslav army's future needs, with Eisenhower exploring the possibility of equipment transfers between Italy and Yugoslavia. Even though, as Eisenhower acknowledged, the Italians and the Yugoslavs "had not always been good friends," Popović said he saw no objection to such a program. The NATO commander then asked Popović "a somewhat awkward question": Would the Yugoslav military "based on the Communistic system, fight shoulder-to-shoulder against the Soviet system with the Western capitalistic system?" Popović replied that "the doctrinaire factor did not weigh very heavily." Yugoslavia had broken with the Soviets because of the "imperialist nature" of the Soviet system; its soldiers would aid "in resisting aggression alongside the soldiers of Western Europe." But Popović repeatedly emphasized that Yugoslavia could be an effective fighting force only if it received the necessary level of military support from the West. He also remained noncommittal when Eisenhower raised the issue of coordinated military planning with the West in advance of the outbreak of hostilities.[101]

For Eisenhower, these questions involved issues beyond the more immediate defense gains envisioned for the wedge strategy. In his diary entry for 11 June, Eisenhower wrote that the problem of European security would only be solved by the creation of "a United States

98. "U.S. Arms Delivered to Yugoslavia for Defense of Her Independence," *New York Times*, 20 June 1951, 1, 7.

99. Joyce to Matthews, 24 May 1951, RG 59, 768.5/5-2451.

100. U.S. House of Representatives, Committee on Foreign Affairs, *Selected Executive Session Hearings of the Committee*, 1951–56, *European Problems*, 15:133, 144.

101. Vernon Walters and D. MacArthur, memorandum of conversation, 10 July 1951, Dwight David Eisenhower Papers, Pre-Presidential Principal File, Conversations— Memos of (SHAPE) 1951–52, Dwight D. Eisenhower Library, Abilene, Kansas.

of Europe" whose membership would include the NATO countries as well as "West Germany and (I think) Sweden, Spain, and Jugoslavia, with Greece definitely in if Jugoslavia is."[102]

At the end of June Tito's government finally made its formal request for military assistance under the MDAP.[103] During subsequent negotiations on the MDAP agreement, the Yugoslavs provided lists of the materials they wanted, but were not forthcoming with details of what they already had or how they intended to use the equipment gained. This put them at odds with what Acheson called "the declarations of democratic faith and explanations of need that Congress had scattered along the approaches" to such assistance. Acheson believed their reticence justified, but acknowledged that the Yugoslavs were withholding the kind of information that was "the lifeblood of Pentagon bureaucrats."[104]

To enhance further Yugoslavia's ability to survive a Soviet attack, Acheson also believed that the United States and its major military partners would have to decide what "operational measures" they and the larger NATO alliance would or would not take in the face of Soviet or Soviet-sponsored aggression against Tito's government.[105] The question was a crucial one since the PPS estimated the combined forces of Yugoslavia, Turkey, and Greece to be greater than all of the European members of the Atlantic alliance and a "formidable bastion against aggression in the eastern Mediterranean area."[106]

Tito appeared anxious for an answer as well. As he explained to Truman's foreign policy adviser W. Averell Harriman when the latter accepted Tito's invitation to visit Yugoslavia while on a mission to Europe in August, a general war could still result from a Soviet miscalculation, such as an act of local aggression to which the Soviets believed the West would not respond. At a press conference following this conversation, Harriman "did not dispute" Tito's contention that an attack on Yugoslavia could not remain a localized conflict. Despite this rather mild statement and Harriman's disclaimer that he came to Yugoslavia "simply . . . as a visitor," the *New York Times* editorialized that Harriman had demonstrated Washington's resolve to warn the

102. Robert H. Ferrell, ed., *The Eisenhower Diaries* (New York: W. W. Norton, 1981), 194–95.
103. Acheson to Embassy in the United Kingdom, 14 July 1951, *FRUS, 1951*, 4(2):1827–29.
104. Acheson, *Present at the Creation*, 333.
105. Acheson to Embassy in the United Kingdom, 14 July 1951, *FRUS, 1951*, 4(2):1827–29.
106. Carlton Savage, memorandum, 23 May 1951, *FRUS, 1951*, 1:834–40.

Kremlin that "they had better not entertain the idea that an attack against Yugoslavia would fare any better than aggression did in Korea."[107] Harriman later reported to Truman that Tito "considers himself definitely a part of the West."[108]

While these discussions were taking place, Congress, after debates and hearings lasting through the summer and into the fall of 1951, passed the Mutual Security Act (MSA) of 1951, which was designed to gather various military and economic aid programs, such as the MDAP and ECA, into an umbrella Mutual Security Program (MSP). The MSA allowed the extension of military and economic aid to NATO members and to any European country the president "determines to be of direct importance to [the] preservation of peace and security" of the North Atlantic area and to the United States. No aid could be furnished to any country unless it agreed to help promote international understanding, maintain the peace, relieve international tensions, and take what measures it could to develop its own defense capabilities. As passage of the bill neared, the Department of State, to improve Yugoslavia's chances of qualifying for military assistance, urged that the law's language be incorporated into the U.S.-Yugoslav military assistance agreement still under negotiation.[109]

The inclusion of Yugoslavia under the MSA and Truman's plan to meet United States's economic obligations under the tripartite agreement through this program[110] aroused the usual debate and demands for concessions in Congress. The administration, also as usual, refused; the United States simply could not subordinate its "national security interests" to conditions such as Stepinac's restoration.[111] On 13 August, Truman informed the Foreign Affairs and Foreign Relations Committees of Congress of his recommendation that $30 million in economic assistance be extended to Yugoslavia, pending approval of the MSA. This amount was part of and not in addition to the estimated $60 million earmarked for Yugoslavia under the act

107. "Statements by Ambassador W. Averell Harriman at Press Conference, Hotel Toplice, Bled, Yugoslavia, Sunday, August 26, 1951, 11:30 a.m.," RG 59, 611.68/9-1451; M. S. Handler, "Accord on Defense with Tito Is Seen in Harriman Talks," *New York Times*, 27 August 1951, 1, 8; editorial, "To Stalin via Tito," ibid., 18.

108. Notes on Cabinet Meeting, 31 August 1951, Connelly Papers, File: Notes on Cabinet, 2 January–31 December 1951.

109. Campbell, *Separate Road*, 25 n. 11; State Department to Belgrade Embassy, 21 September 1951, RG 59, no. 361, 768.5-MAP/9-2151.

110. Acheson, memorandum of conversation, 3 August 1951, *FRUS, 1951*, 4(2):1836–38.

111. Perkins to Acheson, 23 July 1951, RG 59, 611.68/7-2351.

during fiscal year 1952.[112] After the MSA passed in October, the IBRD, having long demanded such aid as a precondition, finally approved a $28 million loan for Yugoslavia.[113]

In the fall, U.S. Army Chief of Staff General J. Lawton Collins visited Yugoslavia at Tito's invitation to review the regime's use of the U.S. military items already provided and to discuss the terms of the nearly completed military assistance agreement. Before agreeing to the trip, Collins had written to Eisenhower, expressing the JCS concern "as to what quid pro quo we could obtain for whatever aid we gave." Collins wanted the NATO commander's reaction to the proposed talks, in order that any concessions made by the Yugoslavs "be in accordance with" NATO's plans and objectives. Eisenhower "heartily" supported Collins's journey. He was encouraged that "Tito is becoming increasingly amenable to identifying himself more closely with the West," but had "no illusions as to his reasons." Eisenhower agreed "that for every commitment that is asked of us we should obtain an appropriate quid pro quo." Every time NATO discussed "plans and forces required for the defense of Southern Europe, especially Italy" the "contribution that Yugoslavia can make towards the security of my southern flank is brought into focus."[114]

The CIA shared Eisenhower's estimate of Yugoslavia's value. While the agency calculated that the Soviets were inferior to the West overall, they had a "preponderance" of strength in Eurasia. However, the association of "Greece, Turkey, Spain, Yugoslavia and Western Germany" with NATO, which "should be consummated in the coming period, will be a major increment in NATO strength." But the agency lamented that "numerous political and psychological obstacles" combined to delay the full contribution that the later three countries could make to the defense of Europe.[115]

The administration hoped that Collins's trip would remove some of those obstacles. In his discussions on the military assistance program, Collins discovered that the Yugoslavs, still mindful of the Soviets' efforts to control them, disliked the idea of U.S. military personnel inspecting their installations. They yielded only when assured by

112. *FRUS, 1951*, 4(2):1844, editorial note.
113. Leroy Stinebower, memorandum of telephone conversation, 11 October 1951, *FRUS, 1951*, 4(2):1853–54.
114. J. Lawton Collins to Eisenhower, 21 August 1951, and Eisenhower to Collins, 25 August 1951, Eisenhower Papers, Pre-Presidential Principal File, File: Collins, J. Lawton.
115. CIA, SE-13, "Special Estimate Probable Developments in the World Situation Through mid-1953," 24 September 1951, in Warner, *CIA under Harry Truman*, 409–33.

Collins that such a requirement was standard and applied to all countries receiving Mutual Security assistance. Tito actually made less of this issue than his military did, telling Collins repeatedly that the question was "not fundamental" and "could easily be solved." However, like Popović in his talks with Eisenhower, Tito would not be drawn into a discussion of coordination with NATO, noting only that such discussions could be held "at the proper time."[116]

In addition, the Yugoslavs, despite NATO insistence on the defense of the Ljubljana Gap ("the historic gateway for barbarian incursions into northern Italy"), instead proposed to "hold a continuous line running the length of Yugoslavia." The most serious difference between the two sides surfaced when Collins asserted that if Yugoslavia were attacked by the Soviet satellites and the war remained localized, the United States would not provide air support. Yet he hastened to add his own opinion that such a conflict could not remain local and might well precipitate a world war. In that case, Yugoslavia "could expect some support depending on the situation." Popović rather dryly replied that "these statements made clear the Yugoslav requirement for a modern air force." He remained adamant on this point, despite Collins's caution about the costs involved.[117] These three issues— Yugoslavia's support for NATO's defense plans, the extent of Western support for Yugoslavia in case of war, and the country's need for assistance in building an air force—would remain irritants in the U.S.-Yugoslav relationship for years to come.

In retrospect, John Campbell believed that "the Yugoslavs probably fooled us a great deal" on the issue of their relationship with NATO and never intended to use the military goods provided by the West for the sole purpose of assisting NATO in defending the Ljubljana Gap. Nevertheless, Collins returned from his trip to Yugoslavia "terribly impressed with the Yugoslavs and the show they put on." Collins concluded the Yugoslavs were making the "best use" of United States equipment, were proven fighters and would "do anything to defend their country."[118] Greece, Turkey, and Yugoslavia had also begun to

116. Interview with Marshall Tito, Prime Minister of Yugoslavia, 14 October 1951, Eisenhower Papers, Pre-Presidential Principal File, File: Collins, J. Lawton (1); Walter H. Waggoner, "U.S. Will Increase Arms to Yugoslavia," *New York Times*, 27 October 1951, 1, 5; C. L. Sulzberger, "U.S. Ready to Sign Tito Arms Accord," ibid., 11 November 1951, 14.

117. Interview with General Popović, Chief of Staff, Yugoslav Army, 14 October 1951, Eisenhower Papers, Pre-Presidential Principal File, File: Collins, J. Lawton (1); Armstrong, *Tito and Goliath*, 284.

118. Campbell, Oral History, Truman Library, 162–63.

discuss joint defense measures, which further inflated Western hopes of a closer affiliation between Yugoslavia and NATO.

On 7 November 1951, President Truman informed the necessary congressional committees that Yugoslavia met the requirements of the Mutual Security law and sent $77.5 million in military aid and additional amounts of economic aid to Tito's government.[119] A week later, the United States and Yugoslavia finally signed the military assistance agreement that made possible the long-term extension of Mutual Security aid. The agreement, which was to run for a year and/ or until either signatory asked in writing to terminate the pact, bound the United States to provide military assistance and Yugoslavia to use that equipment to deter aggression, with both acting in accordance with the principles of the United Nations Charter. The Yugoslavs agreed to receive a U.S. military mission to administer the program, but the United States pledged to keep the number of personnel assigned as "low as possible."[120]

While the United States and Yugoslavia completed negotiations on the military assistance agreement, the buildup of satellite forces on Yugoslavia's borders again increased. Yugoslavia, still unsure of full Western support for its survival, took its case against the Soviets and their satellites to the United Nations when the General Assembly met in October in Paris. As Ambassador Popović explained to State Department officials in late September, the Yugoslavs intended to ask the Assembly to condemn a whole range of Soviet and satellite aggressive acts, from border violations to the Cominform blockade, and to demand that those activities cease. [121]

The Yugoslavs resorted to the UN primarily to rally world opinion to their side. In the words of Ambassador Mates, who served as a member of the Yugoslav delegation in Paris, his country, preparing for but hoping to avoid a satellite attack, thought its "best scenario was to defeat the Soviet Union publicly before the whole world." After obtaining advice on wording and procedures from the Department of State, the Yugoslavs sent a draft of their resolution concerning their disputes with the Soviets to all of the non-bloc delegations for comments. They then prepared an amended draft, which won the support in December of all non-bloc delegates except two who left the chamber rather than cast a vote. Mates recalled they were Iran and Afghani-

119. Webb to Truman, 30 October 1951, *FRUS, 1951*, 4(2):1858–59.

120. *FRUS, 1951*, 4(2):1862–63, editorial note; Allen to Acheson, 14 November 1951, RG 59, 768.5MAP/11-1451; *DSB*, 26 November 1951, 25:863–64.

121. Hickerson, memorandum of conversation, 26 September 1951, *FRUS, 1951*, 4(2):1846–48.

stan. Both had assured the Yugoslavs of their sympathy, but because
of their border with the Soviet Union they could not risk a public
stance and so "they voted by legs." To Mates, his country's success in
the United Nations "was a shattering blow to the morale in Eastern
Europe" and "the climax of our special Cold War with the Soviet
Union." He credited this and the military assistance agreement with
the United States with enabling the Yugoslavs to "have beaten Stalin
while he was still alive."[122]

By the end of the year, Tito had also removed another irritant in his
relations with the United States. In late November, two congressional
delegations visited Yugoslavia, and each raised the Stepinac issue
with Tito. Tito informed the first group that Stepinac would be eligible
for release as soon as he met the requirements of Yugoslav law and
that he could reside anywhere in the country but could not resume his
clerical duties. When the second group, consisting of Congressman
Clement J. Zablocki and Congresswoman Edna F. Kelly (a persistent
foe of U.S. assistance to Yugoslavia, which Acheson later ascribed to
her "Yugoslav antecedents") pressed to see the archbishop, Tito revealed that he would be freed within a month, but repeated that he
would not be allowed to act as a bishop or archbishop. Ambassador
Allen credited the pressure applied by members of Congress for this
development, noting that Tito would not mind if they took credit for
the cleric's release, since that would "get Tito off hook with Serbs."
The Tito regime released Stepinac on 5 December 1951.[123]

Early in 1952, the Yugoslav press declared that their country had
overcome the effects of the Cominform blockade through its ties with
the West, and was a valued and respected member of the United
Nations and a contributor to the Western collective security system.[124]
Tito had indeed survived, but his ties to the West had not prompted
any other state to follow his path to independence. Although Yugoslav
foreign minister Joze Vilfan told a Western correspondent that Czechoslovakia and Poland were nearing a break with the Soviet Union,
the U.S. Embassy in Warsaw discounted his assessment. Discontent
existed, but a "Titoist Poland" remained unlikely. A Poland independent of the Soviets would jeopardize the latter's position in both the
German Democratic Republic and Czechoslovakia; the Soviets would
resort to force to eliminate such a threat.[125]

122. Interview with Mates, September 1988; *FRUS, 1951*, 4(2):1849 n. 1.
123. Acheson, *Present at the Creation*, 332; Allen to Acheson, 29 November 1951,
FRUS, 1951, 4:1866–67.
124. Jacob D. Beam to Acheson, 17 January 1952, RG 59, no. 672, 768.MSP/1-1752.
125. Raymond A. Lisle to the Department of State, 22 January 1952, RG 59, no. 278,
660.61/1-2252.

Nevertheless, the encouragement of dissident movements remained a diplomatic objective for the United States. As the Eastern European chiefs of mission concluded at their March 1952 meeting, the United States should, in its continuing effort to weaken Soviet control of the satellites, exploit feelings of nationalism and "encourage discordant tendencies within ruling groups fostering where feasible trends toward Titoism."[126]

Yugoslavia, now central to Western defense efforts in its part of the world, continued to receive economic and military assistance for the balance of the Truman administration; however, disagreements between the United States, Britain, and France concerning the amounts of economic aid to be furnished under the tripartite aid program slowed the pace of assistance in 1952 and delayed the conclusion of an agreement for the following fiscal year. By late January, the United States, which preferred the tripartite arrangement because it tied "Yugoslavia directly to a larger number of western countries," became concerned that Yugoslavia would see in the delay a lack of Western resolve and insist that reliance on the United States alone was preferable to the uncertainties of the tripartite arrangement.[127]

In the spring of 1952, after several months of consultations, the tripartite powers reaffirmed their conviction that Yugoslavia's existence as an independent and viable entity outside the "Soviet orbit" benefited the West. Since the fragile state of Yugoslavia's economy threatened the West's objectives, tripartite aid would continue through June 1953. However, Yugoslavia must adjust its economic and investment program and reduce its balance of payments deficit; assistance would be granted only under guidelines adopted by the three powers. They agreed to support a second IBRD loan for Yugoslavia equal to the first granted in October 1951, but because of the links between tripartite assistance and the bank loan, the powers believed Yugoslavia should consult with them on the projects to be supported by the IBRD and on any other credit arrangements undertaken abroad.[128]

When the three Western ambassadors presented these views in an aide-memoire to Tito on 10 July 1952, he rejected their scheme as an infringement on his country's sovereignty. If the document became public, Tito said, Yugoslavia's world position would be "untenable."[129] In a meeting with Acheson a few days later, Ambassador Popović

126. Bruce to Acheson, 7 March 1952, *FRUS, 1952–1954*, 8:12–13.

127. James G. Parsons to Campbell, 17 January 1952, RG 59, 768.5MSP/1-1752; James L. Colbert to Frederick E. Nolting, 24 January 1952, RG 59, 768.5MSP/1-2452.

128. Report of the Second Tripartite Conference on Assistance to Yugoslavia, 21 April 1952, *FRUS, 1952–1954*, 8:1284–90.

129. Allen to Acheson, 15 July 1952, RG 59, no. 64, 768.MSP/7-1552.

expressed particular anger over the stipulation that Yugoslavia consult with the tripartite powers before contracting any loan agreements. He also claimed his country had been initiating economic
reforms, but that the three powers had failed to credit them.[130] After
weeks of negotiation, the Yugoslavs agreed to the July statement
with clarifications that mollified their sensibilities but did nothing to
change the substance of the powers' demands.[131]

By the summer of 1952, the hostility of the Soviet bloc toward
Yugoslavia appeared to ease,[132] but allied discussions on military
assistance to Tito's government continued throughout the year. At
issue were such questions as the involvement of NATO and Italy in
Yugoslav assistance, as well as the nature of the military commitment
the West was prepared to make. The British argued that planning
between the United States, Britain, France, and Italy on the Yugoslav
issue should occur outside of the NATO framework.[133] The U.S. Joint
Chiefs of Staff, though willing to accept "extra-NATO planning at this
time," remained firm in their insistence that NATO be involved
"as soon as this is politically possible."[134] However, the "cardinal
substantive issue" between Britain and the United States centered on
the use of "token land forces" to defend Yugoslavia. The British
opposed any commitment of British and American ground troops to
Yugoslavia, while the United States argued that since circumstances
at the time of an attack might make it "necessary or desirable for the
United States and/or other NATO countries to utilize their national
forces in support of Yugoslav forces resisting aggression," no advance
judgments against the use of force should be made.[135]

By April the United States and Britain reached a compromise and
agreed to include the French in what would then become tripartite
strategic planning discussions with Yugoslavia. The "inevitable" and
"desirable" involvement of NATO would be postponed, as would a

130. Campbell, memorandum of conversation, 17 July 1952, RG 59, 768.5MSP/
7-1752.

131. Allen to Acheson, 25 August 1952, *FRUS, 1952–1954*, 8:1301–2; Allen to
Acheson, 25 August 1952, ibid., 1303–4.

132. Turner C. Cameron Jr. to the Department of State, 6 June 1952, RG 59, no.
1119, 661.68/6-652.

133. Reinhardt, memorandum of conversation, 5 September 1951, *FRUS, 1951*,
4:(2)1845–46; Barbour to Perkins, memorandum, 15 January 1952, RG 59, 768.5/1-1552.

134. William C. Foster to Acheson, 22 March 1952, with enclosure, memorandum
from Bradley to the secretary of defense, 18 March 1952, RG 59, 768.5/3-2252.

135. Barbour to Matthews, memorandum, 28 January 1952, RG 59, 768.5/1-2852;
"Negotiating Paper for Politico-Military Discussion with British on Planning for Yugoslavia," 8 April 1952, RG 59, 768.5/4-852.

decision on the use of ground troops to defend Yugoslavia. The three countries' ambassadors would make an approach to Tito regarding talks, with Admiral Robert B. Carney designated to actually conduct the discussions; the Italians would be informed only if Tito's response was positive.[136]

A number of months then elapsed as the French considered these proposals, and the three governments debated the positions they would take and the personnel they would use in their discussions with Tito. By July all had agreed to substitute General Thomas T. Handy for Admiral Carney, because of the latter's NATO affiliation.[137] The Yugoslavs must understand, the United States insisted, that the three powers were making "no . . . advance commitment" to assist Yugoslavia in case of an attack. As soon as possible, however, "contingent planning for YUGO shall be integrated" into NATO, with the "subsidiary objective" of Yugoslavia's "*de facto* MIL integration into NATO."[138] After agreement had been reached on all of these essential points the tripartite representatives sent a final report to each government for approval; additional delays and debates over the timing of the approach to Tito then ensued.

In the interim, various United States military and civilian officials visited Yugoslavia. In talks with Tito in July, Assistant Secretary of Defense Frank Nash, with Allen's approval, indicated that Yugoslavia could expect some additional military aid from the West. Tito replied that while he did not wish to enter into military discussions with NATO, he did welcome the participation of the British and French in discussions between the United States and the Yugoslavs on various strategic and operational questions.[139]

Tito's statements to Nash clearly had given the tripartite powers the pretext to make their formal presentation regarding military discussions; however, all of the necessary agencies in each country had not yet formally approved the summer proposals. In addition, the French government argued that political issues, such as a settlement on Trieste, be linked to the military talks.[140] By early September, U.S.

136. Matthews to Lovett, 16 February 1952, *FRUS, 1952–1954*, 8:1266–67; Summary Transcript of Discussion at a United States–British Politico-Military Meeting, 16 April 1952, ibid., 1276–84.

137. *FRUS, 1952–1954*, 8:1295 n. 3.

138. Acheson to London and Paris, 12 May 1952, RG 59, nos. 5854 and 6685, 768.5/5-1252.

139. Allen to Acheson, 15 July 1952, *FRUS, 1952–1954*, 8:1297–98; Perkins to Acheson, 17 July 1952, RG 59, 768.5-MSP/7-1752.

140. See for example, Secretary to Belgrade Embassy, 15 September 1952, RG 59, no. 379, 768.5/9-1552.

policymakers (whose own JCS had not yet acted) expressed concern that "further delay in a formal reply will sacrifice the psychological advantage arising from Tito's initiative."[141] The Yugoslavs themselves were becoming increasingly uneasy. When British foreign secretary Anthony Eden held talks with Tito in September, Tito expressed surprise that the West had not taken advantage of Yugoslavia's willingness to enter into military discussions.[142]

The three powers finally made their approach to the Yugoslav government in late October. Kardelj responded with enthusiasm, agreeing both with the need for secrecy and for other NATO members to be informed of the talks' existence.[143] The military discussions with General Handy presiding began in mid-November. In the initial sessions, Yugoslavia's past experiences with the bloc and its wish for a more definite defensive commitment from the West undermined the proceedings. Handy began the talks by explaining that they were designed to enable the tripartite powers to learn as much as possible about Yugoslavia's needs, so that they could undertake tripartite military planning to meet those needs when they convened in Washington. The Yugoslavs reacted badly because as Allen told the State Department, they feared the West was using the talks to penetrate their defenses without giving them any information in return. Yugoslavia also worried that the West would pass what it had learned on to other powers. After the three ambassadors met with Kardelj to assure him that Yugoslavia's fears were unfounded, and Handy promised a reciprocal report on the Western military, the talks appeared to proceed more smoothly.[144]

When the military discussions ended on 20 November, Allen reported that their chief utility resided in the fact that the West had acceded to Tito's wish that such talks be held and that the foundation had been laid for future discussions.[145] Even that assessment seemed overly optimistic by year's end. In late December, when the three ambassadors formally presented a copy of Handy's report to Kardelj, he informed them of the Yugoslav view that more progress could not be made without a clearer goal. Kardelj feared Yugoslavia would

141. Raymond L. Thurston to Matthews, 2 September 1952, RG 59, 768.5/9-252.

142. Allen to Acheson, 25 September 1952, *FRUS, 1952–1954,* 8:1312. For an account of Britain's hope that the Eden visit would reduce Tito's "prickly independence," see John Young, "Talking to Tito: The Eden Visit to Yugoslavia, September 1952," *Review of International Studies* 12 (January 1986): 31–41.

143. Allen to Acheson, 21 October 1952, RG 59, no. 578, 768.5/10-2152.

144. Allen to Acheson, 18 November 1952, *FRUS, 1952–1954,* 8:1316–17.

145. Allen to Acheson, 20 November 1952, *FRUS, 1952–1954,* 8:1320–21.

either have to defend itself or "become another Korea," which Allen took to mean a reference to "a localized war with outside assistance."[146] Merely planning for a wide range of contingencies, without a guarantee of full Western support clearly did not meet Yugoslavia's needs.

Before Truman left office, Western delay in signing the new tripartite aid agreement, combined with another drought, provoked a new economic crisis in Yugoslavia. In September 1952, Acheson informed the cabinet that the United States would provide an additional $20 million in drought relief to Yugoslavia.[147] By the end of the year, the tripartite aid agreement had come into effect as well.

While gladly accepting this assistance, Yugoslavia demonstrated anew that aid would not translate into altered policies. Tito first offended the administration by making a number of speeches denigrating United States aid and implying that Yugoslavia would look elsewhere for assistance. Yugoslavia then severed relations with the Vatican, which had repeatedly criticized Tito's religious policy and recently elevated Stepinac to the position of cardinal. Acheson, believing a U.S. response to be necessary, instructed Allen that the Yugoslavs must not misinterpret the drought aid decision to indicate approval of recent "unhelpful Yugo actions." The drought aid was being provided for humanitarian reasons, but its announcement would be accompanied "with some plain talk" to make the Yugoslavs understand that "cooperation is two way street." In addition, both Ambassador Popović and Tito were to be told simultaneously that an improvement in Yugoslav-Italian relations was an "indispensable link" in the Western security system.[148]

Allen thought it unwise to link nationalistic questions such as Yugoslavia's relations with Italy to the aid issue or to claim the United States was providing assistance to Yugoslavia for any reason other than that country's need to remain strong enough to resist Cominform pressure. Nonetheless, he presented the department's views to the Yugoslav government in early January 1953.[149] Although Allen could not say that Tito "ate crow" in their meeting, his attempts to explain away the speeches he had made convinced the ambassador that Tito

146. Allen to Acheson, 22 December 1952, *FRUS, 1952–1954*, 8:1322–23.

147. Cabinet Meeting, 19 September 1952, Connelly Papers, File: Notes on Cabinet, 4 January 1952–16 January 1953.

148. James C. Bonbright to Perkins, 26 December 1952, *FRUS, 1952–1954*, 8:1324–25; Acheson to Allen, 31 December 1952, ibid., 1325–26.

149. Allen to Acheson, 5 January 1953, *FRUS, 1952–1954*, 8:1326–27; the Embassy in Yugoslavia to the Government of Yugoslavia, aide-memoire, 7 January 1953, ibid., 1330–32.

realized his words "had been indiscreet and badly timed." Tito claimed that most of his remarks had been addressed to the Italians, whom he believed wanted U.S. aid to Yugoslavia to cease; his reference to other sources of assistance meant only a Yugoslav resolve to tighten its belt rather than submit to Italian pressure. He had not wished to imply either a return to the Cominform or an embrace of neutralism, the latter being repugnant to Yugoslavia. In the end, Tito accepted Allen's suggestion that he make a public recognition of America's latest aid and a special mention of the fact that the United States attached no conditions to its assistance.[150]

Allen and Tito also discussed the Handy talks, with Tito expressing alarm that tripartite military planning seemed to be based on the assumption that Yugoslavia would be considered "another Korea" in case of an attack. Tito repeated his government's oft-stated belief that an attack on Yugoslavia would lead to a general war; until the West agreed, Yugoslavia would have to prepare for its own defense. Allen replied only that the state of Yugoslav-Italian relations constituted the chief obstacle to collective security arrangements, but advised the State Department of Yugoslavia's deep concern "over lack of definite security arrangements with West."[151]

Overall, Allen remained optimistic about the effect of U.S. policy. In his assessment of the success of the Mutual Security program in Yugoslavia during the last six months of 1952, Allen concluded that Tito had made even greater strides in "orienting Yugoslav foreign policy westward." Allen also acknowledged that while Yugoslavia, Turkey, and Greece had made substantial progress in their relations, the "Balkan defense line" remained unsecured due to continued Yugoslav-Italian friction. Politically, the regime "proclaims its Marxist orthodoxy," but some reforms have occurred, which the Yugoslav public ascribed to U.S. assistance. The economy remained weak, with the drought and the need to divert some assistance to deal with its effects preventing more progress. The reluctance of the Yugoslav government to allow inspection of the uses of U.S. military equipment had also hampered the military assistance effort.[152]

The U.S.-Yugoslav relationship assumed a unique dimension during Truman's presidency, for the United States extended not only economic but military assistance to this still communist regime. While

---

150. Allen to Acheson, 8 January 1953, *FRUS, 1952–1954*, 8:1333–35.
151. Ibid., 8:1335–36.
152. Allen to Acheson, 10 January 1953, *FRUS, 1952–1954*, 8:1336–39.

the United States harbored no illusions about the nature of Tito's government, Truman and his advisers realized that any crack in the Soviet bloc benefited the West. How far Yugoslavia would go in its new relationship with the United States and its allies remained elusive, as did the extent to which the West would defend Yugoslavia against a Soviet attack. In general, the wedge strategy appeared more applicable to the political arena and to bilateral U.S.-Yugoslav relations than to the intricacies of NATO planning. Translating a subtraction from the Soviet bloc's military power into a positive gain for NATO foundered on the West's reluctance to pledge any and all levels of response to a Soviet attack on Yugoslavia and on Yugoslavia's own reluctance to throw open its doors to a Western military presence. Still, the very existence of such an extensive dialogue between Yugoslavia and the United States, while the latter was battling other communist states in Korea and the former was defending its Marxist orthodoxy, demonstrated the ability of both countries to base a foreign policy on national security requirements rather than ideological imperatives.

CHAPTER FOUR

1953–1955
THE "ROLLBACK" OF SOVIET POWER

Harry S. Truman's success in sustaining Tito and drawing his country closer to the West did his party little good in the presidential elections of 1952. The Red Scare and the stalemate in Korea dominated the campaign, with the Republicans criticizing the Democratic version of containment as timid and sterile. Once in power, President Dwight D. Eisenhower and Secretary of State John Foster Dulles promised a "New Look" in foreign policy: a more forceful response to communist aggression, one backed by U.S. superiority in nuclear weapons. Dulles declared that the United States would "roll back" the Iron Curtain and liberate the "captive peoples" of Eastern Europe. Eisenhower was always more careful, both during and after the campaign, to emphasize that the Republicans sought liberation only through "peaceful means,"[1] but both Dulles and Eisenhower shared the goal of reducing Soviet influence around the world.

Continued assistance to Yugoslavia was part of that overall plan of reducing Soviet power, but it conformed to other parts of the administration's philosophy as well. Eisenhower, since his days as

1. For a discussion of the liberation theme during the 1952 campaign, see Robert Divine, *Foreign Policy and U.S. Presidential Elections* (New York: New Viewpoints, 1974), 44–51.

NATO commander, had hoped to improve the Yugoslav-Italian relationship and include Yugoslavia in the North Atlantic alliance. As
president, he held to his strong belief in a collective defense system;
one of his biographers has called the Atlantic Alliance the "issue
closest to his heart." Free world security depended on a united Europe,
and a Yugoslavia oriented toward the West made the continent that
much safer.[2] John Foster Dulles, committed to both unity and liberation, was certain that Tito's heresy would provide the West with the
leverage it needed to pry open the Soviet bloc.

The Eisenhower/Dulles version of the wedge strategy, implemented
after the Korean War had ended and the threat of a Soviet attack
against Yugoslavia had passed, was more aggressive than that pursued by Harry Truman. It also envisioned more military and political
gains for the West. Tito *would* be enticed to join NATO; his military
forces were not to be simply subtracted from Soviet power, they were
to be added to that of the West. Tito *would* also be convinced to inspire,
if not lead, a Titoist liberation movement in the satellites. However,
the administration's need to codify its own foreign policy philosophy,
a task complicated by the death of Stalin and the new Soviet leaders'
"peace offensive," caused uncertainty about how to best accomplish
those objectives. In addition, Tito's willingness to improve relations
with the Soviets, while also joining with third world nations in a
nonaligned movement, made it difficult for the administration to
secure congressional support for the aid packages it deemed indispensable to its plans. Last, the administration's often flamboyant anticommunist rhetoric, which did not match its policy in Yugoslavia, undermined the rationale offered by Eisenhower and Dulles to explain their
support for Tito's brand of communism.

In early February 1953, the Eisenhower administration began a review of national security policy. The review posed a number of questions, relevant to both Eastern Europe and Yugoslavia. Most pressing
was the dilemma of how to reduce Soviet power and influence around
the world and behind the Iron Curtain without resorting to war in the
former case or "deliberate subversion" in the latter. Another question
centered on whether the United States should support a "totalitarian"
government, "provided only that it is independent of Soviet control
and influence," or work exclusively with democratic states.[3] Over all

2. Stephen E. Ambrose, *Eisenhower, Soldier and President* (New York: Simon &
Schuster, 1990), 249, 253–54.
3. Lay, memorandum to the NSC, 6 February 1953, with enclosures, *FRUS, 1952–
1954*, 2(1):223–31.

loomed the quandary Eisenhower had raised during the presidential campaign of how to maintain a strong defense without continuing the current practice of allocating 70 percent of the budget for that purpose and eventually bankrupting the U.S. economy.[4]

Before the administration could develop its answers, Stalin died. The collective leadership that succeeded him included Georgi Malenkov as head of the Council of Ministers, Nikita Khrushchev as first secretary of the Communist Party, Vyacheslav Molotov as foreign minister, Nikolai Bulganin as defense minister, and Lavrenti Beria as head of security. By mid-March, the CIA, in an analysis that proved more wrong than right in regard to Yugoslavia, concluded that although Georgi Malenkov appeared to be in charge in the Soviet Union, a power struggle could eventually develop. The new Soviet leadership, which seemed "vulnerable" and unsure of their ability to maintain power, would continue Stalin's policies of hostility toward the West but would be more cautious in their approach. The Agency predicted that Stalin's death would have no influence on Yugoslav-Soviet relations, since the quarrel had not been "personal, but arose from a genuine clash of Yugoslav national interests with the Soviet Communist Party." Although that proved incorrect, the CIA's belief that the Soviets could not recognize Tito as "an independent Communist ally" without seriously undermining their control of the Eastern European satellites was accurate as far as it went, but did not anticipate the upheavals that would in fact occur. The CIA also did not think that Tito's influence in the satellites would increase, unless there was a protracted power struggle within the USSR.[5]

Secretary Dulles, by contrast, saw opportunities for the United States in the Soviet leader's demise that could be used to reduce the threat posed by the USSR. Stalin had ruled the satellite states in part by transforming their "normal urges of nationalism" into "virtual worship of Stalin as a demi-god." With Stalin dead, that "impulse of nationalism" would be uncontrollable. The United States must "play up this nationalism and discontent for all it was worth" and "break down the monolithic Soviet control of the satellites."[6] The West had to be careful about when and how it seized the opportunities Stalin's passing afforded, but Dulles emphasized that one way of ending the

4. Robert J. Donovan, *Eisenhower: The Inside Story* (New York: Harper & Brothers, 1956), 17; Divine, *Foreign Policy*, 56.

5. SE-39, "Probable Consequences of the Death of Stalin and of the Elevation of Malenkov to Leadership of the USSR," 12 March 1953, *FRUS, 1952–1954*, 8:1125–32.

6. Memorandum of Discussion at the 136th Meeting of the NSC, 11 March 1953, *FRUS, 1952–1954*, 8:1117–24.

threat posed by the Soviet Union was by "inducing the disintegration of Soviet power." The Soviets were already overextended, forcing their "tyrannical rule over unwilling peoples." If the West applied enough pressure, it could achieve either "a collapse of the Kremlin regime" or at the least, a transformation of the bloc "from a union of satellites dedicated to aggression into a coalition for defense only."[7]

However, changes in Soviet foreign policy appeared to negate the secretary's analyses. Shortly after Stalin's death, the team leading the USSR began to seek more cordial relations with the West and to modify their treatment of the satellites. Articles appeared in the Soviet press criticizing Stalin's policies and the Soviets even hinted they would cooperate in achieving a Korean armistice. In response President Eisenhower decided to deliver an address "setting concretely before the world the peaceful intentions" of the United States. In a letter to Winston Churchill, Eisenhower complained that ascertaining the intentions of the Soviets was an endeavor "strewn with very difficult obstacles," but the United States was "deadly serious in our search for peace and are ready to prove this with acts and deeds and not merely assert it in glittering phraseology."[8]

In his speech to the American Society of Newspaper Editors on 16 April 1953, the president eloquently calculated the costs of war and suggested that the Kremlin make more concrete gestures to signal its willingness to achieve a peaceful world. The Soviets subsequently reprinted the speech and eased restrictions on U.S. citizens and diplomats in the Soviet Union. Additional steps involving other countries, including proposals to settle the German question and to exchange ambassadors with Yugoslavia followed as the Soviet "peace offensive" accelerated.[9] Nonetheless, NSC 153/1, the administration's preliminary statement of its national security policy approved in mid-June 1953, labeled the "formidable power and aggressive policy of the communist world led by the USSR" as one of the main threats to U.S. security. The other danger was the "serious weakening of the economy of the United States" that could result from the need to oppose the "Soviet threat over a sustained period."[10]

7. Memorandum of Discussion at a Special Meeting of the NSC, 31 March 1953, *FRUS, 1952–1954,* 2(1):264–81.

8. Eisenhower to Churchill, 6 April 1953, in Peter C. Boyle, ed., *The Churchill-Eisenhower Correspondence, 1953–1955* (Chapel Hill: University of North Carolina Press, 1990), 37–38.

9. Bohlen, *Witness to History,* 347–49; Dwight David Eisenhower, *Mandate for Change, 1953–1956* (Garden City, N.Y.: Doubleday, 1963), 143–49.

10. Lay, Report to the NSC, 10 June 1953, with enclosure, NSC 153/1, 10 June 1953, *FRUS, 1952–1954,* 2(1):378–86.

Ambassador Charles E. Bohlen also cautioned from Moscow that the Soviet Union remained "a totalitarian police dictatorship," but that the new leaders, unable to utilize "Stalin's methods of rule," had to find a new approach for both allies and enemies. In order to avoid war and ease the strains on their economy, Bohlen predicted they would pursue "a return to diplomacy and a lessening of world tension for an indefinite period to time." The Kremlin leaders hoped their gestures toward Yugoslavia in particular would "jettison the more senseless and unproductive positions in which Stalin placed them."[11]

However, the Kremlin had to improve its relationship with Yugoslavia only on the Soviets' terms. The death of Stalin had already been followed by protests in East Germany and Czechoslovakia against the regimes in power there. Soviet overtures to Tito could make the satellites even more rebellious unless those overtures resulted in the resumption of some measure of Soviet control over Yugoslav policy. The reestablishment of party-to-party ties, which to the Soviets involved the recognition by all communist parties of Soviet leadership of the international communist movement, would accomplish that goal, but was that possible? The members of the collective leadership, competing for primacy, had no single answer. Molotov, co-signer of the Cominform's denunciation of Tito, favored only the resumption of state-to-state relations with Yugoslavia. Tito, in his opinion, remained too great a danger to the cohesion of the bloc. Khrushchev, by contrast, argued for party-to-party ties. He conceived of a revived but more fraternal international communist movement, led by the Soviets but tolerant of different forms of socialism, such as those followed by the Yugoslavs and the Chinese. To Khrushchev, such a course was essential if the Soviets were to appeal, as he believed they must, to the emerging nations in the underdeveloped world.[12]

The United States, like the Soviet Union, also had to place its policy toward Yugoslavia in a wider context. Although the Eisenhower administration wanted Yugoslavia to remain oriented toward the West, the United States still had to consider the effects that ties with a country like Yugoslavia would have on the United States's allies. During the 1952 presidential campaign, Eisenhower, in speaking of the relationship of Yugoslavia and Spain to NATO, had said that the United States should make alliances only with countries that shared

11. Bohlen to John Foster Dulles, 7 July 1953, *FRUS, 1952–1954*, 8:1193–96.

12. David J. Dallin, *Soviet Foreign Policy after Stalin* (Philadelphia: J. B. Lippincott, 1961), 341–43; James G. Richter, *Khrushchev's Double Bind: International Pressures and Domestic Coalition Politics* (Baltimore: Johns Hopkins University Press, 1994), 72–73.

its commitment to a free system. It would be "a great victory for the free world" when Spain and Yugoslavia "begin to show what we would consider a little bit more enlightened concern for these basic aspirations and forms of government."[13]

Although Eisenhower's remarks were consistent with the comments he had made to General Popović in 1951, when uttered in public by a presidential candidate they were bound to irritate Yugoslavia's chronically tender sensibilities. Indeed, *Borba* soon declared that "allusions to making political conditions to this country will bear same fruit as did threats from the East." The newspaper, which always spoke for the government, attributed the candidate's words to a desire to obtain the Italian and overall Catholic vote in the November elections.[14]

Alês Bebler, the Yugoslav vice-minister for foreign affairs, sought out Dulles after Eisenhower's campaign speech to ascertain the Republican attitude toward Yugoslavia and the Soviet Union. Dulles assured him that while he could not speak for Eisenhower or for the Republican Party, he believed Yugoslavia deserved Western assistance as the one nation that had successfully defied the Kremlin and as an example to others within the Soviet bloc. Yugoslavia, Dulles told Bebler, was a symbol of the "possibility of breaking up the Soviet empire without war"; the West would not want to see his country "struck down." Dulles warned that assistance might have to be reduced in the future, but no steps would be taken to impair Yugoslav independence or to sacrifice Yugoslavia to the Soviet Union, which to Dulles represented the "despotic terrorism of a new Dark Age." Dulles sent a memorandum of this conversation to Eisenhower with a notation that he would later repeat as secretary of state. The situation in Yugoslavia, Dulles told Eisenhower, was "precarious, and I think we need to sustain their morale." Eisenhower agreed.[15]

After his inauguration but before Stalin's death, Eisenhower, still fixated on the military rather than the political implications of the Yugoslav-Soviet split, quizzed Ambassador Allen on whether the break with Moscow was genuine and how Yugoslavia would react in case of a war between the Soviets and the West. Allen had advised that Yugoslavia would remain neutral as long as possible but that a great

13. Austin Stevens, "Eisenhower Retires with Defense Plea; Explains Air Stand," *New York Times*, 4 June 1952, 1, 23.

14. Allen to Acheson, 10 June 1952, RG 59, no. 1564, 611.68/6-1052.

15. Dulles to Eisenhower, 25 June 1952, with enclosed memorandum of conversation, 24 June 1952; Eisenhower to Dulles, 25 June 1952, Eisenhower Papers, PAP, Ann C. Whitman/Dulles/Herter Series, File: Dulles Prior to Inauguration.

deal depended on the combatants. If the Germans were on the Western side against the Soviet Union, Allen guessed that Tito might be inclined to align "with his fellow Slavs." If Germany was not involved and if Stalin was still in power, Tito, who had a very "bitter personal quarrel with Stalin," would not enter the conflict. In another conversation with Dulles, Allen expressed the hope that his replacement in Yugoslavia would continue the policy he had followed of increasing "the distance between Belgrade and Moscow politically." He proposed George Kennan as an excellent choice for the Yugoslav post, on the grounds that he alone could discover exactly what had occurred between the Yugoslavs and the Soviets in 1948. Nothing came of this suggestion, an outcome Allen attributed to Dulles's personal dislike for Kennan, whom he found "intellectually arrogant."[16]

Even without Kennan, the administration's Yugoslav policy, as Dulles's statement to Bebler indicated, followed the basic path Kennan and the Democrats had established. But Dulles emphasized the liberation of the satellites and Yugoslavia's role there more than his predecessors had. The secretary of state, as U.S. ambassador to Yugoslavia James R. Riddleberger later recalled, was "fascinated by the possibility of breaking the monolithic structure of the Communist world." Yugoslavia could help him achieve that goal. Tito also had thirty divisions under arms, which represented "a subtraction from the Eastern military power." The administration had no illusions about Tito; Dulles simply thought it possible for both countries to gauge when the "vital interests of the United States" coincided with the "vital interests of Tito." Riddleberger remembered that Dulles believed Tito was a "real patriot," who would always act in his country's best interests.[17] What Dulles saw as a virtue in Tito roused only the ire of hardliners in the Kremlin. As the aging Molotov told an interviewer in the 1970s, Tito "is a nationalist, and that is his main defect as a communist . . . he is infected with the bourgeois spirit."[18] Khrushchev wanted to harness that nationalism, lest it lead to upheavals in the satellites and further weaken the cohesion of the bloc. Eisenhower and Dulles, to achieve the very outcome the Kremlin dreaded, sought to nurture Yugoslavia through a sustained program of military and economic assistance.

But a long-term U.S. assistance program, especially a military one,

16. George V. Allen, Oral History, Eisenhower Library, 7–8, 31–32.

17. Riddleberger, Oral History, Princeton, 52, 43.

18. Albert Reiss, ed., *Molotov Remembers: Inside Kremlin Politics* (Chicago: Ivan R. Dee, 1993), 83.

had to have immediate and tangible results to sustain public and congressional support. Military aid had initially been given to Tito because of and during the Korean War; peacetime assistance would not be as easily secured. Current policy decreed that commitments between the United States and other countries, such as Yugoslavia, rest on the assumption that the relationship "would result in a net gain in the broad, collective security picture vis-à-vis the Communist threat." The administration knew that geography alone would ensure that "security agreements exchanged with Yugoslavia might involve the whole of the NAT organization in hostilities"; however, the wisdom of including a communist state within NATO and the effect that would have on the organization's effectiveness remained an open question.[19]

In early 1953, the prospects for increased cooperation between Yugoslavia and some of the United States's NATO allies appeared promising. The rapprochement between Greece, Turkey, and Yugoslavia, which had begun during the Truman administration, culminated in the signing of a Treaty of Friendship and Assistance, also known as the Ankara Pact, between the three on 28 February 1953. Yugoslavia, whose uncertainties about Western support in the case of a Soviet or satellite attack had not been alleviated by the Handy talks, had suggested that the treaty have a military and mutual assistance dimension; however, the United States and Britain insisted that was both premature and likely to meet opposition from other NATO members, notably Italy. The final treaty therefore had no such provision, but did allow for informal consultations between the three countries' general staffs.[20]

Since the Truman administration, most of the military aid sent to Yugoslavia had been designed, at least in the mind of the West, to hold the Ljubljana Gap, a key point for the NATO defense of Italy. The signing of the Ankara Pact between Yugoslavia and two other NATO members and the military talks provided for under the agreement made a Yugoslav association with NATO itself appear more feasible.[21] In late February, just prior to the formal conclusion of the pact, the JCS recommended to Secretary of Defense Charles E. Wilson that "no time should be lost in preparing for additional discussions with

19. Parsons to Bohlen et al., 21 January 1953, with attachment, "The Question of Security Commitments between the United States and Yugoslavia, with particular reference to the North Atlantic Treaty," RG 59, 768.5/1-2153.

20. Dulles to John E. Peurifoy, 21 February 1953, *FRUS, 1952–1954,* 8:624–25; also editorial note on 627; Hoffman and Neal, *Yugoslavia and the New Communism,* 419.

21. Campbell, *Tito's Separate Road,* 27.

Yugoslavia."[22] The planned March visits of Yugoslav chief of staff General Peko Dapčević to the United States and Tito to Great Britain gave the discussions some urgency. The State Department approached the matter with more caution, suggesting only that General Dapčević be informed of the West's wish to resume deliberations "on as early a date as feasible." The State Department also indicated that any such talks should be postponed until after the pending Italian elections and consultation with the other members of NATO.[23]

None of these issues had been resolved by the time Tito visited Britain in mid-March 1953. During his stay, Tito assured his British hosts that he was secure enough internally to accept common defense obligations, but not within the NATO framework. The Soviets had successfully depicted NATO as an instrument of Western aggression, and Tito claimed that Yugoslav membership would lesson his country's appeal to the satellite states.[24] In the end, Tito and the British agreed that NATO membership was not desirable for Yugoslavia at that time, but their joint communiqué emphasized that a war involving Yugoslavia "could hardly remain local in character." According to Ambassador Allen, Tito left Britain "more confident that he is no longer in an isolated position."[25]

When the Soviets accelerated their attempts to establish better relations with Yugoslavia in the spring, Tito demonstrated his security by minimizing their overtures. In an Air Forces Day speech in late May 1953 the Yugoslav leader, surrounded by Western military attachés and their equipment, referred to the United States, the United Kingdom, and France as "our allies" who were assisting both Yugoslavia and the cause of peace. He granted that Soviet propaganda against Yugoslavia had eased, but pointed out that there had been no corresponding improvement in relations between the Soviet bloc and Yugoslavia. Accordingly, Tito concluded, the Yugoslavs had no reason to "fall into the arms of those who have been slandering us and who have hurt us so viciously." He cautioned that his country wished to have "normal tolerable relations" with the Soviets and the other states in Eastern Europe, but "tolerable relations do not . . . mean friendly relations." He stressed the importance of the aid that the West had provided his country "when we were experiencing worst days of our

22. Collins to Charles E. Wilson, 20 February 1953, *FRUS, 1952–1954*, 8:1341–42.
23. Bonbright to Matthews, memorandum, 7 March 1953, RG 59, 768.5/3-753.
24. Oliver M. Marcy, memorandum of conversation, 16 April 1953, RG 59, 768.5/4-1653.
25. Winthrop W. Aldrich to Dulles, 21 March 1953, *FRUS, 1952–1954*, 8:1346–47.

history" and declared that Yugoslavia would never betray its "real friends and allies."[26]

U.S. analysts took Tito at his word, believing that he had little to gain by rejoining the bloc. Tito's commitment to national communism, the stature he had achieved as a world figure since the break, the need of the Yugoslav economy for Western capital and technology, and the Soviet system's inability to tolerate genuine change or multiple centers of power, all mitigated against an alteration in Yugoslav policy.[27]

Nonetheless, the process of establishing "normal" relations between the Soviet Union and Yugoslavia quickly advanced. In June 1953, the Yugoslavs accepted the Soviets' offer to exchange ambassadors for the first time since the Tito-Stalin split. The U.S. embassy in Belgrade saw this Soviet gesture as one "calculated and timed to raise serious problems" for Tito's government, which would have to assure its benefactors in the West that it had not taken the "first step" toward a return to the Cominform. The administration could assist the Yugoslavs in this effort, the embassy advised, by publicly associating "Yugoslavia with Western powers as most recent target of Soviet maneuvers and thereby reinforce idea that Yugoslavia was practicing member Western bloc."[28]

Tito did a little public-relations work of his own. He placed the exchange of ambassadors within the context of Yugoslavia's overall foreign policy by claiming that it had taken place on the Soviets' initiative and represented a victory for Yugoslavia. The Soviet Union's goals toward Yugoslavia had not changed; only Stalin's methods had been modified. Border incidents with the satellites had actually increased since Stalin's death. Tito thus challenged the Soviets to provide proof of their supposed good will: "I do not believe in words, which mean nothing. I believe only in deeds." He assured the West that Yugoslavia's commitment to the Ankara Pact and its ties to Western countries would not diminish.[29] A National Intelligence Estimate (NIE), prepared for Dulles at the end of June, concluded that Yugoslavia would not rejoin the bloc as long as Tito remained in power. Yet the drafters of the report speculated that the Soviets would attempt to weaken Tito's ties with the West "through increasingly conciliatory gestures."[30]

26. Woodruff Wallner to Dulles, 21 May 1953, RG 59, 661.68/5-2153.

27. Wallner to Dulles, 25 May 1953, RG 59, 661.68/5-2553.

28. Wallner to Dulles, 11 June 1953, RG 59, 661.68/6-1153.

29. Wallner to Dulles, 14 June 1953, RG 59, 661.68/6-1453; Cameron to Dulles, 19 June 1953, RG 84, 320 Yugo/USSR.

30. NIE-93, "Probable Developments in Yugoslavia," 26 June 1953, *FRUS, 1952–1954*, 8:1357–59.

In a meeting with Adlai Stevenson on Brioni that same month, Tito gave no indication that the Soviet ploy had succeeded. Acting as a senior international statesman advising the West, Tito again stated that the apparent changes in Soviet policy and the nature of the Soviet system were not genuine. He told Stevenson that he supported the idea of negotiations between the West and the Soviet Union, only because they would deprive the Soviets of the ability to claim that the West was plotting war. He called the recent riots in East Germany the most important postwar event since Yugoslavia's 1948 break with Stalin, since they demonstrated the degree to which the Soviet Union exploited the satellites. Tito also claimed that the initiative for better Italian-Yugoslav relations lay with the Italians, but that he expected little from them. Domestically, with a possible eye toward U.S. public opinion, he stated his wish that Cardinal Stepinac leave the country, and his belief that the peasants were more content since the decollectivization of agriculture. In his final comment to Stevenson, Tito observed that he would like very much to visit the United States, but did not believe Senator Joseph McCarthy would permit it![31]

Tito's comment on Italy reflected how, in the summer of 1953, the chronic dispute over Trieste loomed as more of a threat to relations between Yugoslavia and the West than did the Soviets' overtures. After a serious deterioration in Italian-Yugoslavia relations in the region threatened to lead one or both antagonists to military action, the United States and Britain announced that they would transfer the administration of Zone A to Italy, hoping this would force the Yugoslav and Italian governments to negotiate. The two Western allies also informed the Yugoslavs that they would not oppose Yugoslav control of Zone B and reminded Tito that his country's relations with the West could not improve while the Trieste question remained unsettled. In response, Yugoslav crowds attacked the United States Information Service in Belgrade, and Tito moved his troops to the Italian border.[32]

Djilas, citing Tito's displeasure at his country's dependence on U.S.

31. Llewellyn E. Thompson to Livingston T. Merchant, 10 July 1953, with enclosure Adlai Stevenson to Thompson, 10 July 1953, *FRUS, 1952–1954*, 8:1361–64. In June Ambassador Popović had raised the possibility that Tito visit the U.S. with the State Department, prompting Undersecretary of State Walter Bedell Smith to speculate that Tito, invited to London, "is now extremely anxious to be invited to the United States, and is going to be very sensitive as times goes on and such an invitation is not forthcoming." Smith to Dulles, 20 June 1953, RG 59, 611.68/6-2053.

32. The United States Delegation at the Tripartite Foreign Ministers Conference to the Department of State, 16 October 1953, *FRUS, 1952–1954*, 7(1):692–94; Rabel, *Between East and West*, 150.

aid and the foreign policy adjustments he had already made as a result, later wrote that Tito acted aggressively in 1953 to express his independence of the West. But Tito had also confided to Djilas that Italy would press its claim to Zone B unless the Yugoslavs responded with a show of force.[33] Although Dulles suspected that Tito had responded as he had because the United States and Britain had not consulted him before issuing their ultimatum, he strongly objected to Yugoslavia's actions and asked that they cease.[34] The secretary, in an interesting display of gauging his remarks to his audience, made the same appeal for a lessening of tensions to the Italians, but told them that Yugoslavia, as a communist state, believed "in the use of force to achieve its objectives." The restraints inherent in "a Christian society" were not present there, as they were in Italy.[35]

This crisis, like all the others surrounding Trieste, eventually passed, but it had a negative impact on Yugoslav-Western relations in general and on military ties in particular. In early June, the JCS and the Department of Defense informed the Department of State of their agreement, and that of the British and French, that tripartite military talks be resumed with Yugoslavia "on a covert basis" as soon as possible after the Italian elections. The military representatives of the tripartite powers, after meeting in May in Washington, had decided that while no political guarantees should be given to Yugoslavia during the talks, the military representatives should be authorized by their governments to inform the Yugoslavs that "as military men, they do not believe that a Soviet and/or Satellite attack against Yugoslavia could be limited to a local war." The State Department concurred, providing the military made it clear that the talks were being conducted "on a contingent planning or assumptive basis, and that no commitments of any nature can be made."[36] The United States urged that the talks resume in late June, since the Yugoslavs had begun to question the delay in resuming discussions and seemed to expect their imminent renewal: however, continued wrangling be-

33. Milovan Djilas, *Tito: The Story from Inside* (New York: Harcourt Brace Jovanovich, 1980), 65–66.

34. Barbour, memorandum of conversation, 13 October 1953, *FRUS, 1952–1954,* 8:308–12.

35. Homer M. Byington, memorandum of conversation, 14 October 1953, *FRUS, 1952–1954,* 8:314–17.

36. Frank Nash to Dulles, 3 June 1953, with enclosure, *FRUS, 1952–1954,* 8:1353–57; Matthews to Wilson, 11 June 1953, RG 59, 768.5/6-353; Dulles to London and Paris, 11 June 1953, RG 59, nos. 7889 and 5969, 768.5/6-1153.

tween the tripartite governments over the exact wording of the military representatives' instructions caused additional delays.[37]

The talks finally resumed in Washington in late August. Although the sessions "had gone extremely well," the Western powers declined to schedule additional sessions because the conflict in Trieste rendered "the association of Yugoslavia with NATO difficult," and until a settlement was reached, the "usefulness to NATO of the Greek-Turkish-Yugoslav *entente*" remained limited.[38] When Ambassador Popović complained to Dulles that Yugoslavia had for the first time given full details of its defense plans to the West during those August discussions only to be pilloried in the American press over Trieste, Dulles reminded Popović that the military talks had been secret. The press could only judge Yugoslavia on its public actions.[39]

In October, the administration completed its national security review and issued NSC 162/2, which continued to identify the Soviet Union as the greatest threat to U.S. security. Although post-Stalinist unrest in the satellites showed the "failure of the Soviets fully to subjugate these peoples or to destroy their desire for freedom," the Soviets' military power prevented any significant change. The detachment of the satellites from the bloc did not at that time appear feasible except "by Soviet acquiescence or by war." While such a defection would not seriously diminish the Soviets' military capacity, it "would be a considerable blow to Soviet prestige and might impair in some degree Soviet conventional military capacities in Europe." However, because of the old rivalries among the European states, such as the Italian-Yugoslav dispute over Trieste, Western strength also remained impaired. The United States had to continue to pursue collective security and the possibility of meaningful negotiations with the Soviets, while also taking steps to weaken Soviet prestige and "complicate" the Soviets' control of the satellites."[40]

37. Dulles to London, Paris, and Belgrade, 22 June 1953, RG 59, nos. 8092, 6123, and 1538, 768.5/6-2253, and 23 June 1953, RG 59, nos. 8178, 6190, and 1550, 768.5/6-2353; Aldrich to Dulles, 5 June 1953, RG 59, no. 6426, 768.5/6-553, and 23 June 1953, RG 59, no. 6728, 768.5/6-2353.

38. Merchant to Bonbright, Barbour, and Ridgeway B. Knight, 1 September 1953, RG 59, 768.5/9-153; Paper Prepared in the Office of the Special Assistant to the Secretary of State for Intelligence (W. Park Armstrong), 18 January 1954, *FRUS, 1952–1954,* 8:1365; NIE-99, "Estimate of the World Situation Through 1955," 23 October 1953, *FRUS, 1952–1954,* 2(1):551–57.

39. Henry P. Leverich, memorandum of conversation, 3 September 1953, *FRUS, 1952–1954,* 8:244–47.

40. Report to the NSC by the NSC Planning Board, 30 September 1953, with

The adoption of NSC 174, "U.S. Policy Toward the Soviet Satellites in Eastern Europe," represented the latter policy.[41] During the Truman administration, government analysts had questioned the feasibility of encouraging Titoism in Eastern Europe but little follow-up had occurred until the Eisenhower administration made change in the region one of its priorities.[42] NSC 174, completed in December 1953, acknowledged that although nationalism remained a disruptive force within the Soviet bloc, none of the satellites was likely to duplicate Yugoslavia's history of resistance. Yet that country continued to play an important role in demonstrating "a practical alternative for nationalist communist leaders to submission to Soviet control." The national security interests of the United States demanded a policy of opposition to and eventual termination of Soviet control of the satellites; "feasible" open and covert measures therefore would be used to "create and exploit troublesome problems for the USSR, complicate control in the satellites, and retard the growth of the military and economic potential of the Soviet bloc." These methods included the encouragement of democratic and anticommunist forces within the satellites, as well as the exploitation of "any Titoist tendencies" to demonstrate "that opportunities for survival exist outside the Soviet bloc."[43]

The NSC believed that Tito's continued independence presented a "standing insult to Soviet prestige and a challenge to Soviet infallibility" and that his "political and ideological counteroffensive" was a "disturbing factor within the satellite communist parties." The "mere fact" of Western assistance to Yugoslavia "must have its effect on both communists and non-communists in the satellite countries." The NSC observed that Tito appeared to be moving Yugoslavia "toward closer integration with the defensive system being built up by the free world" and predicted he would ultimately coordinate his military capacity with that of NATO.[44] Little proof for these suppositions existed, but the administration seemed to reason that if it predicted a Titoist

---

enclosure, NSC 162, 30 September 1953, *FRUS, 1952–1954*, 2(1):489–514; Lay, report to the NSC, 30 October 1953, with enclosure, NSC 162/2 and annex, undated, ibid., 577–97.

41. NSC 174, "United States Policy Toward the Soviet Satellites in Eastern Europe," 11 December 1953 (plus attachments), Eisenhower Papers, White House Office (WHO), Office of the Special Assistant for National Security Affairs (OSANSA): Records 1952–61 NSC Series, Policy Papers Subseries, File: NSC 174 Policy Toward the Soviet Satellites in Eastern Europe.

42. *FRUS, 1952–1954*, 8:110–11 n. 1.

43. NSC 174, 11 December 1953, with enclosure, Staff Study by the Planning Board of the NSC, *FRUS, 1952–1954*, 8:110–27.

44. Ibid.

outbreak in the satellites and a Yugoslavia entry into NATO often enough, both were bound to occur.

In reality, the only discernible trend in relations between Yugoslavia and the bloc was one of improvement. By early 1954, border incidents with the satellites had ceased and the Yugoslav press had become less bitter in its criticism of the Soviet Union.[45] Events within Yugoslavia also caused the Eisenhower administration to speculate, just as the Truman administration had, whether Tito's turn to the West had full support within Yugoslavia, or if Tito himself feared the internal implications of his policy. In mid-January 1954, the Yugoslav Central Committee stripped Milovan Djilas of his party positions and forced him to resign as president of the National Assembly. Djilas, a close associate of Tito and one of the leading political theorists in Yugoslavia, had become increasingly critical of the bureaucratization and centralization of the Yugoslav system, which he claimed hampered the growth of democracy. In late 1953, Djilas had written a series of articles for *Borba* in which he had called for a more rapid "withering away" of the party and warned that Stalinism was a danger in any one-party totalitarian state. Tito had known of the series in advance of publication, but after conservative communists criticized Djilas, Tito did as well.[46] Tito finally condemned Djilas, charging that he was willing to pay any price to bring Western democracy to Yugoslavia, including the restoration of capitalism and the destruction of the party.[47]

U.S. analysts believed this controversy brought into the open a conflict that had been raging for some time between more "orthodox" communists within Yugoslavia and those favoring Tito's policies. In the end, Tito had sided with the conservatives because Djilas's criticism threatened the system too much; Tito and his followers were no "more interested in surrendering their power to Western democracy than to Sovietism."[48] The State Department predicted that the whole Djilas affair would have a "negative result on the liberalization process."[49] At the end of January, Ambassador James R. Riddleberger informed Washington that several Yugoslav officials had assured him that there would be no change in Yugoslavia's Western policies, but that many older, more orthodox communists still distrusted the West.[50]

45. Edwin M. J. Kretzmann to Dulles, 5 January 1954, RG 59, 660.68/1-554.
46. Wilson, *Tito's Yugoslavia*, 91–93.
47. Paper Prepared in the Office of the Special Assistant to the Secretary of State for Intelligence (Armstrong), 18 January 1954, *FRUS, 1952–1954*, 8:1365.
48. Ibid.
49. Barbour to Merchant, 18 January 1954, RG 59, 768.00/1-1854.
50. Riddleberger to State, 26 January 1954, RG 59, 768.00/1-2654.

After reviewing its policy toward Yugoslavia in light of the Soviets' continued overtures to Tito and the regime's treatment of Djilas, the administration devised a less optimistic policy statement on Yugoslavia in February 1954. U.S. policymakers remained certain that Yugoslavia would not return to the bloc, but acknowledged that Tito's fear of alienating "doctrinaire Yugoslav Communists and . . . his own unwillingness to have Yugoslav forces serve under non-Yugoslav command" limited the extent of Yugoslavia's participation in Western defense efforts. Some Western nations also remained unwilling to deal with a communist state "as an equal and an ally." The recent Yugoslav-Greek-Turkish treaty, "an example of free association of independent Balkan nations serving as a potential alternative to Soviet rule," was a much more positive development. For the short term, the United States's primary policy objective was still to support Yugoslavia's independence and the appeal of Titoism; aid and other forms of assistance would continue to that end. For the long term, the United States would encourage "political and economic liberalization" within Yugoslavia but only if that did not jeopardize its primary objective. If Soviet or satellite forces attacked Yugoslavia, the United States would "proceed on the assumption that global war is probably imminent." The chances were good that Yugoslavia "even if not initially attacked, would cooperate with the West in event of general war."[51]

In presenting this policy paper to the NSC, Robert Cutler neatly summarized the "tightrope" on which the United States balanced its policy. It consisted, he said, of working for the "immediate objective" of continued Yugoslav independence, despite that state being "a Communist dictatorship," while pursuing the long range goal of establishing a "freely chosen" government there. Assistant Secretary of State Walter Bedell Smith joked that the State Department accomplished its impossible task through "a simple formula" of not letting "the right hand know what the left hand was doing."[52]

The administration, in reality, faced but would not acknowledge a more profound dilemma. If Tito and his followers had no intention of "surrendering their power to Western democracy" then how feasible a policy was the liberating role assigned to Tito in the wedge strategy? Changing the policy's emphasis to stress political rather than military gains did little but beg this more essential question. A purely geopolit-

51. NSC 5406/1, "United States Policy toward Yugoslavia," 6 February 1954, *FRUS, 1952–1954*, 8:1373–77.

52. Memorandum of Discussion at 183d Meeting of the NSC, 4 February 1954, *FRUS, 1952–1954*, 8:1369–72.

ical approach to U.S.-Soviet relations should have led the administration to require only that Tito's independence continue to detract from the Soviets' power. However, the Cold War's cult of anticommunism, which Dulles's rhetoric helped to nourish, demanded the kind of change within Yugoslavia that would render that geopolitical goal unattainable.

In the short run, Yugoslavia continued to improve its ties with the West and its immediate noncommunist neighbors. Military talks between Greece, Turkey, and Yugoslavia had taken place throughout 1953 and continued into 1954, centering on the premise that an attack on the members of the Ankara Pact by Soviet and/or satellite forces would precipitate a world war.[53] The United States welcomed these discussions, insisting only that Greece and Turkey coordinate their proposals with NATO, and that the planning remain on a "contingent basis" with formal political commitments between the three nations to occur later.[54] By the spring of 1954, all three countries suggested that the talks proceed beyond the contingency stage, but the Eisenhower administration remained adamant that concerns about the Italians and the negotiations on Trieste (which at that point appeared promising) precluded more definite arrangements.[55]

The Yugoslavs resented the U.S. position on the Balkan military alliance and sought to change it by appearing conciliatory toward Italy. In a May interview with C. L. Sulzberger of the *New York Times*, Tito offered to propose Italian membership in the Balkan alliance if Italy accepted the Trieste proposal then under discussion (in essence the final settlement that gave Zone A and the city of Trieste to Italy and Zone B, with some economic compensations, to Yugoslavia). He also hinted that Yugoslavia would join Dulles's beloved European Defense Community if it were broadened to be more than a military organization.[56]

Koča Popović, now serving as foreign minister, took a far different tack, complaining to Ambassador Riddleberger that Yugoslavia, by agreeing to negotiate a military alliance with Greece and Turkey and to concessions on Trieste had made "heavy sacrifices for the common defense" but had received little reward for its efforts. The tripartite military discussions had not been resumed, no high-ranking U.S. officials had visited Yugoslavia, and Tito's request to visit the United

53. Cannon to Dulles, 28 November 1953, *FRUS, 1952–1954,* 8:634–36.
54. Smith to Embassy in Greece, 16 December 1953, *FRUS, 1952–1954,* 8:638–39.
55. Smith to Embassy in Greece, 16 February 1954, *FRUS, 1952–1954,* 8:640–42.
56. C. L. Sulzberger, "Trieste Formula Offered by Tito," *New York Times,* 9 May 1954, 20.

States had been abruptly dismissed by Secretary Dulles at a recent press conference. In short, according to Popović, the United States had displayed "a chilly and critical attitude" toward his country. Yugoslavia had little choice but to conclude that United States support was "wavering" and to perhaps "re-assess its policy to take account of the lack of U.S. support, material and moral." Riddleberger attempted to assuage Popović's concerns, but advised Washington of his belief that Yugoslavia's leaders genuinely felt "aggrieved." The ambassador's past conversations with the Yugoslavs on such issues as Trieste and military and economic assistance had featured "hard, tough arguments in which kind and sympathetic words" had not been spoken. That approach had been the correct one, but "perhaps the time has come to apply some balm." Riddleberger suggested closer contacts with Yugoslav military and political leaders and reciprocal high-level visits, including one by Tito to the United States, once the Trieste question had been formally settled.[57]

The United States, Britain, and France did not intend to delay a Balkan alliance indefinitely; their concern centered on the relationship of such a pact to NATO and its effect on Italy and Trieste. The timing and finer details of the alliance rather than its existence were at issue.[58] After some weeks of haggling, Yugoslavia, Greece, and Turkey finally hammered out alliance language compatible with the latter countries' NATO obligations. Although the Trieste negotiations had stalled, Italy dropped her objections to the proposed alliance, since it provided for coordination between the pact members and NATO.[59] Greece, Turkey, and Yugoslavia signed the Treaty of Military Alliance (Balkan Pact) in Bled on 9 August 1954; it entered into force after final ratification by all three governments in 1955. The treaty stipulated that an attack against one of the signatories constituted an attack against all and provided for continuing military discussions and periodic meetings of the foreign ministers of each country.[60]

With this alliance concluded, both Greece and Turkey considered NATO membership for Yugoslavia to be the logical and desirable next step.[61] Tito, who envisioned more of a separation between politics

57. When asked if he knew of any plans to have Tito visit the United States, Dulles had quickly replied in the negative. *FRUS, 1952–1954,* 8:1386 n. 3; Riddleberger to Merchant, 23 June 1954, *FRUS, 1952–1954,* 8:1385–90.

58. Dulles to Riddleberger, 29 June 1954, *FRUS, 1952–1954,* 8:658–59.

59. Dulles to Embassy in United Kingdom, 28 July 1954, *FRUS, 1952–1954,* 8:669–71.

60. Hoffman and Neal, *Yugoslavia and the New Communism,* 422–23.

61. George C. McGhee to Dulles, 6 February 1953, *FRUS, 1952–1954,* 8:616–19.

and defense, did not agree. In a series of speeches in Yugoslavia in September, he reminded the West that his was still a socialist regime. Yugoslavia had long expressed an interest in joining some sort of cooperative European organization, provided it was broadly based rather than strictly military in nature. But Tito saw no place for Yugoslavia in NATO, which he characterized as purely an anticommunist organization. Yugoslavia did not belong in a bloc "with an anti-Socialist tendency." He celebrated the Balkan Pact as an example of the kind of nonideological association that states enter into to preserve their own independence and to deter aggression.[62]

Whatever need Yugoslavia had felt for a Western military alliance in the first years of its quarrel with the Soviets had clearly diminished. Stalin was dead, and the new Soviet leadership seemed determined to repair at least some of the cracks in the Yugoslav-Soviet relationship. If Soviet policy reverted to its Stalinist roots, Yugoslavia's alliance with Greece and Turkey ensured an indirect connection with NATO. Although tripartite economic assistance had ended in June, with both Britain and France asserting that the goal of easing Yugoslavia's transition from an Eastern-oriented to a Western-oriented economy had been attained,[63] the Yugoslavs also were confident of continued U.S. support for their still unstable economy. Tito, in short, had changed the script so carefully crafted for him by Eisenhower and Dulles and had assumed a leading rather than a subordinate role in his relations with the West.

However, that change was less dramatic than it appeared. The Yugoslavs, even when most concerned about a Soviet attack, had always refused to work with the Truman administration on anything other than their own terms. Tito had made "concessions" such as freeing Stepinac or closing the Greek frontier as much for internal reasons as external ones. He was never any more willing to be a junior partner to the West than he was to the Soviets. By the time Eisenhower had assumed the presidency, the U.S. military and economic commitment to Yugoslavia, coupled with the apparent diminution of the Soviet threat, had added a genuine feeling of security to Tito's usual bravado.

But bravado did not ensure self-sufficiency and in the summer of 1954, Yugoslavia submitted an elaborate and long-range economic

62. Jack Raymond, "Yugoslavia Backs Bonn Sovereignty and Right to Rearm," *New York Times,* 20 September 1954, 1, 4.

63. The Department of State to the British Embassy, aide-memoire, 5 April 1954, *FRUS, 1952–1954,* 8:1378–79; the British Embassy to the Department of State, aide-memoire, ibid., 1382–83.

program to the U.S. embassy. The core of the plan centered on a request that the United States, instead of providing assistance on a yearly basis, agree to design a program to meet several years of Yugoslav economic needs, relying on loans rather than the usual grants. The Yugoslav proposal also included requests for additional shipments of wheat and raw materials. Riddleberger advised that the United States could easily meet the requests; pending congressional legislation allowing the sale of agricultural surpluses abroad for local currencies could provide the needed commodities, while additional loans from the Export-Import Bank could fulfill the country's other requirements. The issue to the ambassador was a political one: Did the United States wish to make that kind of a commitment to Yugoslavia? If the United States still intended to maintain Yugoslavia's defensive strength while developing an economy that could support the desired military establishment, the Yugoslav proposal had merit. Long-range planning would provide for a better use of Yugoslav resources and enhance the ability of the United States to influence Yugoslavia's economic and military development.[64]

But would such a program of support enable the United States to influence Yugoslavia's foreign policy? Had it done so in Trieste? By the fall of 1954, most of the issues regarding Trieste had at last been settled; only an impasse over a "tiny bit" of land remained. Eisenhower dispatched Robert Murphy, who was then deputy undersecretary of state for political affairs, to Yugoslavia and Italy to break the deadlock. In the rather warm letter he sent to Tito to explain Murphy's mission, Eisenhower praised Tito's "wisdom and statesmanship" and asked him to "intervene personally" to bring the Trieste negotiations to a successful conclusion. Because of the "close association and cooperation in the economic and military fields" then in existence between Yugoslavia and the United States, and the larger issues "weighing on the free world of which our countries are a part," Eisenhower felt able to call upon Tito "in this friendly fashion." The Yugoslav leader "as a military man" would understand that a better defense of the whole area would be achieved, and U.S. military assistance more effectively spent, if Trieste were settled. Eisenhower closed by noting that he had been told of "certain economic developments and emergencies" in Yugoslavia and that he had asked Murphy to discuss them with Tito "in a spirit of sympathy."[65]

64. Riddleberger to Dulles, 1 July 1954, *FRUS, 1952–1954,* 8:1390–94.
65. Eisenhower to Tito, 10 September 1954, Eisenhower Papers, PAP, Whitman File, International Series, File: Yugoslavia (2).

In the conversations between Tito and Murphy concerning Trieste, Tito proposed a formula for the territory under dispute designed to save face for everyone concerned. The Italians concurred, and all parties signed a memorandum of settlement on 5 October. Murphy had also been authorized, as Eisenhower's letter obliquely indicated, to offer assistance to Yugoslavia if the issue arose. When vice-president Svetozar Vukmanović-Tempo told Murphy of the country's enormous wheat deficit, Murphy agreed the United States could provide 400,000 tons.[66]

Riddleberger credited a number of factors for the final settlement of Trieste, this "thorn in the side" of U.S. relations with both Italy and Yugoslavia. Although Clare Booth Luce, then serving as ambassador to Italy considered the satisfaction of that country's claims "a holy cause," Riddleberger believed Dulles simply wanted a fair and quick settlement. In the end, "drought and diplomacy" carried the day, as Yugoslavia received the impression that U.S. assistance would flow only if both sides came to terms.[67] Luce, who thought Tito to be "a great blackmailer," later claimed that she had suggested to Murphy, during a visit to Washington, that someone "who knew him well enough to twist his arm" be dispatched to Yugoslavia to promise Tito wheat if he agreed to a Trieste accord. After Murphy offered himself as a likely candidate, Luce recalled that she put the question to Eisenhower and Dulles and eventually the bargain was made.[68]

In his memoirs, Eisenhower also implies at least a connection between U.S. assistance and the Trieste settlement. He cites the Yugoslav need for wheat and their desire to enter into talks regarding their general state of indebtedness with giving the United States "a certain leverage" in gaining Yugoslav acceptance for the final agreement.[69] Murphy, by contrast, rejected the suggestion that aid played a role in Tito's thinking. Yugoslavia genuinely wanted to settle the Trieste issue, and Tito was not a man who "would have surrendered on matters of principle for a shipment of wheat."[70] In an oral history of the Trieste negotiations published in the 1970s, Murphy explicitly denied the contention that Tito had been bought off. He recalled that his economic discussions with the Yugoslavs had occurred only after the Trieste issue had been settled, and then with second-

66. Robert Murphy, *Diplomat among Warriors* (Garden City, N.Y.: Doubleday, 1964), 422–24.
67. Riddleberger, Oral History, Princeton, 18–22.
68. Clare Boothe Luce, Oral History, Eisenhower Library, 39–41.
69. Eisenhower, *Mandate for Change,* 419.
70. Murphy, *Diplomat among Warriors,* 424.

rank Yugoslav officials. Murphy believed that what had impressed Tito during the last stage of the negotiations was the fact that "Eisenhower had personally written him on wonderfully friendly terms," and that Murphy had personally delivered the letter.[71] Vladimir Velebit, who represented Yugoslavia in the negotiations and who contributed to the same oral history, agreed with Murphy's recollection. Tito "was pleased that a man like Eisenhower, a big hero of World War II . . . writes him a letter as a friend. . . . It changed the situation at once."[72]

While this personal exchange made some difference, Yugoslavia had also realized that it had nothing to gain by prolonging the conflict over Trieste. According to Velebit, although pressure from the Soviet Union had eased, Tito and his associates remembered the danger Stalin had posed for them and wanted "some form of insurance." If reaching a settlement on "a minor question" like Trieste could help Yugoslavia secure its independence of the Soviets, it was "easier to give up a claim . . . than to jeopardize your very existence."[73] Both the Truman and Eisenhower administrations had always posited Trieste as one of the obstacles to greater cooperation between Yugoslavia and the West, and the link between better relations and better aid had never been minimized. The only problem, as Livingston Merchant explained in a March 1954 memo, was "that it will be difficult long to conceal the step-up in aid for Yugoslavia which we envisage granting after a Trieste settlement." The "discrepancy" between assistance to Yugoslavia and that furnished to Italy would be "even more pronounced" unless the United States took steps to "provide Italy with economic assistance in roughly comparable amount if we get Trieste settlement."[74]

Yugoslavia reaped other benefits from this improvement of relations with the West when the Soviets accelerated their own reconciliation campaign with Tito's government. By the fall of 1954 the Soviets had requested that Yugoslavia send a high-level trade delegation to Moscow, and Tito had agreed. Negotiations had been opened between Yugoslavia and the satellites on short-term barter agreements as well, with longer-range talks to follow. Acting Foreign Minister Bebler informed the Americans that the Soviets also had made some concessions to Yugoslav sensibilities, such as moderating their anti-Yugoslav

71. John C. Campbell, ed., *Successful Negotiation: Trieste, 1954* (Princeton: Princeton University Press, 1976), 133–34, 137.

72. Ibid., 92.

73. Ibid., 106.

74. Merchant to Bonbright, 19 March 1954, RG 59, 768.5-MSP/3-1954.

propaganda, and that the Yugoslavs had made small gestures in return.[75] The United States observed these developments with some concern. Although the embassy in Belgrade continued to accept Tito's assurances that improved relations with the East would not weaken Yugoslavia's ties to the West, the staff warned that the Yugoslavs would attempt "to improve their deal with the west by judicious flirtation with Soviet bloc."[76]

Analysts within the Department of State added a few other elements to the mix, advising Dulles that Tito's wish to improve relations with the Soviets and Eastern Europeans was not surprising; he naturally felt more comfortable in the socialist than in the capitalist camp. Tito understood that while the Soviets may have changed their tactics toward him, their ultimate goal of control remained the same. Yet Tito also seemed to believe that the Soviets' recent behavior indicated a renunciation of military action in Europe, which conformed with his goal of reducing East-West tension and the potential for military conflict. He ultimately hoped to see the emergence of a more independent Europe, one that would serve as a "third force" supporting the USSR and/or the United States only when their policies were deemed acceptable. If it appeared that Tito intended to pursue "excessive free-wheeling between East and West" or to move closer to the bloc, the United States could put its aid on "a discreet short-term, short-tether basis which intentionally aimed at preventing complete Yugoslav viability in the economic and military fields."[77] No one making these recommendations seemed to realize that such a policy was the antithesis of the aid program Yugoslavia had already requested and worked against the imperatives of the wedge strategy as well.

When Foreign Operations Administration (FOA) director Harold E. Stassen visited Yugoslavia in late October, Tito, as though privy to the State Department's analysis, assured him that Yugoslavia's influence with the Balkan satellites would increase because of the Soviets' change in policy toward his country. He spoke of a possible link to the Western European Union if it "develops economic objectives," but foresaw no imminent association with the West on military issues. Tito assessed Yugoslav policy for Stassen by saying that in contrast to India's policy of a "third position through softness," Yugoslavia pursued a "third position through national strength."[78]

75. Wallner to State, 13 October 1954, RG 59, 661.68/10-1354.

76. Wallner to State, 14 October 1954, RG 59, 660.68/10-1454, and 21 October 1954, RG 59, 768.00/10-2154.

77. Ray L. Thurston to Charles B. Elbrick, 26 October 1954, RG 59, 768.00/10-2654.

78. Harold E. Stassen to Dulles, 1 November 1954, *FRUS, 1952–1954,* 8:1414–16.

There is little wonder that Dulles remained convinced, as he told an NSC meeting on October 28, that the Yugoslavs were not "likely to abandon the West and return to their position within the bloc."[79] The president agreed and asked the secretary if there were not some action that the United States could take that would prevent any genuine reconciliation between the Soviet Union and Yugoslavia. The United States, the president said, "must be prepared to do almost anything to keep Tito not only outside the Kremlin orbit but—so far as possible— actively on *our* side."[80]

Dulles responded by suggesting that the administration continue to support Tito "vigorously lest any doubt enter Tito's mind that firm ties to the West are essential for the security and prosperity of Yugoslavia." He also would "hold, as a reserve trump card, an invitation to Tito to visit the U.S."; a move Dulles believed would "cement official relations between the two countries for a substantial period." In the meantime, Dulles confided that he was considering a personal visit to Belgrade.[81] Ever the optimist, Dulles also assured Eisenhower that the way was now clear for further integration of Yugoslavia into Western defense planning and for discussions on the possibility of greater cooperation between NATO and the Balkan Alliance.[82] Tito's disclaimer in his talks with Stassen apparently had had little impact on the secretary of state.

However, both prudence and Congress demanded that continued support for Yugoslavia be subject to a number of new conditions. When a Yugoslav delegation led by Svetozar Vukmanović-Tempo arrived in Washington in November to discuss the summer economic aid proposal, they found more structure and permanence attached to the U.S. foreign aid program. Title 1 of the Agricultural Trade Development and Assistance Act of 1954 (PL 480), passed by Congress and signed by the president a few months before, provided for the sale, in return for local currency, of U.S. agricultural products abroad. Other provisions in the law permitted the donation of food for famine relief or other emergencies and the exchange of surplus products for strategic or more perishable goods.[83] In general, under the provisions of PL 480,

79. NSC Meeting no. 220, 28 October 1954, Eisenhower Papers, PAP, Whitman File, NSC Series, File: NSC Meeting no. 220.

80. Eisenhower to Dulles, 27 October 1954, Eisenhower Papers, PAP, Whitman File, Whitman Diary, File: ACW Diary October 1954 (1).

81. Merchant to Dulles, 2 November 1954, with enclosed memorandum for the president, *FRUS, 1952–1954*, 8:1417–19.

82. Riddleberger to Dulles, 16 November 1954, *FRUS, 1952–1954*, 8:1421–23.

83. Burton I. Kaufman, *Trade and Aid: Eisenhower's Foreign Economic Policy, 1953–1961* (Baltimore: Johns Hopkins University Press, 1982), 28–29.

the aid that the Yugoslavs had expected simply to be given to them by the United States would now have to be purchased.

When Vukmanović-Tempo presented his country's requests for 700,000 tons of wheat and pressed for the acceptance of Yugoslavia's earlier proposals, the United States offered to *sell* him almost half a million tons of wheat, ten million dollars worth of cotton, and one million dollars worth of tobacco. The dinars given in payment would be used to purchase Yugoslav strategic materials and other goods, to supply equipment to the Yugoslav military beyond that given under the MSP, and to support economic development programs within Yugoslavia. The United States made no commitments on the other proposals. Tempo's response was "sharp and bitter." He expressed particular anger about the provisions concerning tobacco, which Yugoslavia also produced and exported and threatened to fly back to Belgrade immediately if better terms were not secured.[84]

In an account of these negotiations published some years later, Tempo recalled the continuing drought that had compelled Yugoslavia to again seek help from the United States. He also related his desire to receive U.S. consent for an internal development scheme to be financed by the sale of the wheat requested from the administration. Under the Mutual Security Act of 1951, the money obtained from selling the foodstuffs acquired from the United States had to be spent on projects mutually agreed upon by the two governments. The Yugoslavs resented these provisions, characterized by Vukmanović-Tempo as "interference in our political economy," but had submitted to them out of necessity. Recent overtures by the Soviets to improve relations with Yugoslavia had caused Tempo to be even more reluctant to engage in simultaneous negotiations with the United States, but Tito and Kardelj had assured him "this was precisely the moment for maintaining good relations" with both powers.[85]

Vukmanović-Tempo's initial discussions in Washington had proceeded smoothly; he recorded that his "meeting with Dulles was a pleasant surprise" and centered on discussions of the past histories of the United States and Yugoslavia. He was therefore "stunned" when the U.S. negotiators presented their counterproposals, which he saw as "blackmail" and an assault on Yugoslavia's independence. He dismissed Robert Murphy's assurances that all countries receiving United States aid were subject to the provisions of PL 480 and stormed

84. Dulles to Riddleberger, 18 November 1954, *FRUS, 1952–1954*, 8:1423–24.
85. Svetozar Vukmanović-Tempo, *Revolucijo Koja Tece: Memoari* (Belgrade: Kommunist, 1971), 2:208–11.

out of the meetings. Tempo claimed that only the importuning of his own staff and FOA director Stassen persuaded him to remain in Washington in hopes that a compromise could be reached.[86]

After additional talks, the two sides negotiated an accord involving only the sale of wheat and cotton, with a U.S. promise to consider additional wheat shipments and to assist Yugoslavia in finding solutions to its other economic problems.[87] Robert Murphy later criticized what he saw as the United States's lack of toughness in dealing with the Yugoslavs. He thought their demands excessive and counseled Stassen to negotiate more aggressively. Stassen demurred, and Murphy, already aware of Tito's ability to manipulate the wedge strategy more effectively than the administration could, believed the United States never received "a bit of satisfaction or benefit" for the aid it provided.[88]

Dulles did not agree. To ensure public support for continued assistance to Tito's government, he attempted to integrate the Yugoslav-Soviet rapprochement into his cherished "liberation of captive peoples" policy. In a speech in Chicago in November 1954, Dulles stated that when Yugoslavia had broken free of the Soviets in 1948 it had "reasserted its own nationalism," only to be "reviled" by its Soviet bloc neighbors. Now that Yugoslavia had successfully sustained its independence, the Soviet Union treated it "with deference," while viewing Hungary, Bulgaria, and Romania and their "puppet governments" with "contempt." Dulles hoped that this difference "may embolden the satellites to demand a measure of independence."[89] At a press conference in December, the secretary returned to this theme, describing the Soviets as "almost fawning in their efforts to win back good relations with Yugoslavia."[90]

The Soviets' fawning quickly showed its limits. Even though Yugoslavia and the bloc continued to negotiate and sign a variety of trade, loan, and credit agreements,[91] the Yugoslavs and the Soviets publicly criticized each others' policies. In early March, Soviet foreign minister Molotov, still opposed to the Soviet overtures to Tito, charged Yugosla-

86. Ibid., 2:214–20.

87. Stassen to Riddleberger, 23 November 1954, *FRUS, 1952–1954,* 8:1426–27.

88. Murphy, *Diplomat among Warriors,* 426–27.

89. Dulles, "The Goal of Our Foreign Policy," address to the National 4-H Club Congress, Chicago, Illinois, 29 November 1954, Department of State for the Press No. 674, Selected Correspondence and Related Materials, box 88, John Foster Dulles Papers, Seeley G. Mudd Manuscript Library, Princeton University, Princeton, New Jersey (hereafter cited as "Dulles Papers, Correspondence [Princeton]," with box number).

90. Radio and Press Conference no. 17, 21 December 1954, Dulles Papers, Correspondence (Princeton), box 88.

91. Hoffman and Neal, *Yugoslavia and the New Communism,* 341–42.

via with being slow to accept Soviet attempts to normalize relations and suggested that Tito probably now regretted the stance he had taken in 1948. Tito's angry reply, in which he demanded that Soviet and bloc leaders admit they had made a mistake in 1948 when they expelled Yugoslavia, cheered Western observers, who believed it demonstrated that Tito was indeed not about to return to the Soviet fold.[92] The *New York Times* of 20 March 1955 probably said it best when it titled its account of the Tito-Molotov exchange: "Tito Stands Off Soviet Advance."[93]

However, rather than turn to the West, Tito continued to develop his "third force." Since the break with Stalin, Tito had cultivated relations with the newly independent and nonaligned states in Asia and Africa. When he traveled to India in late 1954 and early 1955, he plainly proclaimed his opposition to any and all ideological and political blocs. In their joint communiqué, Tito and Indian prime minister Jawaharlal Nehru had also rejected neutralism and proclaimed their adherence to an active nonaligned policy, designed to promote genuine peace and security for all nations of the world.[94]

In an effort to weaken Tito's increasing attachment to nonalignment, the United States eagerly supplied him with millions of dollars of economic and military assistance. Even though Tito had said almost nothing about continuing military talks with the NATO powers for several months, the JCS urged greater efforts "to insure that Yugoslavia's considerable military potential will be a positive asset to the United States and its Allies." The Chiefs disagreed with the State Department's recommendation that this occur through a joint Italy–Balkan Pact–U.S. exchange and instead supported only bilateral contacts with the Yugoslavs to coordinate their defense plans with NATO and to ascertain the kind of military support the West could furnish Yugoslavia in case of an outside attack. The JCS accepted Tito's unwillingness to join NATO, but echoing Dulles's optimism, saw that delay as temporary and suggested that the discussions "should await a more favorable political climate."[95] Tito's government remained silent. The Yugoslavs also refused to allow the American Miliary Assistance Staff (AMAS) personnel to inspect the uses of the military equipment already sent, even though the U.S.-Yugoslav military assis-

92. Reiss, *Molotov Remembers,* 83; "Tito's Strong Tone on Soviet Stressed," *New York Times,* 9 March 1955, 8; "Press in Moscow Prints Tito Blast," ibid., 11 March 1955, 1, 4.
93. Jack Raymond, "Tito Stands Off Soviet Advance," *New York Times,* 20 March 1955, 6E.
94. Rubinstein, *Yugoslavia and the Non-aligned World,* 53–55.
95. JCS to Wilson, 6 January 1955, *FRUS, 1955–1957,* 26:613–15.

tance agreement of 1951 and the MSP legislation passed by Congress required such inspections.[96]

Riddleberger's analysis of Yugoslavia's policy provided some comfort, particularly to an administration itself skilled in using rhetoric to disguise the fact that there often was more continuity than change in its overall containment policy. In late February, the ambassador advised that Yugoslav officials remained "largely conciliatory," despite uncertainties concerning military coordination and the recent Yugoslav decision to reestablish relations with Communist China. Aid and support from the West was of "paramount importance" to Tito's government. The regime would continue its rhetoric against both blocs, since it "provides an easy way of exemplifying how Yugoslavia is "different," is independent, and helps to justify unpopular internal policies." The Yugoslavs, who still felt vulnerable to attack, were unhappy that more far reaching reform had not occurred in the USSR. Tito might engineer a change in foreign policy as a result and the regime's decision on further military cooperation with the West, "a question now reposing with Tito personally" would serve as a guide in that regard.[97]

In late March, Admiral John H. Cassady, commander in chief, naval forces, Eastern Atlantic and Mediterranean, finally held bilateral talks with Tito and other Yugoslav officials, as the JCS had suggested, but they were not definitive. This prompted Jacob Beam, the director of the Office of European Affairs, to ask Riddleberger for another assessment of Yugoslavia's policies. To secure aid for Yugoslavia the United States must know what limits if any, the Yugoslavs had set for their rapprochement with the Soviets and to what extent Yugoslavia would attach itself to NATO.[98]

Riddleberger based his response on the premise that "Yugoslavia is less than an ally, even if at present more than a neutral, and it is always possible that the private reassurances of its leaders to the West may not be genuinely meant." Advantages the West had once sought through its relationship with Yugoslavia, such as the hope that the Balkan Pact would be converted into a military alliance and that Tito would align himself closely with NATO, had become less certain since both the rapprochement with the Soviets and Tito's embrace of the nonaligned movement. However, Yugoslavia's maintenance of its military strength; its resolve to foster good relations with Italy, Greece,

96. Murphy, *Diplomat among Warriors*, 425–26.
97. Riddleberger to Dulles, 21 February 1955, *FRUS, 1955–1957*, 26:615–22.
98. *FRUS, 1955–1957*, 26:631–32 n. 10.

and Turkey; its attempts to build economic ties with Western Europe; and its support of the UN were all advantageous to the West. Yugoslavia's continued independence and its "power of seduction of the satellites" further weakened Soviet power. The pull of "ideological affinity" between Yugoslavia and the Soviet Union was a constant danger, but Riddleberger believed the pro-Western, anticommunist views of the Yugoslav people set "a limit on how far Tito can swing to the East." The Yugoslavs, rather than solidifying their ties with the Soviets, could very well embrace a genuinely neutralist position, despite Tito's claims to the contrary.[99]

Riddleberger conceded that Yugoslavia could be of more use to the Soviets than to the West, but that would not occur as long as the Yugoslavs needed Western assistance and Soviet policy remained a threat to their independence. The Tito regime would "take almost any risk . . . that promised to prevent or avoid war," since it knew full well it could not survive such a conflict. As long as the West pursued policies "of moderation and reasonableness" the Yugoslavs would remain "steady." Yet enough uncertainties existed in the relationship between Yugoslavia and the West, and between Yugoslavia and the Soviet Union, to justify a review of U.S. policy. Riddleberger agreed that continued aid would not be justifiable if Yugoslavia did not involve itself more deeply in Western defense plans and pledged to do whatever he could in that case "to bring home the facts of life to the Yugoslavs."[100]

This he did in a meeting with Tito at the end of April. The State Department, preferring to remain "relatively flexible," had empowered Riddleberger to discuss conditions for resuming tripartite discussions, but only on an interim basis; "some form of NATO planning tie" remained the administration's preference. The United States still valued Yugoslavia, but had to be assured that its "substantial military manpower . . . will fight on our side in major European war, which is primary assumption our present aid programs." While Yugoslav "armed neutrality . . . would be useful," the United States most needed "assurance that Yugoslav forces will protect Ljubljana Gap." Barring that, Riddleberger was to tell Tito, Yugoslavia's promise to cooperate in the defense of Greece and Turkey would be "valuable" and assist the United States in its policy reevaluation.[101]

99. Riddleberger to Beam, 4 April 1955, *FRUS, 1955–1957,* 26:623–32.
100. Ibid.
101. Herbert C. Hoover, Jr., to Riddleberger, 23 April 1955, *FRUS, 1955–1957,* 26:638–40.

Tito did not provide what the administration required. Although he seemed open to future discussions on military coordination (suggesting June as a possible date), he did not clearly indicate whether he preferred multilateral or bilateral talks. His remarks on the Balkan Alliance Riddleberger characterized as "elusive." However, Riddleberger left the meeting certain that Tito understood the linkage between continued assistance and military coordination and that he "was more than a little unhappy" with some aspects of U.S. policy. Nevertheless, the meeting with Tito had "served the purpose of clearing the air."[102]

At an NSC discussion of Yugoslavia in early May, all of the current points of view concerning that country's policies received an airing. CIA director Allen Dulles summarized his agency's most recent assessment, which centered on the failure of the United States to remember that Tito was "after all, a hard-core Moscow-trained Communist." Nonetheless, Yugoslavia would pursue a policy of "benevolent neutralism" toward the West, while seeking to "maintain correct relations" with the Soviets. The Yugoslav people were not happy under communism and would change their regime were they able. Tito "wanted to keep his job," said Dulles, and probably feared that if he associated himself "too closely with the West, Yugoslavia will gradually lose its Communist character and he in turn would lose his job." JCS chairman Radford conveyed his group's conviction that "no new aid commitments" should be made to Yugoslavia "pending clarification of Tito's attitude." Eisenhower agreed that the United States "had better be very cautious in our future dealings with Tito." The group as a whole endorsed a reevaluation of NSC 5406.[103]

As these deliberations proceeded, Tito, after what Riddleberger described as a "somewhat animated interview" with the Soviet ambassador at a diplomatic reception for the Turkish prime minister, suddenly proposed to Riddleberger that talks with the tripartite powers resume in June. Riddleberger and his French and British colleagues agreed to accept Tito's proposal and to include on the agenda the question of military coordination with the West, even though the Yugoslavs had not made clear their intention to tackle this subject in any detail.[104] Because of the continuing problems with the U.S. military aid program, Riddleberger and the head of the AMAS in Yugosla-

102. Riddleberger to Dulles, 25 April 1955, *FRUS, 1955–1957*, 26:641–44.

103. NSC Meeting no. 247, 5 May 1955, Eisenhower Papers, PAP, Whitman File, NSC Series, File: NSC Meeting no. 247; Memorandum of Discussion of NSC Meeting no. 247, 5 May 1955, *FRUS, 1955–1957*, 26:645–47.

104. Riddleberger to Dulles, 6 May 1955, *FRUS, 1955–1957*, 26:647–49.

via, General Peter C. Hains III, had been discussing the suspension of shipments of some military goods to Yugoslavia. Both now decided that a total suspension should be delayed in light of Tito's willingness to hold talks with the tripartite powers.[105] However, Riddleberger warned Vukmanović-Tempo that while the United States was prepared at that time to meet Yugoslavia's wheat requests, "we would have to suspend various shipments" if the military issue were not satisfactorily solved.[106]

Before the proposed discussions took place, even more severe complications surfaced in the Yugoslav-Western relationship. On 13 May, Yugoslav foreign minister Popović, in advance of an announcement in the press, informed Riddleberger and the ambassadors of the United Kingdom, France, Greece, and Turkey that a top-level delegation of Soviet leaders would visit Belgrade at the end of the month in accordance with Yugoslavia's policy of improving relations between the two countries. While his country welcomed this opportunity, Yugoslavia still believed relations between nations had to be based on the principles of equality and noninterference. The meeting would provide a way to ascertain the sincerity of the Soviets' claims regarding the normalization of relations, just as the West and the Soviets were exploring ways to relax tensions between them. Popović also repeatedly emphasized that this step signaled no change in Yugoslavia's attitude toward the West. Indeed, he depicted the Soviet journey to Belgrade as a "victory" for Yugoslavia's independent policy and the United States's support of that policy. Uncertainty surfaced only in Popović's concern that the Western press would put a negative connotation on the meeting; Riddleberger replied that the news would cause a "sensation." Riddleberger attempted but failed to discover if Tito planned a return visit to the Soviet Union, or what the precise agenda of the meeting would be. The foreign minister did reveal, however, that Molotov would not be part of the Soviet delegation, and interpreted this as significant in light of Molotov's role in the Tito-Stalin split.[107]

This seeming rapprochement between Yugoslavia and the Soviet Union made Riddleberger pessimistic that any agreement concerning military coordination could now be reached or that the regime would keep the West appraised of its discussions with the Soviets. Riddleberger judged that the West had already clearly made its case with

105. *FRUS, 1955–1957,* 26:649 n. 8.
106. Riddleberger to Dulles, 8 May 1955, RG 59, no. 915, 768.5-MSP/5-855.
107. Riddleberger to Dulles, 13 May 1955, RG 59, no. 942, 661.68/5-1355.

Tito but had been "rebuffed." He counseled that all military shipments be suspended now, before the Soviets and Yugoslavs conferred, and that the tripartite ambassadors agree on a joint strategy before their June meeting with the Yugoslavs.[108]

Riddleberger's suggestion posed more questions that it answered. Was such a suspension of U.S. military aid on the eve of the Soviet visit a wise policy, particularly if Tito's proposal for the resumption of tripartite military talks had been designed as a counter to that visit? If, as the result of an aid suspension, the Yugoslavs turned to the Soviets rather than to the West, all that the West had gained from the split would disappear. But how extensive were those gains? Had the United States achieved all that it ever would from its relationship with Yugoslavia? Although the Yugoslav government followed its private assurances to Riddleberger with public avowals that the Soviet visit would not in any way alter Yugoslavia's attitude toward the West,[109] it soon became clear that an unrequited wedge strategy had raised congressional concerns. Senators Walter F. George, the Democratic chair of the Senate Foreign Relations Committee, and William Knowland, the Republican minority leader, quickly charged that the Soviets hoped to turn Yugoslavia from its ties to the West and cause Tito to adopt an even more neutral position. Although Senator George expressed doubt that the Soviet ploy would succeed, if it did the United States would have to reevaluate its position regarding aid to Yugoslavia.[110]

In a good summary of the issues bedeviling the administration's policies, the *New York Times* in mid-May acknowledged the understandable "misgivings" generated by the Soviet visit to Belgrade, but nonetheless remained convinced that no "basic change" in Yugoslavia's policy would occur. Yugoslav leaders, having tasted the "heady wine" of freedom and an increase in their popularity because of their "courage" in resisting Stalin, would have no reason to return to the status of "servants of distant Kremlin masters."[111]

During the early years of the Eisenhower administration, Tito appeared to have won in his Cold War game between East and West.

108. Riddleberger to Dulles, 16 May 1955, RG 59, no. 957, 661.68/5-1655.

109. See, for example, "Top Soviet Chiefs to Visit Belgrade on Peace Mission," *New York Times,* 14 May 1955, 1, 2; "Tito Gives Pledge to Shun Any Bloc," ibid., 16 May 1955, 1, 10.

110. Elie Abel, "U.S. Sees Soviet Aiming to Groom Tito as Neutral," *New York Times,* 15 May 1955, 1, 4.

111. Editorial, "Visit to Belgrade," *New York Times,* 19 May 1955, 28.

Each side extended assistance to his regime; each sought his support for their own foreign policy objectives. Although Tito seemed ready only to chose the third path of nonalignment, neither the United States nor the Soviet Union cut him adrift, as each still hoped to influence his policies. To optimists like Dulles, Tito's ties to the West, represented by the Balkan Pact and the amount of Allied economic and military assistance flowing to Yugoslavia seemed to place his nonalignment in a pro-Western context. Dulles was more than willing to continue aid on that premise. Still, by the middle of 1955, the Soviets' attempts to repair the break with Yugoslavia and Tito's unwillingness to increase his participation in Western defense plans caused the Eisenhower administration as a whole to look more closely at what Tito did rather than at what they hoped he would do, and to question its own expectations. Only Dulles, in his zeal to bring change to Eastern Europe, continued to depart from this pattern, but he alone did not make policy.

CHAPTER FIVE

1955–1956
FROM BELGRADE TO BRIONI
TO MOSCOW

Personal diplomacy played a key role in the relationships between Yugoslavia and the United States and Yugoslavia and the Soviet Union in 1955 and 1956. The spectacle of Khrushchev and company traveling to Belgrade in 1955 to make their peace with Tito was matched only by the vision of John Foster Dulles being whisked around a lake in Tito's speedboat later that same year. Despite the Yugoslav-Soviet rapprochement, Dulles remained certain that Tito's foreign policy, like his hospitality, was balanced between East and West but that this posture served the interests of the United States more than it did the aims of the Kremlin. However, Tito's journey to the Soviet capital in 1956 and his reluctance to support anything but socialist liberalization in the satellites tested even Dulles's faith. Tito's neutralism appeared far more pro-Soviet than pro-Western, and Tito's critics in Congress used his neutralism, as they had his communism, to oppose the administration's plans to assist him. As a result, Eisenhower and Dulles had to use all of their persuasive skills to salvage Yugoslavia's place in the wedge strategy.

After the Yugoslav announcement of the pending Soviet trip to Belgrade, Yugoslav ambassador Leo Mates, appearing on *Meet The Press*, gave the administration a boost by contending that the visit was bound to stir the leaders of the Eastern European satellites to strive for greater independence from Moscow. He also firmly declared Yugoslavia's rejection of a neutral international stance.[1] In a subsequent meeting with the ambassador, Dulles hailed the Soviet move as a victory for Yugoslavia's policy of independence, but requested Mates's assurance that that policy had not changed. Mates obliged, stressing that the Soviets, not the Yugoslavs, had requested the visit, and that his government considered this only a preliminary step in the improvement of relations between the two countries. Mates promised that no secret agreements would result from the talks and that all "friendly" governments would be kept apprised of the results.[2]

According to the minutes of this meeting, Dulles said nothing about Riddleberger's proposal to suspend military shipments, but only informed Mates that problems still existed "in connection with the operation" of the military assistance program. Since he did not wish "to get this matter mixed up with the visit of the Soviet leaders to Belgrade," he assured Mates that the United States would not raise the issue now, but that this "was a matter which we felt was important to work out and one to which we would revert in the future."[3]

Dulles subsequently released a statement to the press (having secured Mates's approval of its wording), in which he recalled the "violent hostility" the Soviets had shown to Yugoslavia since 1948. He also congratulated Tito's government on the maintenance of its independence, "a policy which the Government of the United States has been assured by the Yugoslav Government it will continue to follow."[4]

Congress, in the midst of its debate on (and chronic attempts to trim) the Mutual Security Program, had a less sanguine reaction to the proposed Soviet visit. Eisenhower, who had personally observed the contributions made to Western security by both the Marshall Plan and NATO, strongly believed in the Mutual Security Program.[5] In his memoirs he wrote of the anger he felt when shortsighted members of Congress labeled it as nothing more than an attempt to buy the friendship and support of other nations. Gaining funds for the MSP

1. "Tito Envoy Sees East Bloc Astir," *New York Times*, 23 May 1955, 1, 10.
2. Merchant, memorandum of conversation, 23 May 1955, *FRUS, 1955–1957*, 26:652–53.
3. Ibid.
4. Department of State for the Press no. 284, 23 May 1955, Dulles Papers, Correspondence (Princeton), box 98.
5. Donovan, *Inside Story*, 147.

was never easy; throughout his years in office he fought "eight battles" with Congress to protect its appropriation.[6]

Congressional opposition to aid to Yugoslavia had increased steadily since the relief bill of 1950, with Democrat Edna Kelly usually leading the forces in the House, and Republican Knowland playing a similar role in the Senate.[7] Although the Democrats had a slim majority in Congress, Minority Leader Knowland was a particular irritant to Eisenhower. A member of the isolationist wing of the Republican Party, the very group Eisenhower had run for the presidency in part to defeat, Knowland had been chosen by Robert A. Taft to succeed him as Republican leader. Yet the man whom Taft saw as a worthy opponent of the internationalists proved too abrasive and independent to have much more than a negative influence.[8] But that negative influence, wielded by a senator described by Robert Murphy as "an especially formidable opponent of the Yugoslav aid program" proved troublesome.[9] By 1955, empowered by the Yugoslav-Soviet rapprochement, Knowland and his followers could threaten to eliminate or at least greatly reduce funds for Tito's government.

Dulles, in a appearance before the House Foreign Affairs Committee a few days after his meeting with Mates, urged Congress not to deny Yugoslavia assistance under the Mutual Security Program. He used the Soviet visit to Belgrade as an example of the kind of policy changes that had been forced on the Soviets by Yugoslavia's inclusion in the Western defense network. Dulles found it remarkable that "the heads of the Soviet State, who have never yet in time of peace left their home country, go to Belgrade to make their peace. Independence is rewarded, and heresy is condoned. This is bound to have a profound effect throughout the Soviet zone."[10]

The assessments of the Yugoslav-Soviet talks provided by the U.S. ambassadors to Yugoslavia and the Soviet Union should have served to temper the secretary's views. As the Soviets arrived in Belgrade, Riddleberger reported that negative opinions about the meeting prevailed among both the general Yugoslav public (with reactions ranging "from depression through alarm to outright fear") and rank-and-

6. Eisenhower, *Mandate for Change*, 215–16.

7. Campbell, *Tito's Separate Road*, 50.

8. James T. Patterson, *Mr. Republican: A Biography of Robert A. Taft* (Boston: Houghton Mifflin, 1972), 606–7, 615.

9. Murphy, *Diplomat among Warriors*, 426.

10. Department of State for the Press no. 292, "Statement in Support of Mutual Security Bill before House Committee on Foreign Affairs," 25 May 1954, Dulles Papers, Correspondence (Princeton), box 98.

file party members, who expected "directives to rethink their loyalties which had been exclusively oriented toward Tito and Yugoslav party." "Party rapprochement" constituted the main item on the Soviet conference agenda, but the Yugoslavs planned to counter that with a demand that the Soviets recognize more than one road to socialism. The presence of top Soviet leaders in the USSR delegation indicated that the Soviets were not certain of success and unless they made a "spectacular" offer to the Yugoslavs, Riddleberger expected "hard bargaining at conference." Yet he also surmised the Soviets would not have staked their prestige on the meeting unless they were sure they had some proposals, such as those on commonly held foreign policy positions, which the Yugoslavs would accept. Kardelj, however, had already assured him that the Yugoslavs would not agree to any proposals for a neutralized Germany, which would be, they assumed, one of the Soviets' main priorities.[11]

On balance the Soviet visit, which lasted from 27 May to 2 June, did not heal the rift between the USSR and Yugoslavia. Although Khrushchev immediately apologized for the events of 1948, the Soviet leadership, still in the early stages of their de-Stalinization campaign, blamed Stalin's lieutenants for the misdeeds of his rule rather than the man himself. In his airport arrival speech Khrushchev appealed to Yugoslavia to rejoin the communist family of nations but cited Lavrenti Beria rather than Stalin as the instigator of the Soviet-Yugoslav split. Tito made no response, and the assembled crowd did not applaud Khrushchev's words.[12] As the *New York Times* observed, Tito had no other choice: "The insult which had been rendered to his intelligence would have required a reply out of accord with the diplomatic protocol required by the occasion."[13] Ambassador Bohlen agreed, later writing that the Yugoslavs "must have listened to that lie in amazement," knowing all too well that the policy and the threats behind it had been Stalin's.[14]

Bohlen surmised that Khrushchev's "bare-faced" and "embarrassing" remarks at the airport demonstrated that the Soviets, rather than simply hoping to reestablish party relations with the Yugoslavs, actually sought "to bring 'comrade Tito' back into fold on basis shared belief Marxist-Leninist teachings, common goals of socialism and

11. Riddleberger to State, 26 May 1955, RG 59, no. 1021, 661.68/2655.
12. Jack Raymond, "Khrushchev Apologizes to Tito in Belgrade and Bids Him Return," *New York Times*, 27 May 1955, 1, 4.
13. Jack Raymond, "Yugoslavs Aloof as Russian Talks Open in Belgrade," *New York Times*, 28 May 1955, 1, 2.
14. Bohlen, *Witness to History*, 376.

interest in 'international workers movement.' " Nonetheless, the ambassador characterized Khrushchev's speech as the "full Soviet apology for events 1948 and public confession of error" that Tito had
long demanded.[15] Riddleberger agreed that the speech "met stated
Yugoslav requirement that Soviets accept responsibility for 1948
break and make full retraction although manner of doing so leaves
much to be desired." While not certain that the Soviet apology foreshadowed greater autonomy for the satellites, another Yugoslav position, Riddleberger believed the speech endorsed the possibility of
different roads to socialism. But Yugoslav sources had indicated displeasure at Khrushchev's behavior, with Undersecretary of State for
Foreign Affairs Srdja Prica complaining that Khrushchev had "talked
as if he were addressing some local committee in Moscow." Riddleberger remained confident that the Yugoslavs would not rush into the
Soviet embrace.[16]

Khrushchev must have had a similar reaction. In his memoirs, he
recalled that he first realized the "falsity" of his view of Stalin when
the Yugoslavs rejected his airport remarks with scorn and sarcasm.
He credited himself for insisting that overtures to improve relations
be made to Yugoslavia, but complained that the reception in Belgrade
was devoid "of brotherly feeling" and too "restrained." Khrushchev
feared the coldness of his welcome would only encourage those in the
Soviet leadership who opposed rapprochement with Yugoslavia. He
also resented Yugoslavia's trade with the West; nonetheless, the Soviets agreed as a result of the meeting to forgive Yugoslavia's debt and
to extend credits as well.[17]

Tensions between the United States and the Soviet Union intruded
on the Yugoslav-Soviet talks, as least briefly, when Khrushchev inef-
fectually browbeat Riddleberger about U.S. policy toward the USSR.
At a dinner meeting Khrushchev complained that the United States
persistently misjudged Soviet motives and prevented the peaceful
settlement of issues by insisting on negotiating from a "position of
strength." When Riddleberger catalogued several instances in which
the Soviets had used force to gain an advantage, Khrushchev changed
the subject and railed against the failure of both the capitalist United
States and Riddleberger himself to understand the grievances of the
world's working classes. Riddleberger disputed the Soviet leader's

15. Bohlen to Dulles, 27 May 1955, RG 59, no. 2118, 661.68/5-2755.
16. Riddleberger to Dulles, 27 May 1955, RG 59, no. 1025, 661.68/5-2755.
17. Strobe Talbott, ed., *Khrushchev Remembers* (Boston: Little, Brown, 1970), 343,
374–83.

claim by disclosing that "as a young man I had been a farm hand, an iceman, a painter, an apple picker" and that for Khrushchev "there could be no greater illusion than to believe that all Americans whom he happened to meet at parties had no manual labor background." Khrushchev again changed the subject, and as the two argued over U.S. policy toward the upcoming Geneva Conference, Tito interrupted to propose a toast, only to have Riddleberger and Khrushchev wrangle over the wording. Riddleberger believed the whole encounter "was a planned affair but perhaps went further than the Yugoslavs anticipated."[18] The State Department congratulated Riddleberger on his "firm skillful handling" of the episode.[19]

At the end of the visit, Yugoslavia and the Soviet Union issued the Belgrade Declaration, which expressed agreement on a number of foreign policy issues, such as the admission of the People's Republic of China to the UN. Of greatest significance and importance to the Yugoslavs was the Belgrade Declaration's acceptance of the right of each state to find its own road to socialism, without interference by another, and to run its foreign policy in the same independent fashion. As the *New York Times* reported, despite Khrushchev's claim that the declaration had ended the ill will between his country and Yugoslavia, most Western diplomats viewed the communiqué as a clear triumph for Yugoslavia.[20]

Bohlen and Riddleberger agreed that the Soviets had not achieved their objectives in Yugoslavia. The Yugoslavs, according to Bohlen, had resisted Soviet attempts, "so crudely set forth in Khrushchev's airport statement," to tie them to Soviet ideology. However, the Yugoslavs had made some concessions by publicly supporting a number of Soviet foreign policy positions. This created the "appearance of solidarity with Soviet Union on chief questions of current international interest," although the Yugoslavs in fact endorsed no positions they did not already hold.[21]

18. Riddleberger to Dulles, 28 May 1955, RG 59, no. 1035, 661.68/5-2855. In his political biography of Khrushchev, William J. Tompson has written that the visit to Yugoslavia "was full of petty humiliations" for the Soviets. Tito did "everything he could to make his guests look foolish," and they often unwittingly cooperated. William J. Tompson, *Khrushchev: A Political Life* (New York: St. Martin's Press, 1995), 146.

19. Hoover to Riddleberger, 31 May 1955, RG 59, no. 968, 661.68/5-2855.

20. Jack Raymond, "Tito and Russians Concur on China and German Unity," *New York Times*, 3 June 1955, 1, 2; James Reston, "U.S. Sees Warning in Belgrade Accord," ibid.; Jack Raymond, "Soviet Bloc Feud with Tito Ended, Khrushchev Says," *New York Times*, 4 June 1955, 1, 3; Clifton Daniel, "Moscow Sees Broad Effect in Its Yugoslav Agreement," ibid.

21. Bohlen to Dulles, 3 June 1955, RG 59, no. 2154, 661.68/6-355.

Through the Belgrade Declaration, the Soviets had, in Bohlen's words, declared the satellites' right "to follow path of internal developments dictated by their national interest (always, of course, within framework of socialism) and not dictated by Moscow." He theorized that this could be part of a policy of liberalization toward the satellites, a policy for which reconciliation with Tito was a necessary first step. Bohlen also speculated that the establishment of diplomatic relations between Yugoslavia and the People's Republic of China may have worried the Soviets, who then acted to repair the rift with Yugoslavia and prevent Yugoslavia and China from creating a "rival Communist center with resultant effect on Asian neutrals such as India."[22]

Riddleberger's analysis followed the same lines. The Yugoslav officials to whom he spoke were "highly satisfied" with the negotiations and Yugoslavia's ability to resist Soviet pressure. Nonetheless, Riddleberger viewed the joint foreign policy statements as damaging to the free world, and despite the Yugoslav claim to have worded the declaration carefully to protect their interests, thought the "Soviets astutely took advantage of Tito's already demonstrated neutralist tendencies." However, on balance Riddleberger shared Bohlen's view that the conference had widened the gap between the two communist countries. Yugoslav sources had told him that Tito, who had been optimistic about the meeting, was "disillusioned" and no longer as convinced of the Soviets' good intentions. He was reportedly "shocked" at the Soviets' casual talk of the gains they could make through a third world war and at their admission that Stalinist policies continued within the USSR. Many in the Yugoslav leadership also had formed a low opinion of Khrushchev and the other Soviets and doubted their ability to negotiate with the West. Riddleberger and his Western counterparts all agreed that a "conference with tripartite powers should be held if only for purpose of ascertaining real Yugoslav position following this conference."[23] The State Department concurred, giving Riddleberger the discretion to set a definite date in June for tripartite talks with Yugoslavia.[24]

On the way back from Yugoslavia, the Soviets visited Sophia and Bucharest and summoned the leaders of Hungary and Czechoslovakia to meet with them as well. This, coupled with the absence of invitations to Poland and Albania signaled to Bohlen a plan to "establish some gradation among satellites of permissible and non-permissible

22. Ibid.
23. Riddleberger to Dulles, 3 June 1955, RG 59, no. 1066, 661.68/6-355.
24. Dulles to Riddleberger, 4 June 1955, RG 59, no. 986, 661.68/6-355.

relations with Yugoslavia in light of the Belgrade talks."[25] But the U.S. ambassadors to Poland and Czechoslovakia reported that while the sight of Khrushchev "crawling to Tito" might give hope to dissidents in the two countries, most people saw little hope of change.[26]

The level of criticism directed at the administration's aid policy increased after the Soviets' visit to Yugoslavia, with members of Congress demanding that Ambassador Riddleberger reassure them concerning Tito's intentions. "I've never trusted the guy," Republican Congressman Lawrence H. Smith of the House Foreign Affairs Committee told the *New York Times* in early June, after the issuance of the Belgrade Declaration. Dulles, in yet another attempt at damage control, visited the Foreign Affairs Committee chair, Democrat James P. Richards, at his home to press the case for Yugoslav aid. Richards subsequently announced that he would approve the aid requests that the president had submitted, in order to strengthen the United States position at the impending Big Four meeting scheduled for Geneva.[27]

At a news conference on 8 June, a reporter asked Eisenhower if the United States would reevaluate its aid program to Yugoslavia in light of the apparent Soviet-Yugoslav rapprochement. The president, without giving a definite answer, seemed to state that while the United States sought to win neutrals to its side, a country's commitment to neutrality did not lessen U.S. interest in its welfare. Yet he believed that Tito had rejected a neutral position for Yugoslavia.[28] This statement *was* viable because Tito did not see himself as a neutral in the sense of being weak or uninvolved, since such a stance only invited aggression. He pursued a policy of "active coexistence," designed to positively promote the cause of peace.[29] However, Tito's philosophy could be interpreted by Eisenhower's critics as anything from genuinely neutral to pro-Soviet and this made the administration's fight for continued assistance to Yugoslavia that much more difficult.

Riddleberger echoed Dulles's earlier theme when he made what had become a yearly plea for continued aid to Yugoslavia to a Congress that "tolerated rather than approved" the administration's policy.[30] As

25. Bohlen to Dulles, 7 June 1955, *FRUS, 1955–1957*, 25:34–36.

26. U. Alexis Johnson to Dulles, 14 June 1955, *FRUS, 1955–1957*, 25:37–41; Joseph E. Jacobs to Dulles, 20 June 1955, ibid., 39–41.

27. "Assurance Asked on Tito Use of Aid," *New York Times*, 5 June 1955, 3.

28. "Transcript of Presidential Press Conference on Foreign and Domestic Affairs," *New York Times*, 9 June 1955, 16.

29. Hoffman and Neal, *Yugoslavia and the New Communism*, 429.

30. Riddleberger, Oral History, Princeton, 22.

the ambassador told the House Foreign Affairs Committee in mid-June, the Soviets' "public groveling" in Belgrade represented a setback for the international communist movement and the Soviet Union's control of it. Such a public acceptance of Tito's view that there are different roads to socialism "may lead to more cracks in the whole Soviet system."[31] Despite attempts by Congresswoman Kelly to defeat the Yugoslav aid provision, the House Committee approved it.[32]

Yet other members of Congress, shifting from an anti-communist to an anti-neutralist stance, persisted in their attempts to end or restrict aid to all countries, such as India and Yugoslavia, that did not side actively with the West. To counter them, the administration argued that it made little sense to cut off such areas just as the United States sought to "woo" them from their neutralist position. Neutralism was not a policy with which the United States agreed, but such nations were sovereign and independent and it was preferable that they remain neutral rather than fall "under Communist domination."[33]

Yugoslavia probably considered this reasoning to be more insulting than amusing, preferring the simpler wisdom that the "enemy of my enemy is my friend." Dulles, of course, envisioned more of a reciprocal relationship between his country and Tito's. He still cast Yugoslavia as an instrument of the administration's liberation policy, though less and less as a military ally. As the secretary told the legislative leadership in late June 1955, Yugoslavia was "the best leverage" the United States had in winning independence for the satellites. The Soviets had "eaten humble pie" in Belgrade, and the United States should not risk any action that would drive Yugoslavia back into the Soviet camp. Senator Knowland, shifting a bit from his anti-neutralist stance, agreed that neither India nor Yugoslavia should be cut completely from the program but proclaimed it essential for the United States to carry out the regular equipment inspections required under the law on the matériel sent to Yugoslavia. Dulles, playing his role as conciliator, assured Knowland that the United States was negotiating the inspection issue with Tito and that congressional pressure in this area would be helpful.[34] In the end, Congress agreed to continue the Mutual Security Program in support of the administration's claim

31. "Yugoslavia Held 'Good Risk' on Aid," *New York Times*, 16 June 1955, 27.

32. Allen Drury, "House Unit Beats Curbs on Tito Aid," *New York Times*, 24 June 1955, 11.

33. Stassen to Wilton B. Persons, 27 June 1955, *FRUS, 1955–1957*, 10:11–13.

34. Legislative Leadership Meeting, Supplementary Notes, 28 June 1955, L. A. Minnich Jr., Eisenhower Papers, PAP, Whitman File, Legislative Meetings, File: Legislative Meetings 1955 (3) May–June.

that the MSP was responsible for the post-Stalin change in policy by the Soviet Union.[35]

The administration's private views were more realistic than Dulles's public pronouncements. The State Department, in analyzing Yugoslavia's drift toward neutralism, acknowledged that Tito's ties to the West had always been "pragmatic" and in many ways "basically distasteful to the Yugoslav regime." Since relations between Yugoslavia and the Soviet Union had improved, Yugoslavia would most likely "steer a more independent course between East and West." Tito's policy of "active coexistence" allowed his country to "play a role on the world stage out of proportion to Yugoslavia's size and strength" and to establish ties with the newly independent nations of Asia and Africa. In short, Yugoslavia's brand of neutralism was "an attempt to exert influence in international affairs by enhancing the nation's bargaining position rather than an attempt to escape from the facts of life."[36]

The Eisenhower administration realized that a number of factors, ranging from the fear of nuclear war and genuine pacifism to antagonism toward U.S. leadership, caused many Europeans to seek security "with a minimum of burdens, risks and responsibilities." Yugoslavia presented the best example of "the calculated pursuit of maximum security at minimum cost," but other countries, such as Ireland, Sweden, and Switzerland also enjoyed the protection of NATO security programs without charge. Such a "free ride" made neutrality even more appealing. While the communists did not approve of a neutral Yugoslavia, they did seek to increase neutralist sentiment in the noncommunist countries of Europe, and it was imperative that the United States develop measures to counter that tactic.[37] A wedge strategy that resulted only in an increase in neutralism was neither fundable nor desirable.

But could the wedge strategy still draw Yugoslavia into the Western defense network? When the tripartite talks resumed in late June, the Yugoslavs discussed technical issues, such as their need for specific equipment and a detailed delivery timetable of military supplies, but again resisted military coordination between their forces and NATO.[38]

35. Minnich to Rowland R. Hughes, 28 June 1955, Eisenhower Papers, PAP, Whitman File, Legislative Meetings, File: Legislative Meetings 1955 (3) May–June.

36. "The Yugoslav Position on Neutrality," 20 June 1955, Eisenhower Papers, WHO, NSC Staff: Papers 1948–61, Planning Co-ordinating Group (PCG) Series, File no. 9 Bandung (4).

37. "Neutralism in Europe: Summary Report," undated, Eisenhower Papers, WHO, NSC Staff, PCG, File: Bandung (2).

38. "Yugoslavia Seeks to Reassure West," *New York Times*, 25 June 1955, 2.

As the discussions ended, Prica suggested that "high level military talks" between Yugoslavia and the West could be held only after the diplomats from the countries involved had agreed on a precise agenda. Riddleberger attributed this stance to the Yugoslavs' hope for continued assistance without commitment and to their desire to keep "the ball in play until the diplomatic events of the summer have revealed more clearly what the future holds." He still believed it feasible to engage Yugoslavia in a "makeshift arrangement" in connection with the Mutual Security Program that would yield some information for the West, but doubted that genuine joint military planning was possible. However, it might be useful to hold discussions on the agenda for a conference such as Prica suggested, for such talks would either result in "substantial expectation re solution of problems or an impasse which might force US to take a decision as to future aid program for Yugoslavia."[39]

The final communiqué of the tripartite meeting declared only that the parties involved, in an atmosphere of "cordiality and mutual confidence" had discussed and reached agreements on a wide range of international issues. The four nations endorsed the Balkan Pact as "an important contribution to peace and stability" as well as the right of all nations to "independence, equality, self-defense and collective security in conformity with the Charter of the United Nations." The Yugoslav government, still juggling East and West, coupled this with an announcement that the Soviets had invited Tito to visit the Soviet Union during their recent stay in Yugoslavia and he had accepted. The *New York Times*, which saw the conference statement on the Balkan Pact as particularly significant, editorialized that if Khrushchev's mission to Belgrade had been designed to isolate Yugoslavia from the West, he had not succeeded. Even the Yugoslav announcement of a Tito visit to the Soviet Union at some future date did not bode ill if the Pact served to strengthen Tito's hand.[40]

Yet all of these "ifs" about Yugoslavia's behavior began to seem overwhelming. As the fiscal 1956 MSA bill and the Yugoslav appropriation included within it made its way through the Senate, the Yugoslavs continued to refuse thorough inspections of the equipment already received or to provide the Defense Department with information necessary to the military procurement program. These actions, combined with the new Yugoslav-Soviet relationship and the recent Soviet

39. Riddleberger to Dulles, 28 June 1955, *FRUS, 1955–1957*, 26:659–60.
40. Jack Raymond, "Tito Will Visit the Soviet Union; Talks with West End in Accord," *New York Times*, 28 June 1955, 1, 4; editorial, "News from Belgrade," ibid., 26.

offer to renew party ties, caused the United States to severely limit military shipments to Tito's government. By mid-June, the Department of State and Defense had agreed to accord the lowest priority to MDAP shipments to Yugoslavia, except for material already in the pipeline, or essential spare parts for equipment already furnished.[41] Aid would be resumed only if Yugoslavia allowed the necessary inspections and alleviated U.S. concern about its relationship with the Soviet Union. The administration made this decision even as Dulles was pressing Knowland and other critics to fund continuation of the aid policy, so that he could retain the flexibility he needed to manipulate this key component of the wedge strategy. The United States did not intend to cease its aid, but the need to control the rate and volume of that aid to ensure what Kennan earlier had called "a loyal and cooperative" attitude on the part of Yugoslavia had become more urgent.

Tito aggravated an already strained situation by declaring in a speech in Croatia at the end of July that Yugoslavia had complied with the inspections required under the military assistance program and that the United States was incorrectly demanding to see installations equipped from other sources. Yugoslavia would not allow additional inspection or control of the military equipment acquired from the West. He would not be bound by U.S. law, only Yugoslav. If the West chose to deny him aid because he had said "there will be no war," so be it. Tito claimed that he had no further need of military assistance and that his country's resolve to maintain good relations with the West would not suffer if aid ceased. Tito also revealed that Yugoslavia had rejected Western demands to make "some military arrangement which would be connected with the Atlantic Pact, or let us say strengthening of the Balkan Pact from the military point of view."[42]

Riddleberger denied all of Tito's charges and surmised that he was "conditioning his people and the world to a cessation of aid" and fixing the blame on unfair Western rules.[43] But as the *New York Times* observed in a late July editorial, Tito's remarks would "strengthen the suspicions of those who distrust Yugoslavia's good faith," and were therefore not in the best interests of a nation so in need of Western aid.[44]

41. Progress Report on NSC 5406/1, 23 November 1955, *FRUS, 1955–1957*, 26:704–6.
42. Riddleberger to Dulles, 28 July 1955, RG 59, no. 80, 768.5-MSP/7-2855.
43. Riddleberger to Dulles, 28 July 1955, RG 59, no. 81, 768.5-MSP/7-2855.
44. Jack Raymond, "U.S. Rein on Arms Rejected by Tito," *New York Times*, 28 July 1955, 1, 6.

The Soviets proved as resistant to pressure as the Yugoslavs. At the Four Power summit meeting held in Geneva in July, Eisenhower and Dulles intended to press the Soviets on their control of the satellites. Neither Britain nor France shared Washington's enthusiasm for such an approach, but NSC 5524/1, which presented the U.S. position to be followed at the summit, listed withdrawal of Soviet forces from the region as an objective of U.S. policy.[45] However, Eisenhower and Dulles failed to achieve their objective; the Soviets simply refused to discuss conditions in Eastern Europe. Throughout the meetings, however, the Soviet leaders assured their Western counterparts of their sincerity in seeking to improve relations with other states, and usually used the normalization of relations with Yugoslavia as proof of their intentions.[46] Dulles remained certain, as he told West German chancellor Konrad Adenauer, that the Soviet attitude toward the satellite issue sprang from fear that their peace with Tito might cause some of the Eastern Europeans to "follow his example and establish, in accordance with Yugoslavia, a Communist nationalistic bloc competitive with the bloc Moscow rules."[47]

Although neither side gave ground at Geneva, each claimed victory. Nikita Khrushchev, who referred to Dulles in his memoirs as "that vicious cur," boasted that the Soviets had shown they could "hold their own" against the pressures exerted by the West.[48] Dulles, by contrast, considered the summit a success for the United States, although a perilous one. As he told the NSC, the USSR had been placed on the defensive but the cost had been a "blurring of the moral barrier between the Soviet bloc and the free world." As evidence of this Dulles cited the earlier statement made by Tito that the danger of war had all but disappeared, and that Yugoslavia therefore had no further need for Western military assistance. To Dulles, such a lessened sense of danger did little but give impetus to neutralism. It also posed a dilemma for U.S. policy, for if there were less dependence on United States military assistance, the United States could not continue to rely on its military alliances. Eisenhower did not completely share Dulles's pessimism; a "blurring of the distinction between the USSR

45. *FRUS, 1955–1957*, 25:46–47, editorial note; "Basic U.S. Policy in Relation to Four-Power Negotiations," 11 July 1955, *FRUS, 1955–1957*, 5:287–98.
46. Memorandum for the Record of the President's Dinner, 18 July 1955, *FRUS, 1955–1957*, 5:372–76; Memorandum of Conversation at the President's Breakfast, 20 July 1955, ibid., 398–403.
47. Dulles to Konrad Adenauer, 15 August 1955, *FRUS, 1955–1957*, 5:547–50.
48. Talbott, *Khrushchev Remembers*, 398, 400.

and the free world" might be in the offing, but Geneva had served to correct that "false picture." Dulles immediately agreed.[49]

Another image that needed clarification was that involving Yugoslavia's place in U.S. defense planning. In mid-August, Dulles informed Eisenhower that the Joint Chiefs of Staff "had choked off the military pipeline" and "saw no future in military aid to Yugoslavia," now that the prospects for Yugoslavia's closer association with NATO appeared dim. Dulles surmised, as other analysts had, that Tito, rather than returning "under the yoke of Moscow leadership" aspired to lead a bloc of nonaligned communist states. He saw Tito as a "Bukharin" communist, who believed "you could have Communism on a national basis and that Communist countries need not necessarily be under the iron discipline of the Soviet Communist Party as the leader of the world proletariat." If this indeed was Tito's ambition, "it was one we could afford quietly to countenance." Still, Eisenhower and Dulles thought it prudent to take "new soundings" regarding Tito, and that Robert Murphy be dispatched to do so. Murphy could "at his discretion and if he thought it was important" invite Tito, at Eisenhower's behest, to visit the United States later that year, but this was not to be done "unless it seemed really necessary."[50]

Although it had been Tito's ambition for some time to be invited to the United States ("a mark of being accepted in good society" as Dulles claimed), the administration knew his presence would be opposed by many Americans. However, since Eisenhower and Dulles had recently met with "top Communists" and survived "unscarred," they believed a visit by Tito to be possible. In any case the fact remained, as Dulles said, that Tito "would be travelling to see us—it might be a good trial balloon" for an eventual visit by the Soviet Union's leaders. But the president still advised caution, since he did not want to risk the embarrassment "of being turned down."[51]

Before Murphy undertook his mission, the Soviet Union and Yugoslavia held a series of economic negotiations and in early September announced a wide-ranging trade and credit accord. Under the agreements, most of which were to be finalized in January 1956, trade between the two states would amount to $70 million a year for the

49. Bromley Smith, memorandum of discussion of the 256th Meeting of the NSC, 28 July 1955, *FRUS, 1955–1957,* 5:529–35.

50. Memorandum of conversation, 11 August 1955, John Foster Dulles Papers, White House Memoranda Series, File: Meetings with the President, 1955 (2), Eisenhower Library (hereafter cited as "Dulles Papers, Memoranda Series").

51. Dulles to Eisenhower, 11 August 1955, Dulles Papers (Eisenhower Library), Telephone Conversations (hereafter cited as "Dulles Telcons.").

next three years, with the Soviets providing additional millions in loans and credits. Despite Yugoslavia's claim of remaining free of any bloc, Ambassador Bohlen counseled that these negotiations could, "if they lead western governments to re-examine aid programs to Yugoslavia, . . . have effect of forcing Yugoslavia willy-nilly into ever closer relationship with USSR."[52]

Murphy and Dulles agreed before the former's departure for Belgrade that Yugoslavia's material ties to the West remained sufficient to offset most of the attractions of the renewed Yugoslav-Soviet relationship. Despite the recent economic agreement with the Soviets, over two-thirds of Yugoslavia's trade and assistance came from the West. The Soviet bloc still represented the most severe threat to Yugoslavia's security while its defense depended on the equipment furnished by the United States. In addition, "Tito's quest for international prestige and importance" would be diminished if he succumbed to Soviet influence. To remain strong and independent, the regime had adopted "a policy of playing one side off against the other to extract the maximum gain possible for itself." The United States approved of this tactic, because of its own support for Yugoslavia's independence. However, U.S. interests demanded that Murphy ascertain "the fundamentals of the Yugoslav position" and "explore the seriousness of the regime's intentions and expectations for a disruption of Soviet domination of the satellites" while discussing additional economic aid under the MSA. If authorized by Dulles at the time, Murphy could extend Eisenhower's invitation to Tito to visit the United States; otherwise Murphy could indicate Dulles's willingness to visit Tito at some future date.[53]

Dulles chose the latter option. When he met with Mates and Popović at the UN a few days before the planned talks in Yugoslavia, he spoke of his plan to "drop down to Yugoslavia during the Geneva Conference." He also reaffirmed U.S. support for Yugoslav independence, while acknowledging the likelihood of a diminished military aid program. Popović did not object, since Tito himself had already indicated in his July speech that a sound U.S.-Yugoslav relationship did not depend on military aid.[54]

During his visit to Yugoslavia, which lasted from 27 September to 1 October, Murphy discussed both military and economic aid with Tito

52. Bohlen to Dulles, 2 September 1955, RG 59, no. 549, 661.68/9-255.

53. Murphy to Dulles, 16 September 1955, *FRUS, 1955–1957*, 26:664–68.

54. Norman Armour Jr., memorandum of conversation, 22 September 1955, *FRUS, 1955–1957*, 26:670–72.

and other Yugoslav officials. Tito expressed his certainty that the changes currently under way in the Soviet Union were "substantial and long-term and not merely tactical," and that the danger of war had definitely lessened. He believed the Soviets were currently preoccupied with Germany, and were simply not able to accept a reunited Germany as a NATO member. On the other hand, Yugoslavia did not intend to recognize the East German government at that time. Murphy in turn conveyed the United States's special interest in Yugoslavia's position vis-à-vis the satellites and asked Tito if he would consider working with the administration to promote his brand of national communism there. Tito responded with enthusiasm. He also welcomed the prospect of a visit by Secretary Dulles and confidently predicted that a word from him to his military personnel would remedy the supply and inspection problems that so troubled the United States.[55]

In his discussions with other Yugoslav officials, Murphy always associated economic and military aid issues, without explicitly linking the two. This tactic, coupled with the obvious willingness of both sides to continue their cooperation (Murphy surmised that Vukmanović-Tempo's recent visit to Moscow for economic talks "may have eliminated certain illusions about relations with Soviets") produced favorable results.[56] The Murphy mission ended with each side affirming their desire for "friendly cooperation" in economic and military matters; the United States pledged additional economic assistance and the delivery of "specific military equipment," while the Yugoslavs agreed to an increased presence for the U.S. military assistance staff. Economic discussions, which resulted in an additional $260 million for the Yugoslavs, were concluded later in Washington.[57]

To even an impartial observer, it might have appeared that the United States was once again bidding for Yugoslavia's favor, with Murphy in his familiar role as the administration's buyer. Dulles, however, expressed his pleasure with the outcome of Murphy's mission, telling Eisenhower in mid-October that Murphy had "pretty well cleared up the concrete points of friction between us."[58] Dulles also reported that all of the U.S. military authorities agreed that the shipment of military supplies to Yugoslavia should resume, but that

---

55. Riddleberger to Dulles, 27 September 1955, *FRUS, 1955–1957*, 26:672–74.

56. Riddleberger to Dulles, 28 September 1955, *FRUS, 1955–1957*, 26:674–76.

57. Murphy to Alfred Greunther, 6 October 1955, with enclosure, Confidential Memorandum, 1 October 1955, Alfred Greunther Papers, NATO Series, File: Murphy, Robert, 1954–1956, Eisenhower Library; Murphy, *Diplomat among Warriors*, 422–30.

58. Memorandum of conversation, 11 October 1955, Dulles Papers, Memoranda Series, File: Meetings with the President, 1955 (2).

the program was being reviewed to effect "substantial economies without interfering with our political objectives in the area."[59]

The secretary of state, accompanied by his wife and a number of State Department officials, visited Tito at his retreat on Brioni in November 1955, during a break in the foreign ministers' meetings at Geneva. Ambassador and Mrs. Riddleberger joined the party in Yugoslavia. In the breaks between lunch, dinner, and a ride in Tito's two-seater speedboat, Dulles and Tito discussed and debated issues ranging from Germany to the Middle East to Asia. The lengthy record of their three-hour talk on Tito's nearby Vanga Island hideaway shows that Dulles clearly appreciated Tito as a man of some wisdom in international affairs and expressed particular interest in hearing Tito's views on the Balkan alliance and the future of the satellite governments. When Dulles briefed Tito on the results of the four-power talks at the Geneva Conference and disputes there concerning German unification, Tito expressed his strongly held view that some solution had to found that would allow Germany to reunify, while assuring that it not be an "expansionist" state. The United States, because it feared Soviet aggression, could not blind itself to the very real dangers of German aggression. Dulles agreed but insisted that the four powers had to act to unify Germany, lest the result be achieved by the violent actions of the Germans themselves, as in the past.

In turning to the Middle East, Tito bemoaned the creation of military alliances in the area, which he believed further fragmented the Arab world. He was particularly critical of the Baghdad Pact. While Dulles disputed this, the two agreed on the pressing need to settle the Arab-Israeli dispute before it led to a general war, but Dulles was more censorious of the Egyptians and the Soviets, while Tito saw the Israelis as the greater irritant. Tito, in response to Dulles's musings about the role he could play in bringing peace to the Middle East, promised to have "frank" discussions with the leaders of both Egypt and Israel on his next visits to each country.

When their discussion moved to Asia, Tito cautioned Dulles that the West should not make the mistake of thinking of Communist China as a Soviet satellite. The Soviets had always found the Chinese difficult to handle, and were China not isolated by the West and forced to rely solely on the USSR, its policies might be more flexible than Dulles realized. In general, the Yugoslavs drew parallels between their own struggle for independence from the Soviets and that of the Chinese,

59. Dulles to Eisenhower, undated, *FRUS, 1955–1957*, 26:678–79.

just as U.S. analysts had done since the late 1940s. Dulles explained the hostile sentiment that existed in the United States toward China because of their aggression in Korea and Indochina, but noted that if China renounced the use of force, the two countries could make some progress in improving their relations. Yet Dulles reminded Tito that the United States also had an obligation not to abandon its ally Chiang Kai-shek.

As their talks veered back to Yugoslavia's part of the world, Tito assured Dulles that while he did not wish to eliminate the military components of the Balkan Pact, the recent relaxation in world tensions made that aspect of the agreement less central. A "new orientation" was also occurring in the relationship between the Soviet Union and their satellites, as the Soviet leadership realized the futility of Stalin's policies and attempted to change their course. This new path "did not involve a renunciation by the Soviets of the desire to have influence in the satellites, but was a change from the previous policy of iron control." Stalinist sentiments still existed within the Soviet Union, but Tito believed the West could lessen their influence by supporting the more moderate Soviets in their desire for reform. Even more Stalinists existed among the satellite leadership, but Tito believed the satellites' own people would force a change and that new leaders would come to power. Tito agreed with Dulles's assertion that Yugoslavia's example of independence exerted a powerful pull on the satellites, but cautioned that their path would be a slower one. Tito also confided that those parts of the Belgrade Declaration that stressed each country's right to choose its own path to socialism and to assert its independence had been added only at Yugoslavia's insistence. As the discussion ended, Dulles expressed his belief that the bonds between the Soviets and their satellites were weakening, and again praised the Yugoslavs for their part in that process. Popović later told Dulles that his statement on the loosening of ties between the Soviets and the satellites had been most "significant" and had meshed with the Yugoslavs' own assessment.[60]

In his report to Eisenhower, Dulles said that the "day with Tito was one of the most interesting I have ever spent." The visit confirmed the secretary's view that Tito had "no intention whatever of falling back into clutches" of the Soviets.[61] Yet although Dulles seemed not to realize it, the differences between the two men's goals in Eastern

60. Record of the Meeting between Secretary of State Dulles and President Tito on the Island of Vanga, 6 November 1955, 3–5:40 p.m., *FRUS, 1955–1957*, 26:680–97.

61. Dulles to Eisenhower, 7 November 1955, *FRUS, 1955–1957*, 26:698–99.

Europe were substantial. Dulles, for all his support of Tito's nationalism, preferred noncommunist regimes to come to power in the satellite states. The Yugoslavs, by contrast, were never willing to countenance change that would end in the dissolution of socialist rule; they simply wished each nation to be free to implement the Belgrade Declaration. Tito made that clear in his response to Dulles's remarks at a news conference at the end of his visit, when the secretary called on the people of Eastern Europe "to develop their own social and economic orders in ways of their own choice."[62] Tito indicated his agreement with Dulles's pronouncement at the news conference itself, but Yugoslav press reports either did not mention that or explained it away.[63] Dulles, though, chose to hear only his own words. Upon his return he wrote to *Foreign Affairs* editor Hamilton Fish Armstrong, who had earlier published a book urging support for Tito's disruptive influence on the Soviet bloc, that "the note we struck on the satellites will have very real significance."[64]

The passage of time only increased Dulles's euphoria. At an NSC meeting on 21 November, Dulles declared that the statement he and Tito had issued concerning the satellites "was in itself worth the whole trip." Their "joint communiqué had really rocked the Russians back on their heels, and they were currently extremely angry at Tito." He recounted Tito's views about the current state of Soviet-satellite relations, but again read his own hopes into what had occurred, saying that Tito "was confident that the Soviets could not hold out much longer, and the changes in these regimes would occur in the not too distant future, perhaps in a matter of months or a year's time." (Tito, as the United States's own record of the meeting showed, had said nothing that optimistic.) Dulles acknowledged that Tito hoped to derive the most he could from a relationship with both East and West, but there was no evidence he "had secretly rejoined the Soviet bloc."[65]

Not everyone agreed that that was enough to justify continued U.S. support. In NSC discussions on a new policy statement on Yugoslavia, the State Department argued for continued aid, even though a Yugoslav association with NATO appeared remote, because Tito's ties to the West increased his "prestige" as an "example to the satellite

62. Campbell, *Tito's Separate Road*, 35–36.

63. *FRUS, 1955–1957*, 26:699 n. 5; Jack Raymond, "Tito Differences with Dulles Seen," *New York Times*, 8 November 1955, 6.

64. Dulles to Armstrong, 8 November 1955, Dulles Papers, Correspondence (Princeton), box 98.

65. Memorandum of Discussion at the 267th Meeting of the NSC, 21 November 1955, *FRUS, 1955–1957*, 26:703–4.

countries." The Department of Defense and the JCS, whose support for assistance always had hinged on Yugoslavia's participation in Western defense schemes, countered that Tito's recent actions had "weakened the prospects for an effective defense of Southern Europe." In their view, if the United States continued to assist Yugoslavia while Tito increased his ties to the Soviet Union, the other allies of the United States would be forced to "conclude that neutralism can be as profitable as collaboration with us."[66] The Defense Department agreed to continue aid, but since the United States was also "desperately seeking to find money for assisting the Turks and Pakistan," the department recommended that the "rate of flow" of goods to Tito's government required adjustment. After remarks by Secretary Dulles, when he again said that the statement he and Tito had made at their press conference "had created a terrific stir in the satellite world," the NSC referred the issue back to the Planning Board for additional work.[67]

Early in 1956, the NSC completed its draft of NSC 5601, "United States Policy Toward Yugoslavia." Adopted on 18 January, the document reflected the State Department's concentration on the political issues involved in Yugoslav policy, with military aid posited as a means to achieve the administration's political goals. The report was more pessimistic than those previously issued, even with its assertion that the United States's short-term policy of bolstering Yugoslavia's independence had succeeded. But that very success, coupled with Tito's conviction that changes in Soviet behavior rendered an attack on Yugoslavia unlikely, had altered the Yugoslav relationship with the West. As a result, the long-term objective of "tying Yugoslavia into the Western system and insuring its effective contribution to free world power in case of war in Europe . . . has not been attained and there is no sound indication that it is obtainable."

Earlier conjecture about Yugoslavia's Western orientation was replaced in this NSC statement with the growing conviction that if war occurred, Yugoslavia would probably remain neutral. Tito would use his troops to ensure his country's own survival rather than to assist NATO, although he had promised not to allow the passage of foreign troops as a nonbelligerent. Yugoslavia's future overall position also

66. Briefing Note, NSC Meeting no. 271, 22 December 1955, Item 4, "U.S. Policy Toward Yugoslavia—A New Policy Paper," Eisenhower Papers, WHO, OSANSA Records 1952–61, Special Assistant Series, Chronological Subseries, File: NSC Meeting no. 271.

67. NSC Meeting no. 271, 22 December 1955, Eisenhower Papers, PAP, Whitman File, NSC Series, File: NSC Meeting no. 271. The minutes, though declassified, are heavily censored.

would be that of a neutral—at times supporting Soviet positions and at others supporting the United States. Tito had clearly achieved his objective of "freedom of action vis-à-vis both sides," and would strengthen this by increasing his country's ties with third world and nonaligned states. He hoped to influence developments in the satellites as well and believed he could do that more effectively if Yugoslavia remained an independent communist state. Nonetheless, it remained in the United States's interest to keep Yugoslavia independent in order to maximize that country's "effectiveness in encouraging separation of the satellites from the Soviet bloc," while pursuing the long-term goal of liberalizing the regime and enticing Yugoslavia to participate "fully in free world community."

To achieve these goals, NSC 5601 recommended that the administration revise the military assistance program to be "more austere." The United States would provide the minimum necessary for the maintenance of Yugoslav independence and regulate the rates of delivery in accordance with the "degree of Yugoslavia's cooperation." Additional aid would be available in the event that Tito's government furnished more detailed information on its defenses or participated in joint NATO planning, but the NSC recognized "that political objectives justify the provision of military assistance that would not be justifiable on strictly military considerations." Such aid would be intended not to endorse or undermine the government but to "exploit the Tito regime's reliance on the West for assistance by seeking to induce it to adopt policies which will contribute to the attainment of U.S. objectives."[68] In essence, the policy enunciated by Kennan in PPS 35, which posited "a loyal and cooperative attitude" on the part of Yugoslavia as a requisite for aid had simply been updated. Political rather than military considerations also had reasserted their dominance in the wedge strategy.

NSC 5601 and its recommendations on military assistance, rather than the agreements reached between Murphy and the Yugoslavs in their October 1955 meeting, were now to guide U.S. policy, much to the annoyance of Ambassador Riddleberger. When informed of the discussions and differences of opinion surrounding the drafting of the NSC report by the Office of Eastern European Affairs's Henry Leverich, Riddleberger expressed his "astonishment" and anger at the violation of the October accords reached with the Yugoslavs on mili-

68. NSC 5601, "United States Policy Toward Yugoslavia," 9 January 1956, *FRUS, 1955–1957*, 26:707–14 (see the editorial note on 714–15 for information concerning the adoption of NSC 5601).

tary aid. In a letter written to Leverich on 9 January 1956, while the final draft of NSC 5601 circulated in Washington, Riddleberger, referring to the December 1955 disputes between State and Defense, asked why if such "a division over basic policy" existed in Washington, had the administration raised "the hoopla and holler last summer over the difficulties of the military program?" If the United States was thinking of abandoning aid, then what difference did it make how many AMAS personnel were stationed in Yugoslavia? If a "retreat" from that agreement was in the making, Riddleberger had to be fully briefed to conduct it.

Draft instructions concerning the substantial reduction in military assistance called for in the NSC policy statement also irritated the ambassador. What he and Murphy had discussed, he told Leverich, was "a review of the program" and "a stretch-out in deliveries," which might "effect some savings." This was very different from a decision to cut out a certain percentage of supplies and then negotiate a new agreement with the Yugoslavs. Yugoslavia regarded the agreed-upon levels of assistance as a firm "commitment," or at the very least "a statement of intention on which they had a right to rely." The failure by the United States to resume a full delivery schedule during the last three months had already made the administration vulnerable to the charge that it had not negotiated in good faith. Murphy had not intended that the military assistance program be stopped, but that "it go forward—granted at a decelerated pace—" while the United States and Yugoslavia continued to discuss its future. During those negotiations, the United States could inform the Yugoslavs that since they themselves have stated that the world situation is less dangerous, "*we* agree that their rearmament program is less urgent." For now, the ambassador advised that the previous "recommendations made for the reactivization of the program be met," particularly those regarding deliveries of the F-86E aircraft often requested by the Yugoslavs. The draft instruction he had received did not need to be reconsidered as much as its emphasis had to be changed to more closely reflect the original recommendations.[69]

Although the Yugoslavs had been pressing the United States for jets for years, the status of the F-86E aircraft that Riddleberger alluded to was less clear than he believed. After his return from Yugoslavia in October 1955, Murphy had assured Assistant Secretary of Defense Gordon Gray that no firm commitment on the delivery of the planes to Tito had been made. A "mobile training team" was to be dispatched to

---

69. Riddleberger to Leverich, 9 January 1956, RG 59, 661.68/1-956.

Yugoslavia by late November to facilitate use of the aircraft, but as Murphy told Gray, he and General Haines estimated that four to five months could elapse before the Yugoslavs had been properly trained and would "be in a position to take deliveries. During that time we would be able to make a general appraisal of the problem." In the interim the United States would make no promises to the Yugoslavs concerning the F-86Es.[70]

When asked at a news conference in late January about reports of Yugoslav complaints of a continued slowdown in military deliveries, Dulles skirted the issue by replying that most of the goods destined for Yugoslavia under the military assistance program had already been delivered, implying that there had been no actual reduction in aid.[71] In a telegram to Riddleberger sent at the same time, however, Dulles stated, in a perfect example of Orwellian "doublespeak," that while "in general status quo prior program suspensions of last spring restored" deliveries to Yugoslavia had been assigned a "third priority" and the "timing" of future deliveries would be fixed by the chief of AMAS. The mobile training teams had not yet been sent to Yugoslavia, but Dulles hoped to soon remedy that.[72]

These exchanges demonstrated that after three years of attempting to build a closer relationship with Yugoslavia, the Eisenhower administration's concerns about Tito's neutralism had almost replaced fears that he would return to the bloc. Dulles still nursed the hope that Tito would inspire the Eastern Europeans to more independence, but evidence to justify that remained slim. The military assistance program had became the index of the administration's concerns; the virtual suspension of deliveries put into place in the summer of 1955 remained in effect, despite the seeming success of the Murphy mission, because uncertainties about Tito's policies were too great. Goods would flow again only if and when Tito showed himself to be a better friend to the West than to nonaligned movement or to the East.

At this inopportune moment, the Kremlin made additional conciliatory gestures toward Yugoslavia. On 1 February, Riddleberger reported that the two countries were rumored to be negotiating a date for Tito's visit to the Soviet Union, announced the previous June. Although talks concerning the resumption of party relations had

70. Murphy, memorandum of telephone conversation, 8 October 1955, RG 59, 768.56/10-555.
71. Jack Raymond, "Reports from Europe, Africa and Asia on Effects of U.S. Foreign Aid Program," *New York Times*, 23 January 1956, 8; Dulles to Riddleberger, 24 January 1956, RG 59, no. 595, 768.5-MSP/1-2456.
72. Dulles to Riddleberger, 24 January 1956, RG 59, no. 592, 768.5MSP/1-2456.

so far been inconclusive, the Yugoslav Communist Party also had apparently been invited to attend the Twentieth Party Congress in the USSR.[73] However, the appointment of Veljko Mićunović, the former undersecretary for foreign affairs, as the new Yugoslav ambassador to the Soviet Union appeared to be a more promising development. Riddleberger considered Mićunović a skilled and astute specialist on Soviet and satellite affairs who was well liked and respected by the Western diplomatic community. The appointment of Mićunović, who according to Riddleberger, was "no fool and dedicated to Yugoslav interests," reflected the importance Tito attached to Yugoslav-Soviet relations. He would fulfill the need to "have skillful representative who can cope with Soviet maneuvers in person" as well as handle their pressure on the Yugoslavs for closer ties.[74]

The United States did not expect the Twentieth Party Congress mentioned by Riddleberger to produce "any surprises on policy issues." Preliminary analyses of the proceedings by the CIA depicted a Congress dominated by continued attempts to replace Stalin's policy with one stressing "collective leadership" and "peaceful coexistence" as well as a "peaceful transition to socialism" for other nations. Allen Dulles, echoing his brother's determination, to interpret everything as beneficial to the administration's policy, believed that many communists would find the Soviets' line difficult to accept and that "widespread dangers of Titoism" would result. Tito, noted the intelligence chief, must think the "Soviet Union has bought his doctrines lock, stock and barrel."[75]

At the Congress, Khrushchev went much further than the CIA had predicted when he delivered his "secret speech" condemning Stalin and his terror and advancing his own views on Soviet domestic and foreign policy. The latter included a commitment to peaceful coexistence and the ability of socialist states to adapt Marxism to their own history and conditions. Tito had decided not to attend the Congress, but the Soviets provided Mićunović a detailed summary of Khrushchev's remarks, which Mićunović then delivered to Tito in person.[76] In subsequent discussions with Riddleberger, Yugoslav officials expressed the "not unnatural pride that Soviets have adopted number of

73. Riddleberger to Dulles, 1 February 1956, RG 59, no. 880, 661.68/2-156.

74. Riddleberger to Dulles, 17 February 1956, RG 59, no. 967, 661.68/2-1756.

75. Policy Information Statement of the United States Information Agency, 8 February 1956, *FRUS, 1955–1957*, 24:56–58; also editorial note on 58; Memorandum of Discussion at the 277th Meeting of the NSC, 27 February 1956, ibid., 59–61.

76. Tompson, *Khrushchev*, 159–60; Hoffman and Neal, *Yugoslavia and the New Communism*, 431; Wilson, *Tito's Yugoslavia*, 99; *FRUS, 1955–1957*, 24:72, editorial note.

Yugoslav ideas" and the conviction that additional and genuine change would now come to the USSR.[77] Privately, however, the Yugoslav leadership wondered why, if Khrushchev really meant to initiate sweeping change, he had kept the details of his speech secret. Yet on balance they concluded that the speech, secret or not, probably boded well for the Yugoslav-Soviet relationship.[78]

The NSC met on 22 March 1956 to analyze "the dramatic news from Moscow." Allen Dulles offered a number of explanations for the apparent shift in policy, ranging from the "communist penchant for self-criticism" to Khrushchev's drunkenness. Regardless of the motives, Dulles theorized that because of the length of Stalin's rule and his enormous influence, the new Soviet leadership would find it "very difficult to create a new tradition." Eisenhower agreed, but observed that if the Soviets wanted the world to accept the new tactics they had recently adopted, they had no choice but to repudiate Stalin. Their quest for a philosophy to replace his would not be easy, since in Secretary Dulles's words, "there was no handbook of Leninism." Still, all present at the NSC meeting agreed that the developments in the Soviet Union "would be definitely advantageous for the United States."[79]

A Yugoslavia assisted by the Mutual Security Program appeared to be the best way to secure that advantage, and in March, the United States resumed "previously programmed deliveries" of military goods to Yugoslavia. Yet the extent to which such shipments could be used to influence Tito's behavior remained in doubt because of uncertainties concerning both the Yugoslav attitude toward additional Western military assistance and the future delivery schedule of U.S. goods. In April, after the Soviets announced the dissolution of the already moribund Cominform, Tito announced his intention to visit the Soviet Union in June. These events prompted both Riddleberger and the United States military representatives in Belgrade to suggest that the delivery of two F-86Es aircraft to Yugoslavia before the Tito visit to Moscow "may have a beneficial effect."[80]

But would such a gesture be welcomed? As Prica told Riddleberger in mid-April, in yet another version of the conversation that had been occurring for some months between the United States and Yugoslavia,

77. Riddleberger to Dulles, 23 March 1956, *FRUS, 1955–1957*, 26:715–18.

78. Veljko Mićunović, *Moscow Diary* (Garden City, N.Y.: Doubleday, 1980), 11–12.

79. Memorandum of Discussion at the 280th Meeting of the NSC, 22 March 1956, *FRUS*, 1955–1957, 24:72–75.

80. CHAMAY Belgrade to Dulles, 13 April 1956, RG 59, AMAS 684, 768.5622/4-1356; Report Prepared by the Operations Coordinating Board, 24 April 1957, Progress Report on NSC 5601, "United States Policy Toward Yugoslavia," *FRUS*, 1955–1957, 26:768–73.

changes within the Soviet Union had reduced world tension and made
disarmament a genuine possibility. The need for military aid thus
appeared "less urgent." Yugoslavia did not wish to abandon its military cooperation with the United States, and Prica hoped that the
latter would not link military assistance to economic aid. He suggested
that economic discussions proceed, while the two countries deliberate
the "political overtones" of military assistance.[81]

In early May, Prica finally informed Riddleberger that Yugoslavia
did not wish to fully implement the agreements reached with Robert
Murphy in October 1955 calling for an increase in the number of
AMAS personnel within the country. Nor did Tito's government plan
to hold discussions on future military aid. Although Prica claimed this
step to be in accord with Yugoslavia's policy of promoting "nonmili-
tary" cooperation between states, Riddleberger believed that the Yugoslavs had taken the action assuming the United States would continue
its military aid in any case.[82]

The Yugoslavs seemed determined to limit the implementation of the
wedge strategy, but the administration was equally determined to
remain the dominant partner in the U.S.-Yugoslav relationship. The
State Department, suspecting Prica's announcement had some connection to Tito's upcoming visit to Moscow, advised Riddleberger to
deliver a "frank, firm and swift response" to the Yugoslavs before Tito
departed for the Soviet Union. The Murphy talks had provided the
basis for U.S.-Yugoslav relations, and the Eisenhower administration
had, over the past several months, overlooked the "increasingly pro-
Soviet public stance" of Yugoslavia in favor of the Yugoslavs' private
assurances that their policy toward the West had not changed. The
military aid issue did not stand alone; cancellation of the military
assistance program would make Congress less willing to support
additional economic aid. Since Yugoslavia's defense needs seemed as
great as ever, the United States concluded that Yugoslavia intended
to obtain military equipment from the East. Dulles informed Riddleberger that until he had discussed these points with the Yugoslavs,
aircraft deliveries scheduled for that month would be suspended.
Dulles added that shipments of all other military goods might be
suspended as well if a "satisfactory conclusion" of this dispute could
not be reached. These actions, coupled with the ambassador's dé-

81. Riddleberger to Dulles, 19 April 1956, *FRUS, 1955–1957,* 26:719–20.
82. *FRUS, 1955–1957,* 26:720–21 n. 2.

marche, should make it "clear to Yugoslavs US position contains no element bluff."[83]

The United States, though in effect suspending a program that had not fully resumed, had enough cards to defeat the Yugoslavs' much weaker hand. Riddleberger followed Dulles's instructions, only to have Prica contend that the Yugoslav military believed the United States had never intended to carry out the provisions of the Murphy memo of understanding, citing as evidence the $60 million decrease in military deliveries since June of 1955. Riddleberger challenged Prica's assessment, but also repeated his warning that deliveries would be delayed if the United States and Yugoslavia did not settle their "difficulties." The ambassador offered to discuss Prica's complaints with the Yugoslav military, only to have Prica retreat and suggest the interview be continued after he had consulted his government. As a result, Riddleberger sensed that the Yugoslavs were having "sober second thoughts." In a similar talk on economic issues with Vukmanović-Tempo, Riddleberger cited the connection between defense and economic issues laid out in the Murphy memorandum; Vukmanović-Tempo agreed that such a connection existed and promised to consult his colleagues. Riddleberger recommended to the State Department that the suspension of the aircraft shipments remain in effect until he ascertained the result of the Yugoslav discussions in his next series of meetings.[84]

After additional talks with the foreign minister, Riddleberger's "salutary jolt" produced the desired results. Popović assured him that his government wished to carry out the "mutually advantageous" military assistance program, which had also served to moderate Soviet policy. Disputes over the Murphy memorandum were of only "secondary importance" and could easily be solved. To that end, the Yugoslavs proposed to allow five new personnel to be added to the AMAS; as deliveries of equipment resumed, additional personnel issues could be discussed. The Yugoslavs, however, still wished to postpone discussions on future military aid agreements, the implication being that such talks would complicate the Yugoslav-Soviet relationship. Riddleberger advised that this "face saving" device be accepted, since it more or less met the U.S. demand that Yugoslavia comply with Murphy's October agreement. The ambassador, along with the military, recommended that the suspended aircraft deliveries be resumed. Riddleberger also suggested, as Prica had requested, that economic discus-

83. Dulles to Riddleberger, 9 May 1956, *FRUS, 1955–1957*, 26:720–22.
84. Riddleberger to Dulles, 11 May 1956, RG 59, no. 1386, 768.5 MSP/5-1156.

sions, especially those concerning Yugoslavia's chronic wheat shortages, proceed, even though Congress had not yet passed the PL 480 or MSP appropriations for 1957.[85]

However, Congress, virtually on the eve of Tito's visit to the Soviet Union, limited the administration's flexibility by reducing the FY57 Mutual Security request for Yugoslavia. Tito then expressed Yugoslavia's preference, now that conditions within the country had improved, for loans rather than grant assistance, because the former were negotiated on an "equal footing" and were more certain and predictable. As proof he cited the Senate committee's action in cutting the grant request in half, noting that such uncertainties made it difficult for the Yugoslavs to engage in effective military planning. Tito also found the conditions attached to the "gratis aid" and the comments made in the Congress to be "insulting" and "disagreeable."[86]

Even though insulted, the Yugoslavs continued to press Riddleberger for enough wheat to cover their projected deficit and for development financing. Yugoslavia also disclosed that it had been forced to negotiate a confidential exchange agreement with the Soviets, because of the vagaries of the U.S. aid program. Riddleberger speculated that either Tito had received such generous offers of aid from the Soviets that "in spite of long history of US assistance he is now willing to jeopardize US support rather than wait several more weeks," or that he believed his position with the United States to be so secure that a deal with the USSR would not endanger it. In any case, Riddleberger counseled that further discussions on economic aid be delayed until the outcome of Tito's Soviet visit could be assessed.[87]

Immediately before Tito's arrival in Moscow in early June, Bulganin and Khrushchev forced Molotov, who had co-signed Stalin's denunciation of Tito in 1948 and continued to oppose the rapprochement with Yugoslavia, to resign from his post as minister of foreign affairs.[88] But even this gesture did not allay the Yugoslavs' suspicions of the Soviets. Kardelj, always pessimistic about Soviet intentions, never thought that Khrushchev and the others actually subscribed to the principles of the Belgrade Declaration. Mićunović shared his concern. He observed in his diary that while Yugoslavia viewed the Belgrade Declaration "as a sort of socialist Magna Carta" applicable to Soviet relations with the satellites as well as with Yugoslavia, the Soviets

85. Riddleberger to Dulles, 16 May 1956, FRUS, 1955–1957, 26:724–26.
86. Riddleberger to Dulles, 25 May 1956, RG 59, no. 1444, 768.5-MSP/5-2556.
87. Riddleberger to Dulles, 28 May 1956, RG 59, no. 1450, 768.5-MSP/5-2856.
88. Bohlen to Dulles, 2 June 1956, FRUS, 1955–1957, 24:108–9.

considered it only another "ephemeral agreement concerning relations between two countries" without "any special or lasting significance." He anticipated that Tito's visit to the USSR would reveal whether the Soviets genuinely intended to treat Yugoslavia as an equal and to moderate their approach to the satellites.[89]

During Tito's lengthy stay (he was in the USSR from the second to the twentieth of June), he and the Soviets argued over the Balkan Pact, Yugoslavia's acceptance of Western aid, and Tito's refusal to conduct his relations with the satellites through the USSR or to recognize the government of East Germany. According to Mićunović, Khrushchev especially resented Tito's influence with the Eastern Europeans and his continued rejection of the principle of ideological conformity. Nonetheless, the visit ended with an agreement on party and interstate cooperation and with the issuance of the Moscow Declaration, which reaffirmed the idea of different roads to socialism. As soon as Tito left Moscow, however, the Soviets summoned satellite leaders to discuss the recently concluded talks. The Moscow Declaration was not even mentioned during those discussions, proving to Mićunović that Yugoslav-Soviet relations had no positive bearing, in the Soviet mind, on the satellites.[90]

The Eisenhower administration, in the thick of its annual battle with Congress over the foreign aid bill and its already threatened appropriation for Yugoslavia, remained publicly unruffled by Tito's Soviet visit. In an early June meeting with congressional leaders, the president argued for passage of his full foreign aid appropriation, including the $30 million in economic aid requested for Yugoslavia, on the grounds that to do otherwise would endanger national security. Senators Knowland and Styles Bridges warned that the bill's provisions concerning both Yugoslavia and India would engender much debate; Senator Joseph R. McCarthy had already introduced a measure in the Senate to suspend all aid to Yugoslavia, with Congressman Michael A. Feighan, an Ohio Democrat, intending to do the same.[91]

At his press conference on 6 June, the president sidestepped the issue of U.S. aid to Yugoslavia, while making even more ambiguous comments on neutralism. Tito had been received so well in Moscow because of his success in challenging the Soviet leadership; "to get him

89. Mićunović, *Moscow Diary*, 7, 43.

90. Ibid., 63–76.

91. Notes of Congressional Leadership Meeting, 5 June 1956, Bryce Harlow Papers, Pre-Acc, File: Leadership Meetings, 1955–56, Eisenhower Library; Dana Adams Schmidt, "President Sees Peril in Aid Cuts; Backs Tito Fund," *New York Times*, 6 June 1956, 1, 18.

back at all," Eisenhower said, "they had to make great concessions." Concern that the satellites might follow Tito's independent example probably motivated Soviet behavior. All in all, the president concluded: "I think that the Tito incident is not wholly and entirely a loss." But he admitted the United States would have to reevaluate its policy toward "this individual." Eisenhower also discussed the U.S. view of neutralism, claiming that in trying to keep the peace, one could not "be too particular sometimes about the special attitudes that different countries take." Neutral nations, he said, were not indifferent to right and wrong, but simply wished to avoid attachment to any military alliances. If such a nation is attacked, world opinion is outraged, which might not be the case if members of one bloc or another are subject to attack.[92]

Dulles found the president's remarks on Tito "disturbing"; in his opinion they seemed to signal a change in policy. The statement on alliances caused an even greater stir, with neutral nations especially pleased but with the NATO partners and Dulles himself concerned about its implications. The White House quickly issued a clarification, saying the president had not repudiated the NATO alliance and had simply attempted to show the American people that neutralism was not a negative concept.[93]

The administration's views on neutralism became even more muddied a few days later when Dulles made his infamous speech equating neutralism with immorality. Although the press interpreted the secretary's remarks as an additional attempt to clarify Eisenhower's press conference statement,[94] they actually constituted more of a repudiation of the president's words. Dulles defined neutralism as a principle that "pretends that a nation can best gain safety for itself by being indifferent to the fate of others," a position which outside of "very exceptional circumstances" Dulles found "immoral and shortsighted." At the same time, however, Dulles criticized Congress's attempts to cut the administrations's foreign aid request and in particular defended aid for Tito's Yugoslavia.[95]

Clare Boothe Luce did not agree. In mid-June, Luce, still serving as

92. *Papers of the Presidents*, Eisenhower, 1956, 555–58.

93. Dulles to James Hagerty, 6 and 7 June 1956, Dulles Telcons.; Dana Adams Schmidt, "Eisenhower Sees Merit in Attitude of Neutral Lands," *New York Times*, 7 June 1956, 1, 10.

94. "Dulles Declares Neutrality Pose Is Obsolete Idea," *New York Times*, 10 June 1956, 1, 24.

95. "Text of Dulles Speech Explaining U.S. 'Peace Insurance Policy,'" *New York Times*, 10 June 1956, 24.

ambassador in Italy and still critical of Tito, wrote to Dulles to oppose continued Yugoslav aid. In her letter, Luce reviewed the history of the European socialists (particularly in France and Italy) who had broken with the Soviet Union because of their distaste of Stalinism, their fear of "Russian imperialism and militarism," and the economic depriva- tion of the postwar period, which had been relieved by the Marshall Plan. Luce claimed that a Marxist affinity still existed between these leftists and the communist parties of their respective countries, and that the de-Stalinization campaign of the Soviet Union had strength- ened those ties. The exchange of visits between Tito and the Soviets had further alleviated socialist fears of Soviet hegemony; Tito had become the symbol "of a reformed, reconverted and peacefully evolving communism." As a result, the re-creation of popular front governments in Europe was a near certainty; all the Soviets needed to do was convince the French and Italians that such a turn to Moscow would not cost them their U.S. military assistance. Luce charged that contin- uing U.S. aid to Yugoslavia would accomplish that task for them.[96]

Yet Tito did little to improve his country's chance for assistance. Before leaving the Soviet Union, he affirmed that the Yugoslav and Soviet Communist parties would reestablish ties. He also stated that the two governments shared a number of common views, including the need to recognize the existence of two Germanys and to admit China to the UN.[97] The PPS, in its analysis of Tito's stay in the Soviet Union, acknowledged that relations between Yugoslavia and the Soviet Union had been brought "into closer harmony," but viewed Yugoslavia as a "fellow-traveler" rather than a member of the bloc. Only two "new developments" had occurred during the talks: the reestablishment of party-to-party relations; and Yugoslavia's further willingness to en- dorse many Soviet foreign policy positions, with the exception of the recognition of East Germany. The Soviets had made every effort to convey the impression that relations between the two states had been repaired; the Yugoslavs "leaned hard the other way" to reassure the West that their ties would not suffer. The effect of the Yugoslav- Soviet reconciliation on the satellites remained unclear. The Soviets obviously sought to "blur Tito's independent status in satellite eyes," but they had moved first to mend relations and had therefore afforded "a special status" to their relationship with Yugoslavia. The agree-

96. Luce to Dulles, 18 June 1956, with enclosure, Luce to Eisenhower, 15 June 1956, Dulles Papers (Eisenhower Library), General Correspondence, File: Strictly Confiden- tial L.

97. Jack Raymond, "Tito, Khrushchev Cite Mutual Aims at Moscow Rally," *New York Times*, 20 June 1956, 1, 4.

ment to reestablish party-to-party ties thus was the "main visible concrete gain" for the Soviet Union; however, this too had occurred "on Tito's terms," with Yugoslavia hoping to use party-to-party relations to increase its influence with the satellites.[98]

Riddleberger and Bohlen again provided less positive assessments. The former considered the Yugoslav-Soviet visit to be "discouraging and depressing," despite Yugoslavia's continued claim to independence. He saw the final communiqué as an embrace by Tito of a number of Soviet foreign policy positions, including the previously avoided Soviet position on Germany. Prica and Vukmanović-Tempo had assured Riddleberger that Yugoslavia did not at that time contemplate extending recognition to East Germany, and had attempted to explain away other portions of the document about which he had raised concerns. They had also pressed Riddleberger for discussions on economic assistance, mostly in the form of long-term loans, and for promised deliveries of military material. Vukmanović-Tempo acknowledged to Riddleberger that the United States was correct to base its assistance to Yugoslavia on its own national interest, but insisted that an independent Yugoslavia continued to serve those interests. Yet Riddleberger remained convinced that a "striking parallelism" in foreign policy now existed between the Soviet Union and Yugoslavia.[99]

Bohlen agreed that Tito had "rejoined Communist community." Although he had done so "on his own terms" and there was no indication that he intended to sacrifice Yugoslavia's independence, Bohlen believed that Tito had "limited his freedom of action." A cessation in aid by the United States could easily be justified on those grounds alone, but did carry the risk of forcing Yugoslavia to greater dependence on Moscow. On the other hand, Bohlen did not believe that a continuation of assistance would slow down the Soviet-Yugoslav rapprochement. The ambassador also told Dulles that he had heard that Tito had urged the Soviets to restore the independence of the Eastern European states and that Khrushchev had agreed, but only if such steps could be taken over time to avoid upheaval.[100] As usual, nothing seemed certain in the U.S.-Yugoslav relationship.

Bohlen's view of the Yugoslavs found its way into Ambassador Mićunović's diary, who recorded that the Americans "are worse disposed toward us" as a result of Tito's visit to the Soviet Union. The

98. Intelligence Brief No. 1952, 22 June 1956, *FRUS, 1955–1957*, 26:728–30.
99. Riddleberger to Dulles, 22 June 1956, RG 59, no. 1550, 661.68/6-2256.
100. Bohlen to Dulles, 23 June 1956, *FRUS, 1955–1957*, 26:731–33; Bohlen, *Witness to History*, 403.

United States appeared certain that Yugoslavia would now have to be subordinate to the Soviets, while the Soviets were unhappy because Yugoslavia had not surrendered enough. It appeared to Mićunović that his country had pleased no one.[101]

When Ambassador Mates met with Dulles in late June, he assured the secretary of Tito's conviction that genuine changes were under way in the Soviet Union and that more independence was evident in the satellites. Yet he cautioned that these regimes were not adopting Western style governments or policies hostile to the Soviet Union. Dulles expressed his understanding with a remarkable declaration that demonstrated the great difference that often existed between the secretary's public and private utterances. As Dulles told Mates, a "post–World War I idea of a *cordon sanitaire* of hostile states around the Soviet Union was completely outmoded." The Soviet Union was a major power, "entitled to have friendly governments surrounding it" such as Finland and Yugoslavia. Europe would be much healthier if the Soviets were surrounded by friendly, rather than "servile or dependent" states; however, the Soviets could not be allowed to extend their "sovereignty to the center of Europe." The expansion of Soviet frontiers after the war had taken "care of all of Russia's legitimate needs"; the rest of Europe had to remain independent. Mates and Dulles agreed that Tito held similar views and that Yugoslavia served as a model of independence for the satellite countries. Mates also expressed the hope that the Soviets would not hold on to their policy in the satellites for too long, lest upheavals occur there that had an anti-Soviet thrust.[102]

The unrest that Mates feared occurred on 28 June when workers rioted in the Polish city of Poznan. The riots, caused by the general unpopularity of the communist leadership as well as by severe economic problems, were also inspired in part by the de-Stalinization program and by the Soviet embrace of Yugoslavia. Yet when the regime crushed the riot with military force, Tito praised the response of the Polish government. While Stalinists were temporarily heartened, a more moderate but still reformist communist government eventually took power. The Polish Communist Party thus retained control of the de-Stalinization process.[103]

Turmoil continued, however, as the presses of other communist

101. Mićunović, *Moscow Diary*, 79–80.
102. David E. Mark, memorandum of conversation, 29 June 1956, RG 59, 661.68/6-2956.
103. Wilson, *Tito's Yugoslavia*, 102.

parties began printing articles attacking the Soviet leadership. The members of the NSC pondered the implications of this: did the Soviets not understand the effects the denunciation of Stalin would have, or was this all some kind of clever plot to convince the world that the Soviets had no control over communist parties in other countries? Secretary Dulles complained that Soviet behavior had become less predictable under Khrushchev than it had been under Stalin. Stalin had always carefully weighed the results of his actions; his only serious blunder had occurred in Korea, but that "could readily be forgiven him," since the Truman administration had appeared indifferent to Korea's fate. Khrushchev by contrast could be "expected to commit irrational acts," caused in part by his constant inebriation. The Soviet leadership was clearly in a state of crisis and had unleashed forces they could not control; however, the secretary of state credited much of the change that had occurred within the Soviet Union to U.S. policy. Allen Dulles speculated that Tito may also have played a role in urging other communist parties to be more critical of the Soviet Union.[104]

The NSC concluded that while Titoism remained a disruptive force, the Soviet reconciliation with Yugoslavia had somewhat neutralized his appeal to the satellite governments. The de-Stalinization campaign and the Soviet acceptance of Tito continued to create problems for the Soviets but the administration saw little hope for the immediate diminution of Soviet control in Eastern Europe. Yet, the West's ability to bring about change was still enhanced by an independent Yugoslavia.[105]

In its analysis, the CIA warned that Khrushchev's criticism of Stalin did not indicate any deviation from the principles of Marxism-Leninism. New and better tactics, such as some measure of decentralization and independence within the bloc and the increased use of popular front and socialist movements would simply be used to achieve the same goals. Such flexibility in means made the "danger of Communist encroachment" even greater, because their maneuvers could not be easily matched "by the more cumbersome parliamentary machineries of the West." The CIA believed "the Titoist gamble of the Soviet leaders appears to have a good chance of success." The Agency, in short, did not see a crisis within the communist movement, but

104. Memorandum of Discussion at the 289th Meeting of the NSC, 28 June 1956, *FRUS, 1955–1957*, 24:118–23.

105. NSC Report, 3 July 1956, with enclosure, "Draft Statement of Policy by the National Security Council on United States Policy Toward the Soviet Satellites in Eastern Europe," *FRUS, 1955–1957*, 25:190–94.

opportunities for an increase in Soviet power, based in part on Soviet manipulations of Titoism, all of which had negative implications for the West.[106]

This uncertainty about Tito's attitude toward both the Soviets and the West caused Eisenhower and Dulles to implement the policy called for in NSC 5601 and suspend most of the recently resumed U.S. military assistance program to Yugoslavia.[107] Dulles's estimate of Tito's resolve to remain independent had not changed; Riddleberger later recalled that Dulles had never doubted that and had expected Tito to visit Moscow after the Soviet visit to Yugoslavia.[108] However, continued military assistance would be more difficult to justify in the face of the most recent Yugoslav-Soviet exchanges. The administration choose to act before Congress compelled it to, in the hope of maintaining some of its ability to manipulate both Congress and the Yugoslavs.

The final outcome of the MSA debate in Congress at least preserved the administration's cherished flexibility. Although the Senate rejected the attempt led by Senator Bridges to cut off all aid to Yugoslavia, by July the lawmakers had banned all new military funds, except those for spare parts and equipment. Congress also mandated that all assistance to Yugoslavia under the Mutual Security Program be terminated within ninety days unless the president issued a finding declaring that Yugoslavia had not returned to the Soviet camp and that aid to Tito's government remained in the security interests of the United States.[109] The administration had had to fight to achieve even this. When Dulles had asked Riddleberger how much support the administration could count on in Congress for its assistance programs in 1956, the ambassador had replied that Dulles would have to choose between funding the Aswan Dam for Egypt and assisting Tito; Congress would not approve both. Dulles had then concluded that he would fight for aid to Tito even if, as Riddleberger recalled, we "get licked."[110]

In waging his campaign, the secretary, through countless phone

106. CIA, CIA/SRS-2, "The Present Communist Controversy: Its Ramifications and Possible Repercussions," 15 July 1956, Eisenhower Papers, PAP, Whitman File, Administrative Series, File: Dulles, Allen (3). The cover page bears Eisenhower's initials.

107. Report by the Operations Coordinating Board, 24 April 1957, Progress Report on NSC 5601, "United States Policy Toward Yugoslavia," *FRUS, 1955–1957*, 26:768–73.

108. Riddleberger, Oral History, Princeton, 43, 65.

109. William S. White, "Senate Rejects Foreign Aid Cut of $1,700,000,000," *New York Times*, 29 June 1956, 1, 6; William S. White, "Conferees Accept 4 Billion Aid Bill: House Cut Pushed," ibid., 7 July 1956, 1, 4.

110. Riddleberger, Oral History, Princeton, 34.

calls to both Republican and Democratic legislators, had stressed the need for the administration to retain some discretion in its dealings with Yugoslavia. He cited the recent unrest in Poland as an example of his faith that "if we can hold the line these others will crack."[111] Dulles also had predicted that if the United States continued to supply military goods to Yugoslavia, it could keep a "strong tether on Yugoslav military machine and remain in position prevent use armed forces in actions contrary US interests."[112] After Senator Joseph R. McCarthy and others in Congress suggested that the Yugoslavs had the capacity to produce their own spare parts, rendering Dulles's assertion of control "largely illusory," the secretary supplied a Defense Department study detailing the Yugoslavs' industrial inadequacies, a condition Dulles transformed into a policy deliberately fashioned by Tito with the United States in mind. The "Yugoslavs accept dependence on us for the servicing of their military machine," he told McCarthy, because "we have no aggressive designs against them." This "reflects a clear policy decision on the part of President Tito and his choice to accept such a relationship with the United States rather than the Soviet Union." While Tito might choose to change that policy, Dulles warned that "we should not force that change upon him."[113]

In private conversations, however, Dulles revealed a more ambiguous attitude. In a discussion with Knowland on their inability to agree on aid for Yugoslavia, Dulles acknowledged that he was not certain Knowland's position was an incorrect one, but he clung to the idea that the fluidity in Eastern Europe demanded that the administration retain its flexibility. Knowland sympathized with Dulles, declaring that if he "were where the Sec. sits, he might feel the same."[114] During a lunch meeting with Henry Luce and C. D. Jackson, Dulles admitted, in Jackson's words, that he "had his fingers crossed on Tito."[115] Yet in a talking paper provided to Senator Everett Dirksen for his use in arguing the administration's position in the Congress, Dulles offered Tito's refusal to recognize the East German regime as proof of his independence. He also noted that while the United States preferred

111. Dulles to Lyndon Baines Johnson and Charles O'Mahoney, 29 June 1956, Dulles Telcons.

112. Dulles to Riddleberger, 26 June 1956, RG 59, no. 1009, 768.5-MSP/6-2656.

113. Ibid.; Dulles to Joseph R. McCarthy, 27 June 1956, RG 59, 768.5-MSP/6-2756, with enclosure, "Yugoslav Capabilities for the Production Domestically of Spare Parts for U.S.-Supplied Military Equipment."

114. William Knowland to Dulles, 13 July 1956, Dulles Telcons.

115. Log, 20 July 1956, C. D. Jackson Papers, File: Time, Inc. F, Eisenhower Library.

democracy to any form of communism, a system of national communism was at least a step in the right direction.[116]

In the end Dulles, to placate his critics and to appease his own ambivalence, pledged key senators that shipments of military goods to Yugoslavia would remain minimal until the president issued his finding. Acting Secretary of State Herbert Hoover Jr. also entered a letter into the *Congressional Record* certifying that no additional jet planes would be sent to Yugoslavia in the interim.[117] The law did not actually require such a policy but the administration clearly believed this a prudent course.

There was no certainty that the suspension of military aid, coming after months when little material had been delivered to Yugoslavia, would have any effect on Tito's policies. Like Bohlen, the intelligence community was convinced that U.S. aid had no influence on Tito's ties with the communist world. If Tito were convinced that aid was to be stopped, he might attempt to "mollify the West" but his overall policy would not change.[118] Tito, however, had no such fears. On 1 August, the Belgrade embassy reported that the Yugoslavs were convinced that "requirements US global policy will dictate continuation American aid Yugoslavia." The fight waged by the administration on Yugoslavia's behalf in Congress only strengthened that belief. The Yugoslavs were confident that Eisenhower would issue a finding that approved continued aid, "since otherwise administration would be repudiating itself." The Yugoslavs had no clear understanding of the role played by Congress in the U.S. system of government and simply assumed that since both the president and secretary of state had spoken on their behalf, aid would continue.[119]

Admonitions from the embassy that the finding was "not merely matter of form" but resulted from "very real reservations on the part of majority of Congress" concerning Yugoslavia's policies had little impact. Since no wheat or any other additional assistance would be shipped until the president acted, the State Department hoped that "negative response at this time on wheat, coupled with emphasis on Congressional mandate on President, may have salutary effect inducing realistic assessment by Yugoslavs of impact US policies and public opinion of Yugoslavia's trend on all fronts away from West and toward

116. Dulles to Everett Dirksen, 17 July 1956, Dulles Papers (Eisenhower Library), General Correspondence, File: C-D(3).

117. Hoover to Riddleberger, 21 July 1956, RG 59, no. 79, 768.5MSP/7-2156.

118. NIE-31-56, "Yugoslavia's International Position," 24 July 1956, *FRUS, 1955–1957*, 26:736–37.

119. Belgrade to Dulles, 1 August 1956, RG 59, no. 165, 768.5-MSP/8-156.

USSR."[120] But the Yugoslavs simply said they would obtain wheat from other sources, naming the USSR and Syria as likely possibilities. According to U.S. diplomats, Yugoslavia "evidenced a desire not to allow this problem to cause a worsening of relations." Even the news of a suspension of arms shipments had been received "calmly" by Tito's government. Indeed, Yugoslavia continued to tilt toward the Communist world. In September 1956 the Yugoslav government announced that it had signed a long-term agreement with the Soviets and the East Germans for the development of its aluminum production. This moved Yugoslavia that much closer to the GDR and the Soviet bloc and made similar ties with the West less attractive to investors.[121]

The United States could not even be certain of the extent or nature of Tito's influence over the satellites, the hook on which so much of its policy hung. As the Operations Coordinating Board (OCB) explained, both the hope and the dilemma were that "because they are Communists, the Yugoslavs can get a hearing among those Communist ruling groups who desire improved living conditions and greater national autonomy. But because they are Communists, the Yugoslavs do not espouse causes and movements which would threaten Communism itself." Yugoslavia's expanding commercial ties to the Soviet bloc, Tito's visit to Moscow, and his deepening relationship with the GDR, which in itself "demonstrates a willingness to flout one of the central tenets of Western policy," were all unfavorable developments. Tito's current foreign policy, in short, did "not give grounds for optimism," and his neutralist stance remained "contrary to U.S. interests" in the example it set for other countries. Yet the danger remained that a cutoff of U.S. aid would only force him more deeply into the Soviet orbit.[122]

After years of providing economic and military assistance, the United States was no closer to controlling Tito's policies in 1956 than it had been in 1950. The accuracy of Ambassador Allen's observation, that the United States should not regret Tito's independent spirit, since it was that very spirit which had caused his rift with Stalin, became more evident as the years passed. But the most profound hope of U.S.

120. Department of State to Belgrade Embassy, 18 August 1956, RG 59, no. 148, 768.5-MSP/8-1356.

121. Beam to Dulles, 4 September 1956, RG 59, 611.68/9-456.

122. Report Prepared by the OCB, Progress Report on NSC 5601, "United States Policy toward Yugoslavia," 5 September 1956, *FRUS, 1955–1957*, 26:740–46.

policy, that Tito would bring independence to the Eastern European satellites, had not yet been tested. On that test of "liberation" and "rollback" hung the future of the relationship between Yugoslavia and the United States.

CHAPTER SIX

1956–1957
"... OUR BEST FRIEND IN THE UNITED STATES"

By 1956 the Eisenhower administration, even though it had ample evidence of Tito's resolve to follow his own course in foreign and domestic affairs, continued to believe that adjustments in the flow of U.S. military aid would influence his relations with both the Soviet bloc and the West. Those adjustments became the hallmark of the administration's policy toward Yugoslavia, but they did little either to alter Tito's behavior or to promote the liberation of the Eastern European satellites. When the Hungarians attempted to free themselves from Soviet control in 1956, both the United States and Yugoslavia had to reconsider their respective goals for Eastern Europe. The Eisenhower administration, despite its talk of liberation, did not assist the rebellion and soon muted its rhetoric to emphasize its support for more gradual, "Titoist" change. Tito, faced with the prospect of a nonsocialist government in Hungary, supported the Soviets' intervention while condemning the policies that rendered it necessary. Tito's actions, while not fully in keeping with the role assigned to him in the wedge strategy, put him temporarily at odds with the Soviets and back in the good graces of the Americans; however, the eventual outcome of the events of 1956 led to a subtle but significant change in the U.S.-Yugoslav relationship.

As Eisenhower pondered his finding on aid to Yugoslavia, Tito sent him a long letter that—perhaps intentionally—paid homage to the wedge strategy and to the problems it posed. When Tito penned his missive on 26 August, he did so in the hope of alleviating the "elements" that had served to "impair our friendly cooperation," but first thanked Eisenhower for the past assistance "extended with no conditions attached and no danger for our independence involved." He expressed "regret," however, over the discussions then under way in the United States "as to whether the Government of Yugoslavia is still behaving well or not, and whether our country should or should not be given military and economic aid in the future, and under what conditions." Tito assured Eisenhower that Yugoslavia's policy toward the West had not altered, and its improved relations with the Soviets and Eastern Europeans had "contributed to the termination of an unhealthy situation in this part of the world." His "voyage of peace" to the Soviet Union had been designed to continue that process; he and his government were capable of taking such steps "without endangering our independence."

But it would "not be logical," Tito asserted, for Yugoslavia to accept more U.S. military aid while pursuing its attempts to exert "a positive influence" on international relations. Tito appreciated the administration's efforts to obtain such aid from the Congress but since this had proved "so arduous a problem," the program's termination might serve to ensure continued good relations. Avenues of cooperation that "would not create difficulties for your administration or place us time and again in a humiliating position" but would ensure Yugoslavia the agricultural supplies and "above all . . . modern jet aircraft" it needed could then be found. Tito closed by asking for the president's views on his proposals, but Eisenhower did not answer him until well after issuing his finding.[1]

Despite Tito's disclaimer, the Soviets continued their attempts to draw him into their orbit. At the end of August 1956, Khrushchev suggested to Mićunović that he would visit Tito in mid-September, while he and his family were vacationing in the Crimea. Khrushchev intended to invite Tito to return to the Crimea with him, along with Mićunović and his wife, on the grounds that all could profit from a week's rest. Although Khrushchev left a quid pro quo unstated, Mićunović was certain that Tito's acceptance of the vacation trip was a precondition to the Soviet visit. Tito, who according to Mićunović

---

1. Tito to Eisenhower, 26 August 1956, Eisenhower Papers, PAP, Whitman File, International Series.

"accepts all Khrushchev's suggestions," agreed but only after a week's delay and a prompting from Mićunović.[2]

Before Khrushchev arrived in Yugoslavia, reports reached the United States from Yugoslavia and elsewhere in Eastern Europe of an anti-Tito missive sent by the Soviets to the satellites. The circular reaffirmed the primacy of the Communist Party of the Soviet Union (CPSU) and directed that other parties be judged by their "more or less intimate relations" with the CPSU. While the principle of "national differences in the building of Socialism was to be respected," the leadership role of the CPSU and adherence to Marxist-Leninist principles could not be abandoned. Having advanced this philosophy, the letter denied that Tito was a genuine communist, warned the satellites not to follow his example, and condemned Yugoslavia for its close ties to the West.[3]

A few weeks later, Yugoslavia, apparently now less sanguine about alternative means of supply, pressed the United States for the badly needed wheat shipments. This request came to the West just as Khrushchev visited Belgrade. The Eisenhower administration remained unsure of the exact reason for Khrushchev's journey, but speculated that it might have resulted from continuing Soviet-Yugoslav disagreements over the satellites. On 18 September, Acting Secretary of State Hoover advised Dulles, who was in London in connection with the Suez crisis, that the Yugoslavs, with a food situation "so nearly desperate," would have difficulty resisting Soviet pressure on any given issue if they had "no recourse but to turn to Soviets immediately or in few weeks for basic food supply." Hoover realized that Dulles could not formulate the department's response to Congress's demand that Yugoslavia be certified as worthy of aid until his return to Washington; but he feared that the delay could be harmful if the Yugoslavs made "virtually irretrievable . . . decisions" in the interim. Hoover therefore asked Dulles to approve a confidential approach through Ambassador Riddleberger to the highest Yugoslav officials to assure them that the secretary of state, barring any "adverse developments" planned to advise the president to issue a finding favorable to Yugoslavia and to continued assistance.[4]

2. Mićunović, *Moscow Diary*, 102–4.

3. *FRUS, 1955–1957*, 25:242–43, editorial note; Clissold, *Yugoslavia and the Soviet Union*, 263.

4. Hoover to Dulles, 18 September 1956, RG 59, no. 6, 768.5-MSP/9-1656. The *New York Times*, on 30 September 1956, indicated that Dulles had sent a message regarding the presidential finding to Tito on 19 September. "Dulles Message Confirmed," *New York Times*, 30 September 1956, 29.

As U.S. analysts attempted to ascertain whether Khrushchev had gone to Yugoslavia to consult Tito or to warn him about an impending Soviet action, they noticed that Tito and Khrushchev suddenly flew to Yalta for discussions with others in the Soviet leadership and with Hungarian Workers' Party head Ernö Gerö. While this provoked "a flood of intelligence material alleging new and serious rifts over the Yugoslav problem among the Soviet leaders," the CIA doubted any such splits.[5] The Yugoslav government added to the mystery by acknowledging that on 29 September Tito and Khrushchev had discussed a number of "ideological" issues, and implying that those issues involved more than bilateral Soviet-Yugoslav relations.[6]

At least one Yugoslav shared the Americans' unease. Although the trip to the Crimea had been presented by Khrushchev as a vacation, Mićunović considered the circular letter to be a repudiation of the Moscow Declaration and this had made him wary. The appearance of Gerö and the others in the Crimea had also surprised Mićunović until he surmised that Khrushchev intended to involve Yugoslavia more deeply in the unfolding crisis in Hungary.[7]

In mid-1955, Mátyás Rákosi had succeeded reformist Imre Nagy as the ruler of Hungary, after Nagy had attempted prematurely to implement a number of non-Stalinist economic policies and in general to follow Tito's example of creating an independent, more moderate regime. Public support for Nagy and his reforms continued, however, and gained even more momentum after the Belgrade Declaration. By early 1956, after Nagy had enunciated a reform program that went well beyond the principles of the Declaration, Rákosi announced plans to arrest the reformer and hundreds of his supporters. The Soviets, fearing another upheaval such as that in Poland, forced Rákosi to resign. In their quest for an acceptable successor, the Soviets consulted Tito, who recommended Ernö Gerö. Tito did so with some reluctance, however, because he believed that Gerö had little popular support.[8]

During the Crimea visit, Khrushchev arranged for Gerö and other Hungarian leaders to visit Yugoslavia in mid-October, a move Mićunović saw as designed to "improve their political standing in their own

---

5. NSC Meeting no. 297, 20 September 1956, Eisenhower Papers, PAP, Whitman Files, NSC Series, File: NSC Meeting no. 297; NSC Meeting no. 298, 28 September 1956, ibid., File: NSC Meeting no. 298.

6. Elie Abel, "Yugoslavs Tell of Doctrinal Drift with the Soviet," *New York Times*, 30 September 1956, 1, 29.

7. Mićunović, *Moscow Diary*, 108, 116.

8. Wilson, *Tito's Yugoslavia*, 103; Hoffman and Neal, *Yugoslavia and the New Communism*, 466.

country."[9] The tactic failed; demonstrations against the regime broke out in Budapest while the Hungarian delegation was still in Yugoslavia.

The United States, struggling to make sense of all of these developments, arrived at a fairly accurate assessment. At a news conference on 2 October, Dulles opined that Tito had not gone to the USSR for a "vacation" but for a discussion of the relationship between the CPSU and the Eastern European satellites. He recalled what he said was Tito's concurrence when they met in Yugoslavia in 1955 that the satellites should be independent; he assumed Tito was now discussing that with the Soviets.[10]

Bohlen also surmised the Soviets sought either to curtail Yugoslavia's appeal to the satellites or to obtain Tito's permission for a pending change in Soviet-bloc relations. He was certain that the Soviets and Yugoslavs were continuing to quarrel over their dissimilar interpretations of the Belgrade Declaration, with the Soviets particularly fearful that the satellites would duplicate Tito's example of establishing economic ties with the West. The Soviets "may be telling Tito that his position of attempting to keep one foot in each camp is unrealistic and is causing great harm to communist cause as a whole and he, therefore must make his choice." The ambassador predicted that in the end the Soviets would not win, because Yugoslavia occupied so strong a position, and the two states would have to compromise their differences.[11]

Against this background, Dulles met with Eisenhower on 11 October and informed him of the State Department's unanimous opinion that the president's finding on aid to Yugoslavia be in the affirmative. Dulles conceded that the United States did not have as much information as it would like on the recent Tito-Khrushchev meetings, but he held to his conviction that Tito would do nothing to compromise his country's independence. Yugoslavia needed assistance, especially wheat, and if the United States did not resume economic and some military aid, that would surely leave the Yugoslavs with no alternative but the Soviets. As Dulles told the president, "they might have to go on their knees to Moscow and there might indeed lose their independence." The secretary believed the U.S. policy of assisting Tito had contributed to the restiveness of the satellites; if the Soviets believed this as well and were applying pressure to Tito then U.S. aid

9. Mićunović, *Moscow Diary*, 117, 121.
10. *DSB*, 15 October 1956, 3:574–78.
11. Bohlen to Dulles, 3 October 1956, RG 59, no. 732, 661.68/10-356.

became even more crucial. But Dulles reiterated his view that a resumption of economic aid was most urgent; "important military aid" had been suspended since the summer and "this suspension could probably be continued for the time being without dangerous consequences." The president, focusing more on the military aid than the economic, concurred with Dulles's assessment, but believed military assistance to be significant because the receiving nation became "dependent upon United States ammunition and spare parts." A Yugoslav dependence on the United States was preferable to a dependence on the Soviet Union.[12]

After meeting with Eisenhower, Dulles consulted with his staff on the text and timing of the presidential finding. The secretary expressed his preference "for a shorter statement . . . which would avoid excessive detail which might lead later to controversy." The text should avoid any mention of a Soviet military threat to Yugoslavia and should not imply continuing congressional monitoring of aid shipments, while "making it clear that shipments of jet aircraft and heavy equipment are suspended pending developments."[13]

In sending the details of the finding to Riddleberger, Hoover acknowledged that it settled nothing in the U.S.-Yugoslav relationship and promised a "constant review" of U.S. policy. Hoover, pinpointing the contradiction in the administration's application of the wedge strategy, feared that the goal of keeping Yugoslavia dependent on the West for its military supplies might be compromised by the suspension of aircraft deliveries. But he believed the United States needed more information about the nature of the Yugoslav-Soviet relationship before such deliveries could proceed. He advised Riddleberger to remind Yugoslav officials (a discussion with Tito would be "most profitable") of the "peculiarly sensitive" nature of the military aid issue, and of the concern the United States had previously expressed when Yugoslavia appeared to desire "military ties simultaneously with both Soviets and West." Once the Yugoslavs were more forthcoming about their discussions with the Soviets, the "mutual confidence" necessary for "useful military cooperation" could be restored.[14]

When Eisenhower issued his finding to Congress on 16 October, he called for the resumption of aid on the grounds that Yugoslavia met the conditions imposed by the Congress under the Mutual Security

12. Memorandum of Conversation with the President, 11 October 1956, Dulles Papers, Memoranda Series, File: August through December 1956 (4).

13. Joseph N. Greene, informal record of meeting, 11 October 1956, RG 59, 768.5-MSP/10-1256.

14. Hoover to Riddleberger, 12 October 1956, RG 59, no. 282, 768.5-MSP/10-1226.

Act. However, in accordance with Dulles' recommendation, only economic aid and negotiations on future economic agreements would be resumed in their entirety. Military aid, which since the congressional action in July had been limited to "small, routine and long-planned deliveries of equipment," would continue only at that level; no jet aircraft or heavy military equipment would be sent. The "balance of available evidence" convinced Eisenhower that the Yugoslavs were attempting to maintain their independence of the Soviets, but he harbored doubts about Yugoslavia's ability to discern the true designs that the Soviets had on them. For that reason U.S.-Yugoslav relations would remain under review, and military deliveries kept at a minimum.[15]

In essence, little had changed since the original suspension of military aid in the summer of 1955. Although political rather than military considerations served as the basis for the administration's aid program for Yugoslavia, the hope that Tito could be enticed to move closer to the West persisted. The need to have some control over negotiations with the Congress, as well as the fear that equipment sent to Yugoslavia could somehow fall into Soviet hands had prompted the suspension of the barely resumed military aid program in the summer of 1956. The greater concern that a rejection of Yugoslavia by the United States would force Tito into a closer relationship with the Soviets and erase the damage his defection had caused the USSR eventually prevailed, but the full volume of military aid was not restored, lest Tito prove unresponsive to U.S. pressure. Thus the Soviet Union remained the real arbiter of the U.S.-Yugoslav relationship. Yet the tactics used by the administration seemed little more than a return to the "pinpricks" so lamented by John Cabot before the momentous events of 1948.

Tito, in an echo of his statements to Eisenhower about the insults Yugoslavia perceived in congressional debates on aid, objected to the president's conditions for assistance, asserting that he saw no Soviet threat to Yugoslav independence. It was the United States, not the Soviet Union, he declared, which failed to respect the principles of equality and cooperation between nations. In a meeting with Riddleberger, Popović, the Yugoslav foreign minister, reiterated that Yugoslavia had already asked that a less demeaning system of credits and long-term financial agreements replace the current grant aid. He also

15. Dana Adams Schmidt, "President Lets Aid to Tito Go On; Withholds Arms," *New York Times*, 16 October 1956, 1, 5; "Text of Eisenhower's Decision on Aid," ibid., 4; *DSB*, 29 October 1956, 35:664–65.

charged that shipments of military aid to Yugoslavia had virtually ceased in any case and disclosed that Tito had informed Eisenhower privately several weeks before that if military aid proved difficult for the administration, its cancellation would not affect the good relations in existence between the two states.[16]

Riddleberger characterized the Yugoslav response to the finding as a "typical example of Yugoslav hyper-sensitivity and bad temper," but understood that Tito, after apparently asserting his independence in his recent exchanges with the Soviets, was especially unwilling to accept criticism from the United States. While he believed the Yugoslav stance was simply the prelude to negotiations rather than a genuine rejection of military and economic aid, Riddleberger did think it significant that Yugoslavia had again stressed its preference for long-term aid agreements, while publicly disclosing Tito's suggestion that military aid be terminated. The latter confirmed Riddleberger's fear that with Yugoslavia's interest in military aid diminishing, it would be increasingly difficult to maintain a "western monopoly" over Yugoslavia's military supplies. In any case, military aid had in fact *not* ceased, and a total of $38.2 million in supplies had been delivered since January.[17]

Riddleberger also believed that "Tito's vanity" had been wounded by Eisenhower's statements concerning the inability of the Yugoslavs to see the Soviets as a danger and also by the administration's refusal to accept their interpretation of their recent talks with the Soviets "at face value." He suggested that Eisenhower "apply some ointment to their bruises" by assuring Yugoslavia of continued economic aid and requesting Tito's "confidential comment on how Western policy should be adapted to changing circumstances in Soviet orbit." A visit to convey such a missive would also provide Riddleberger with a "good opportunity to extract more solid information on Yugoslav-Soviet relations and influence Yugoslav policy."[18]

The administration was struggling to maintain its link to Yugoslavia, but on its own terms. As Dulles explained to a citizens' committee appointed by Eisenhower to review the Mutual Security Program, the United States had expended great effort to prevent a return of Soviet influence to Yugoslavia, and now that "the Soviets are making an economic thrust there, we must keep our hand in because Yugoslavia

16. Elie Abel, "Yugoslavs Chide U.S. over Limits on Continued Aid," *New York Times*, 18 October 1956, 1, 3; Riddleberger to Dulles, 17 October 1956, RG 59, no. 492, 768.5-MSP/10-1756.

17. Riddleberger to Dulles, 18 October 1956, RG 59, no. 500, 768.5-MSP/10-1856.

18. Riddleberger to Dulles, 23 October 1956, RG 59, no. 530, 768.5-MSP/10-2356.

provides a notable example of national independence in Eastern Europe." When asked by a member of the committee whether the Soviets might not consider U.S. aid to Yugoslavia as helpful to them, Dulles replied in the negative and pointed out that requests from Yugoslavia were actually declining. "Tito," Dulles cynically concluded, "was most useful as an exhibit."[19]

Tito had fewer illusions about the Soviets than the United States realized, largely because the Belgrade and Moscow Declarations had not translated into any change in the Soviets' policy toward the satellites. Ambassador Mićunović, after observing the Soviets throughout the summer and fall of 1956 concluded that "Soviet domination of Eastern Europe is as dear to Khrushchev as to any Stalinist."[20] His U.S. colleague Chip Bohlen agreed that the Soviets foresaw only "increasing independence and greater equality for the East European countries . . . within the general framework of, and subordinate to, the general Communist bloc," while Yugoslavia envisioned something akin to its own brand of national communism.[21]

For the next several years, the Soviets and the Yugoslavs alternated between rapprochement and estrangement. Leo Mates later described Yugoslavia's relations with the Soviet Union as a "yo-yo," a constant "up and down" process caused by Tito's emotional attachment to the Soviet Union and his genuine desire to improve relations without sacrificing Yugoslav independence. In Mates's words: "He de-stabilized continually our relations with the Soviet Union because he went always too far in the periods of thaw and he was always too violent in the periods of freezing."[22]

The depth of the disagreement between the Soviet Union and Yugoslavia, the limits Tito placed on satellite reform, and the futility of Dulles's liberation policy all publicly surfaced during the Hungarian Revolution of 1956. While proof of conflict between the Soviets and Yugoslavs advanced the administration's case for assistance for Yugoslavia, the unwillingness of Tito to sanction an end to socialism in Eastern Europe compromised his standing in Dulles's liberation scheme, which was itself undermined by the events in Hungary.

Tito's earlier assessment of Gerö's inability to rule Hungary was quickly proven correct. After the Hungarians, hoping to bring a more

19. Fairless Committee Citizens Advisors on Mutual Security, summary of discussion with John Foster Dulles, 25 October 1956, File: Summaries of Testimonies and Briefings, Eisenhower Library.
20. Mićunović, *Moscow Diary*, 124.
21. Bohlen, *Witness to History*, 407.
22. Interview with Mates, September 1988.

nationalistic leader to power without provoking Soviet intervention, began to demonstrate against the Gerö regime in October, Nagy returned to power as premier. Gerö, however, remained head of the party. The Hungarian politburo then appealed to the Soviets for assistance in suppressing what they characterized as a right-wing revolution. In late October the Soviets intervened militarily, ostensibly to support the Nagy government. Within a few days, Nagy had negotiated a cease-fire, the Soviets had agreed to withdraw, and Tito had condemned the Soviet intervention while appealing to Nagy to end the unrest, lest it have international repercussions.[23]

When the Soviets issued new rules for relations between socialist nations that reflected the principles of both the "secret speech" and the Belgrade Declaration, Nagy responded by proclaiming that Hungary wished to withdraw from the Warsaw Pact and declare its neutrality. At that point, with the rest of the world distracted by the Suez Crisis in the Middle East, the Soviets moved to forcibly suppress Nagy.[24] On 2 November, before the Soviets acted but after speaking to the leaders of the bloc, Khrushchev and Malenkov traveled to Brioni to consult Tito, Kardelj, Ranković, and Mićunović. Mićunović had returned to Belgrade on the eve of the first intervention with a message from Khrushchev, declaring that the Soviets were ready to pursue a political solution in Hungary if one could be found. During these meetings, Khrushchev expressed the fear that capitalism was about to be restored to Hungary and that the Soviets had no choice but to move militarily. Although Tito made clear his conviction that Soviet policies had precipitated the crisis in Hungary, he acquiesced in a second Soviet intervention.[25]

When the Soviets invaded Hungary on 4 November, Nagy sought and received asylum in the Yugoslav Embassy in Budapest, and the Soviets quickly accused Yugoslavia of supporting the Hungarian counterrevolution.[26] In a speech in Pula on 11 November, Tito publicly

23. Wilson, *Tito's Yugoslavia*, 104; Mićunović, *Moscow Diary*, 128.

24. Wilson, *Tito's Yugoslavia*, 105–6.

25. Mićunović, *Moscow Diary*, 127, 131–40.

26. Ibid., 143–45. Documents recently found in the Community Party archives of the former Soviet Union indicate that Khrushchev and Tito had agreed on 2 November that the Yugoslavs would attempt to convince Nagy to support the post-intervention János Kádár regime. See Johanna Granville, "Imre Nagy, Hesitant Revolutionary," *Cold War International History Project Bulletin* 5 (Spring 1995): 23, 27–28. In his diary, Mićunović makes a cryptic reference to an agreement reached for the purpose of "reducing the degree of resistance by the Nagy government" and cites the sheltering of Nagy as having in itself accomplished that. Mićunović, *Moscow Diary*, 150.

condemned the first Soviet intervention and the Soviet and Hungarian policies that had caused it, while portraying the second as a necessary evil to save the socialist system and prevent Western intervention. Tito also criticized the power that Stalinists still retained within the Kremlin leadership.[27]

Soviet leaders subsequently summoned Mićunović to inform him that all friendly relations between their two countries had come to an end.[28] The Soviets also rejected all of Tito's criticisms, while cataloging the deficiencies of the Yugoslav system and its ties to Western capitalism, which rendered Yugoslavia a poor model for other socialist states.[29] At the end of November, the recriminations exchanged by the two became even more heated. Yugoslavia, after receiving assurances from Hungary that Nagy and his associates would not be arrested or tried, allowed the Hungarians to leave the embassy. Soviet authorities immediately arrested Nagy and his companions and took them to Romania.[30]

The Eisenhower administration, in contemplating UN action against the first Soviet intervention, recognized that Tito "might find it awkward to join with us" but hoped Yugoslavia would use its influence with the Soviets to minimize the bloodshed in Hungary.[31] Yugoslavia declined, doubting the usefulness of such an approach, and abstained on a vote to bring the crisis in Hungary before the Security Council.[32]

On 31 October, before the second Soviet intervention, the NSC reviewed its policy of encouraging Titoist regimes to emerge in the satellites, in light of the unrest in both Poland and Hungary. Although large segments of the populations in each country had displayed "anti-Russian and anti-communist sentiments," the Soviets had shown in Hungary that they would use force to prevent any change in a satellite's "close military and political alliance with the USSR." However, the absence of such an intervention in Poland was a more positive development, since it indicated that a communist government that remained "loyal to its military and political alliance with the USSR" could "pursue its own internal road to communism." In any case, the

27. Clissold, *Yugoslavia and the Soviet Union*, 263–68.
28. Mićunović, *Moscow Diary*, 162.
29. Clissold, *Yugoslavia and the Soviet Union*, 266–70.
30. Ridley, *Tito: A Biography*, 345.
31. Dulles to Embassy in the United Kingdom, 25 October 1956, *FRUS, 1955–1957*, 25:292–93.
32. *FRUS, 1955–1957*, 25:298 n. 11 and 316 n. 5.

NSC advised that a review of U.S. policy toward Eastern Europe was in order.[33]

The Suez Crisis in the Middle East proved more pressing. Before the NSC met on 1 November, Dulles advised the president that the crisis in Hungary, which was to have been the focal point of the meeting, appeared to have passed, and both agreed that the NSC should concentrate its deliberations on the Middle East. Eisenhower opened the NSC meeting with those instructions, and the council duly deferred any action on the satellite issue.[34] For the next several days Suez rather than Hungary commanded most of the administration's attention.

Dulles could claim that the situation in Hungary had stabilized because the Soviets had proclaimed their new set of rules governing relations with the satellites and their willingness to withdraw their forces from Hungary. To the State Department, these actions were more proof of Soviet resolve to tolerate national communism in Eastern Europe, lest anti-Soviet feeling there rise to even higher levels.[35] Yet within a few days of the NSC meeting, it became clear that the USSR was increasing its troop strength in Hungary, which to Bohlen pointed to a "basic decision to use of force if necessary to keep Hungary in Soviet camp."[36]

When the Soviets invaded Hungary on 4 November, the United States again worked through the UN, with Yugoslavia now supporting the administration's call for an emergency meeting of the General Assembly.[37] At an NSC meeting on 8 November, still concerned largely with events in the Middle East, Eisenhower agreed that the Soviets' brutal suppression of the Hungarians "was indeed a bitter pill for us to swallow"; however, he saw little "constructive" action that the United States could take, other than to use the incident to highlight the oppressive nature of the Soviet system.[38]

Dulles, who had been hospitalized for cancer surgery just as the Soviets mounted their second invasion, did not take part in these last

33. NSC 5616, "U.S. Policy on Developments in Poland and Hungary," 31 October 1956, *FRUS, 1955–1957*, 25:354–58.

34. Memorandum of Discussion at the 302d Meeting of the National Security Council, 1 November 1956, *FRUS, 1955–1957*, 25:358–59.

35. Circular Telegram from the Department of State to Certain Diplomatic Missions, 2 November 1956, *FRUS, 1955–1957*, 25:366–67.

36. Bohlen to Dulles, 3 November 1956, *FRUS, 1955–1957*, 25:370–71.

37. *FRUS, 1955–1957*, 25:388–89, editorial note.

38. Memorandum of Discussion at the 303d Meeting of the National Security Council, 8 November 1956, *FRUS, 1955–1957*, 25:418–21.

deliberations. When Eisenhower spoke to Dulles in his hospital room at Walter Reed on 9 November, the president told him of charges being leveled in the UN that the United States had excited "the Hungarians through our Radio Free Europe" only to now abandon them. Dulles assured the president that "we have always been against violent rebellion" and that Eisenhower had done all he could to pressure the Soviets on the Hungarians' behalf. The United States was not guilty of "turning our backs" on the Hungarians.[39] But even less than impartial investigations of Radio Free Europe's behavior, conducted by the CIA and the West German government demonstrated that the broadcasts had led the Hungarians to expect that the United States would intervene if a revolution took place.[40]

Despite Dulles's facile disclaimer, the administration took the next several months to examine both the policies and the rhetoric it had been using in Eastern Europe. In an analysis of the events within the Soviet bloc in 1956, the Operations Coordinating Board obliquely acknowledged errors in policy. Positive changes had occurred only in Poland, and although U.S. policy had "undoubtedly" made a difference there, "internal factors" had been the main catalysts for reform. Poland thus served as a good example of the "evolutionary progress" taking place not only in Eastern Europe but in the Soviet Union itself. In Hungary though, the world had witnessed "the forcible reassertion by the Soviets of their political and military control." The administration, in crafting its approach to Eastern Europe, faced a number of difficulties. The most central remained the need "to straddle the contradiction between the traditional anticommunist posture of the United States and the interim NSC objective of encouraging the development of "national communism" as a positive first step in the evolution away from Communist domination." Recent events in the region had provided "a more precise definition" of the term "national communism," but the United States had to be clearer about its willingness to support change through only "evolutionary means."[41]

These considerations served to enhance Tito's role as a peaceful alternative to Soviet domination and prompted Eisenhower to answer Tito's August letter. In addition to applying the balm Riddleberger had suggested in October, the Middle East and Eastern European

39. Memorandum of Telephone Conversations with the President, 9 November 1956, *FRUS, 1955–1957*, 25:424–26.
40. John Ranelagh, *The Agency: The Rise and Decline of the CIA* (New York: Simon & Schuster, 1986), 308–9.
41. "Progress Report on the Soviet Satellites in Eastern Europe," 20 November 1957, *FRUS, 1955–1957*, 25:690–98.

crises also made a "confidential" reply to Tito appear in order.[42] In his
12 November letter to Tito, Eisenhower attributed the recent events
in Eastern Europe to Tito's efforts at change, which had unfortunately
been stymied by Soviet armed force. The United States, although it
sought the independence of Eastern Europe, had not encouraged the
rebellion in Hungary, nor did the administration seek to gain "potential military allies" among the Eastern European states. However, as
it had demonstrated in Yugoslavia, the United States stood ready "to
furnish assistance without political conditions" to those states that
"have started on the path to true national independence." Eisenhower
regretted that Yugoslavia had not completely rejected the Soviets'
actions but appreciated Tito's support for the UN's call on the Soviets
to withdraw from Hungary. He ended his letter with the request that
Tito "visit me in Washington sometime during the coming year."[43]
Tito immediately accepted.[44]

As events unfolded in Hungary and the Mideast, Ambassador Mates
met with Robert Murphy to explain Yugoslavia's policy in Eastern
Europe and to warn of the dangers that had arisen in the wake of the
Hungarian rebellion. At their first meeting, on 16 November, Mates
recounted the Soviets' belief that the West intended to provoke a war
and that the Hungarian revolt had been fomented by the United
States as a first step. If Poland erupted as well, a conflict between the
United States and the USSR was "inevitable." Tito's remarks at Pula
on 11 November had been designed to influence the Soviets' Polish
policy in support of the changes being implemented by the reformist
Gomulka regime. Mates appealed for the United States to moderate
its criticism of the new regime in Hungary, lest it further provoke the
Soviets. The two men also discussed the Suez Crisis, with Mates
claiming that the Soviets' belligerent statements about the Western
role there were designed only to deflect attention from Hungary.
Murphy sent a memorandum of this talk to the president on the
grounds that the "Yugoslav estimate is worthy of our urgent and very
serious consideration."[45]

42. Hoover to Eisenhower, 11 November 1956, Eisenhower Papers, Whitman File,
International Series, File: Yugoslavia 2.
43. Eisenhower to Tito, 12 November 1956, *FRUS, 1955–1957*, 26:754–56.
44. Tito to Eisenhower, 20 November 1956, *FRUS, 1955–1957*, 26:756–57.
45. Murphy to Andrew J. Goodpastor, 17 November 1956, with enclosed memorandum of conversation, 16 November 1956, Eisenhower Papers, WHO, Office of the
Staff Secretary, Subject: State, File: State Department, October–November 1956 (4).
Although it is clear that Murphy is talking to a Yugoslav, Mates's name is excised from
the copy of the document released by the Eisenhower Library. However a second
document, cited in the following footnote, in which Mates is identified and in which

When Mates called on Murphy again, he conveyed the Yugoslav belief that "because of the respect the leaders have for his authority, honesty and of course the power he wields," President Eisenhower was the only world leader capable of influencing the Soviet leadership. Murphy again passed this on to the president.[46]

By mid-November the administration, confident that it had a "clearer picture of independent nature Yugoslav position and confirmation Yugoslav role in promoting evolutionary developments satellites," considered resuming the deliveries of military aid, including jet aircraft, to Yugoslavia. The resumption, intended as both a reward and an inducement, would occur on an extended schedule in order to "maintain Yugoslav military orientation westward for as long as possible." Because of the large number of Soviet forces currently in Hungary, the United States believed the Yugoslavs might consider "increased military cooperation" in the future, but for the same reason be reluctant to make any gesture toward the United States at present.[47]

In early December, Dulles and Eisenhower discussed dispatching the aircraft to Yugoslavia, using the rationale that Tito should not be forced to obtain such equipment from the Soviets. The president had the authority to act on his own under existing mutual security legislation, but Dulles still intended to raise the matter with members of Congress.[48] However, the attitude of the Yugoslavs remained crucial. They had not pressed the United States to resume deliveries, and Murphy thought it possible they would seek a postponement of same "in view of the extremely cautious attitude Tito has recently assumed incident to developments in Hungary."[49] This uncertainty also caused the administration to question the wisdom of, and solicit Riddleberger's advice on, the inclusion of a request for Yugoslavia in the FY58 Mutual Security Program. The question was debatable, since Yugoslavia's current economic needs could be covered under PL 480, and the

---

reference is made to the occasion and substance of a conversation he had had the previous day with Murphy, implies that Mates was the Yugoslav in question on 16 November. A handwritten notation on the source text of the Murphy to Goodpastor memo reads "Noted by President."

46. Murphy to Goodpastor, 17 November 1956, with enclosed memorandum of conversation, 17 November 1956, Eisenhower Papers, WHO, Office of the Staff Secretary, Subject: State, File: State Department, October–November 1956 (4). A handwritten notation on the source text reads "Noted by President."

47. Hoover to Riddleberger, 16 November 1956, RG 59, no. 397, 768.5-MSP/11-1656.

48. Dulles to Eisenhower, 6 December 1956, Dulles Telcons.

49. Murphy to Dulles and Hoover, 14 December 1956, RG 59, 768.5-MSP/12-1456.

absence of Yugoslavia from the MSP would "avoid further unpleasant fight in Congress."[50]

When Riddleberger raised the latter issue with the Velebit, he received a "favorable reaction." The Yugoslavs were equally anxious to avoid additional debate in Congress and Velebit rashly predicted that Yugoslavia's economy would improve enough by 1958 to make continued grant aid unnecessary.[51] Foreign Minister Popović appeared "somewhat reserved in his comments" when Riddleberger broached the resumption of military deliveries, but Riddleberger did not find this surprising. Tito was continuing his efforts to influence Soviet policy in Hungary; the resumption of military aid shipments "may raise problem of timing for Yugoslavs." Riddleberger doubted that Yugoslavia had really lost interest in the military assistance program and theorized that either events in Hungary had shown Yugoslavia the need to raise its living standards and thus minimize discontent, or that the Soviets were demanding a lessening of U.S.-Yugoslav ties as the "price for concessions in Hungary."[52]

The Yugoslavs, months after Tito had first broached the idea to Eisenhower, finally ended this torturous speculation. At the end of December, Defense Minister Ivan Gosnjak announced that his country would not receive additional United States military assistance and cited both changed international conditions and the uncertainty of the aid program as factors.[53] The reasons advanced, though vaguely phrased, accurately represented Tito's attitude. The danger of a Soviet attack on Yugoslavia had long since passed. Tito's self-appointed role as a bridge between East and West demanded that his policies be hostage to neither power. The United States was alone in its failure to realize that it could not encourage Tito's independence of the East without suffering similar consequences in the West.

Tito's decision to forgo U.S. military aid reduced the administration's leverage on his regime. Additional limitations on both countries' policies surfaced when renewed prospects for a Tito visit became known to the American public and raised alarms both in the United States and Yugoslavia. On 17 December the *New York Times* reported that the Eisenhower administration had told Tito that it was ready for him to visit the country.[54] The Yugoslav Embassy in Washington

50. Dulles to Riddleberger, 8 December 1956, RG 59, no. 456, 768.5-MSP/12-856.

51. Riddleberger to Dulles, 21 December 1956, RG 59, no. 879, 768.5 MSP/12-2156.

52. Riddleberger to Dulles, 24 December 1956, *FRUS, 1955–1957*, 26:757–59.

53. Belgrade to Secretary of State, 28 December 1956, RG 59, no. 918, 768.5 MSP/12-2856.

54. Jack Raymond, "Eisenhower to Ask Tito to Visit U.S." *New York Times*, 17 December 1956, 1, 6.

immediately complained about this "leak" and the serious impact it could have on Yugoslav-Soviet relations. The State Department apologized to the Yugoslavs for the "obviously premature moment" at which the story had been printed and advised the White House to simply say that a visit had been under consideration but that no arrangements had been made.[55] At his news conference on 18 December, Dulles suggested that a trip by Tito to the United States for talks would be "useful" and that "sympathetic consideration" was being given to the idea.[56]

In a subsequent memo to Eisenhower, Dulles, after reviewing "the tentative worldwide schedule of suitably spaced state visits," suggested a ten-day sojourn for Tito in late March or early April, featuring "conversations and negotiations" as well as the customary "ceremonial excursions" and state dinners. After three days in Washington, Tito would tour the country in order to obtain "some overall idea of American life." To avoid "the sizable groups among the American public in opposition to Tito," Dulles advised that the Yugoslav delegation not visit cities in the Northeast or Midwest with large Eastern European populations. To blunt the criticism certain to come with a formal announcement of Tito's visit, Dulles suggested that the president make a statement explaining "the trip in terms of the general foreign policy of the US."[57]

This argument carried little weight with Senator Knowland, who wrote to Dulles in December of 1956 that "I cannot help but believe that a "red carpet" welcome to Dictator Tito will take the heart out of a lot of non-Communists behind the Iron Curtain."[58] Other members of Congress as well as various Catholic organizations, citing both Tito's communism and his treatment of Cardinal Stepinac, also announced their opposition to the visit.[59] In yet another confessional phone conversation with Knowland, this time before Christmas, Dulles acknowledged that even though the visit would provoke criticism, Tito had agreed to come and the administration was committed to

55. State to Belgrade, 17 December 1956, no. 484, Eisenhower Papers, WHO, Office of Staff Secretary: Records, 1952–1961, Subject Series: State Department Subseries, File: State Department, November 1957–January 1958 (3).

56. "Transcript of Comments by Secretary Dulles on World Affairs at News Conference," *New York Times*, 19 December 1956, 14.

57. Dulles to Eisenhower, undated, Eisenhower Papers, PAP, Whitman File, International Series, File: Yugoslavia (3).

58. Knowland to Dulles, 19 December 1956, Dulles Papers (Eisenhower Library), General Correspondence, File: I–K(2).

59. Jack Raymond, "2 in Congress Balk over Expected Bid for a Visit by Tito," *New York Times*, 22 December 1956, 1, 6.

receiving him; perhaps Spain's Francisco Franco or China's Chiang Kai-shek could be invited as well to offset Tito's presence. He confided to Knowland that had he been at the Department rather than in the hospital the invitation might not have been made.[60]

On 1 January 1957, Dulles suggested to Eisenhower that Tito's visit be confined to official talks in Washington; a tour of the United States would probably provoke incidents that would jeopardize the U.S.-Yugoslav relationship. The president agreed with Dulles's assessment.[61] Dulles then told Riddleberger that only a West Coast trip, away from Catholic and Eastern European population centers, remained possible and suggested that he advise the Tito regime to "make some gesture . . . which would tend mollify American opposition groups and create atmosphere good feeling throughout this country."[62]

Tito did not make the needed concessions, and it soon became clear that even a limited visit was impossible in the Red Scare climate of the day. By mid-January, at least one member of Congress had pledged to resign his seat if Tito, whom he called a "common criminal," were allowed entry to the United States.[63] After additional discussions with Eisenhower, Dulles informed Yugoslav ambassador Mates that while late April remained an acceptable date for the visit, anything other than talks in Washington could not take place because of the "certainty of demonstrations and possibility of danger." Mates conveyed his regret that U.S.-Yugoslav relations were "not on a very solid basis." Dulles in turn found it unfortunate that Tito had chosen not "to make any gesture to mitigate the opposition . . . but that is of course his affair and we should not press him."[64]

The furor against the visit continued unabated. At the end of January, a bipartisan group of members of the House of Representatives, citing protests by Catholic and veterans groups, drafted a petition to Eisenhower against the Tito visit. If Tito were still to come, the petitioners declared they would engineer a prolonged congressional recess when Tito visited the capital.[65] A few days later, a resolution

60. Knowland to Dulles, 22 December 1956, Dulles Telcons.

61. Memorandum of Conversation with the President, 1 January 1957, Dulles Papers (Eisenhower Library), File: Meetings with the President 1957 (8).

62. Dulles to Riddleberger, 5 January 1957, *FRUS, 1955–1957*, 26:761–62.

63. "O'Konski Says He'll Quit If Tito Comes as Guest," *New York Times*, 17 January 1957, 21.

64. Memorandum of Conversation with the President, 17 January 1957, Dulles Papers (Eisenhower Library), White House Memos, File: Meetings with the President 1957 (8); Dulles to Riddleberger, 17 January 1957, *FRUS, 1955–1957*, 26:762–63.

65. "House Bloc Seeks Ban on Tito Visit," *New York Times*, 27 January 1956, 3.

was introduced in Congress barring the use of Federal funds not only for Tito's visit, but for that of any communist official.[66]

Finally, the United States and Yugoslavia agreed that Tito would not come; Dulles and Mates would "just ease out without a formal announcement."[67] The Yugoslav government resented the undignified treatment to which Tito had been subjected, and the Yugoslav press publicized Tito's unwillingness to visit the United States under such unfavorable conditions. The regime took care not to blame the administration or the American people for the insult, but cited the influence of "destructive forces in the American political life" as the culprits.[68]

Eisenhower also voiced his irritation in a news conference in January 1957 when he was asked his view of the opposition aroused by both Tito's projected visit and that of King Saud of Saudi Arabia, already under way. The president stated that one did not advance the prospects for peace "by talking only to people with whom you agree." Discussions with leaders with whom the United States had differences were also essential if common ground and peaceful solutions to disputes were to be found. Eisenhower was "always obliged to any man, any head of state, who will come and talk to me when we think we have solutions that might be advanced by this kind of meeting." He therefore deplored "any discourtesy shown to a visitor who comes to us as a representative of a government or a people . . . ," rather than demanding that Eisenhower come to them, to help advance the settlement of the world's problems.[69]

New York Times analyst James Reston concluded that the administration had been caught off guard by the depth of reaction against Tito. He saw the episode as a serious setback for the president who had been attempting, since the Soviet crackdown in Hungary, to open new lines of communication between the United States and the satellite states in Eastern Europe. Such incidents made it appear that the United States really did not wish close ties with governments with different social or political systems. Although the Eisenhower administration now insisted otherwise, Reston accurately noted that both Truman and Eisenhower had used rhetoric in the past that fostered that very assumption.[70]

66. Charles G. Bennett, "Mayor Bars Fete For Saud, Here Today on State Visit," *New York Times*, 29 January 1957, 1, 4.
67. *FRUS, 1955–1957*, 26:763 n. 2; Dulles to Eisenhower, 29 January 1958, Dulles Telcons.
68. Elie Abel, "Tito Will Reject Undignified Visit," *New York Times*, 30 January 1957, 1, 5.
69. *Papers of the Presidents*, Eisenhower, 1957, 97–98.
70. James Reston, "A Policy Boomerangs," *New York Times*, 4 February 1957, 7.

While the visit controversy played itself out, the Yugoslavs, again fully at odds with the Soviets after Hungary, reversed themselves in January 1957 and pressed the United States for the delivery of military equipment under the established program.[71] To Riddleberger, the Yugoslav decision to rebut the charges leveled by the Soviets and satellites after Hungary showed their willingness to engage in a "prolonged struggle with Kremlin over issues which they consider basic to their future existence." Tito's championing of the theory of "different roads to socialism" had propelled him into a world leadership role and made a major impact on the communist world; it was not a position he was likely to abandon. Tito had probably believed the Soviets were sincere when both had signed the Moscow Declaration; but by the time of his Yalta trip he had realized that de-Stalinization had not caused a genuine change in the Kremlin's thinking or policy. Tito's acceptance of the second intervention in Hungary, lest communism there be destroyed, did not illustrate to Riddleberger that there was any lessening of the differences between Titoism and Soviet ideology; but it did indicate to Tito what his fate would be if the Soviets succeeded in isolating him from the West.[72]

Despite this analysis, which seemed in accordance with Dulles's own views, and the Department of State's assurance to Riddleberger in January that a decision on the resumption of military aid to Yugoslavia was imminent, months passed without any such action. By mid-March 1957, Riddleberger advised that this had led to "confusion, uncertainty and misunderstanding on part Yugoslav military." The state of readiness and expertise achieved with the military aid the United States had sent in the past was being lost; this problem was especially acute in the air force, which depended on U.S. equipment for its training. The costs involved in storing the supplies that could not be delivered were mounting as well. Riddleberger strongly believed that the continuing rift between the Yugoslavs and the Soviets provided an opportunity for the United States to "consolidate Yugoslav military ties with West." The completion of the military aid program also would present a "strong contrast" to the Soviets' refusal to honor their economic commitments to Yugoslavia.[73]

On 1 April, Dulles decided to resume some aircraft deliveries. He directed that a press release be prepared that emphasized the train-

71. Riddleberger to Dulles, 10 January 1957, RG 59, no. 987, 768.5-MSP/1-1057; *FRUS, 1955–1957*, 26:765 n. 2.
72. Riddleberger to Dulles, 18 February 1957, RG 59, no. 1161, 768.00/2-1857.
73. Riddleberger to Dulles, 12 March 1957, *FRUS, 1955–1957*, 26:765–67.

ing aspects involved in providing the planes in order to blunt any domestic criticism of his action.[74] In an additional attempt at damage control, Dulles met with Archbishop Patrick A. O'Boyle of Washington to explain that the decision to assist Yugoslavia did not indicate approval of the regime, but a recognition of that country's usefulness in furthering U.S. aims in Eastern Europe. The archbishop thanked the secretary for his explanation and assured him that he would convey it to his fellow prelates, who were meeting in Washington the following week.[75]

U.S. analysts' opinions of Tito's policies were more positive than Dulles's limited actions indicated. An OCB progress report on NSC 5601, prepared in April 1957, claimed that although the Soviets once again threatened Yugoslavia's independence, the United States was more certain of Tito's ability to resist that it had been in 1956 when "the Yugoslavs were eagerly reciprocating the Soviet-initiated rapprochement." The Soviets, instead of using incentives to woo Yugoslavia, had resorted, as they had after the Tito-Stalin split, to economic and ideological pressure by canceling or delaying the implementation of newly negotiated trade agreements and blaming the unrest in Poland and Hungary on Tito and his ideology. Tito's example had played a role in both countries' ferment, and continued strains in the Yugoslav-Soviet relationship arose from Tito's resolve to bring "national communism" to the satellite regimes.[76]

By contrast, Yugoslavia's overall foreign policy, in light of the NSC objective "that Yugoslavia not actively further Soviet-Communist cold war objectives and that Yugoslav potentialities be developed on behalf" of the free world, called "neither for great concern nor for enthusiastic approval." The regime's internal policies remained distasteful; the most recent arrest and conviction of Milovan Djilas highlighted "the lack of political freedom that prevails" under Tito. Yugoslavia's trade with the bloc had increased since the rapprochement began, but the regime still looked to the West and particularly to the United States for its major economic needs.[77]

---

74. *FRUS, 1955–1957*, 26:768, editorial note.

75. Murphy, memorandum of conversation, 26 April 1957, RG 59, 768.56/4-2657.

76. Report Prepared by the OCB, Progress Report on NSC 5601, "United States Policy Toward Yugoslavia," 24 April 1957, *FRUS, 1955–1957*, 26:768–73.

77. Ibid. Djilas had been tried and imprisoned for publishing articles critical of the Tito regime's support for Soviet actions during the Hungarian rebellion. After his book *The New Class* was smuggled out of Yugoslavia and printed in the West, Djilas was tried again, even though he was still in jail for his articles written at the time of the Hungarian rebellion and given an additional prison term. "22 Senators Join Plea for

This analysis provided an excellent example of both the merits and errors of the administration's policy. Tito would not return to the Soviet bloc; that resolve was and would remain the centerpiece of his policy. The support of the United States and its allies had enabled Tito to sustain his independence and that blow to the Soviets alone justified continued assistance. But Tito had done little to foster the cause of national communism elsewhere and seemed more aware than the Soviets of the perils of encouraging too much change in the satellites. Yet, the administration persisted in seeing more progress than had occurred and in acting accordingly.

To further strengthen Yugoslavia's ties to the West, the Eisenhower administration finally shipped the long-delayed jet planes and released other MSA funds in the spring of 1957. Eisenhower and Dulles realized that those members of Congress who opposed all aid to Yugoslavia would not countenance these actions; the president also wanted the U.S. Catholic hierarchy (he mentioned in particular "Spellman, McIntyre and Mooney") to understand that the administration's continuing aid was not designed to "help Tito persecute the Catholics." Regardless of the consequences Dulles told the president in late April, in an echo of the advice he had given in 1952, Tito's "relations with Moscow are strained and he needs a boost."[78] As Ambassador Mates later recalled: "This man who is known as the most violent Cold War warrior was our best friend in the United States."[79]

News accounts of the administration's decision to release $1 million in military aid, including dozens of jet aircraft to Yugoslavia appeared in mid-May. The State Department, in anticipation of both public and congressional criticism, confirmed in its press release that the president, under legislation passed by Congress in 1956, had the right to resume such shipments if convinced that Yugoslavia was maintaining its independence. Since the Cominform arms embargo had been imposed on Yugoslavia, that country, which was again being harassed by the Soviets, was at a disadvantage because its Warsaw Pact neighbors were still receiving modern equipment from the Soviet Union. The material furnished by the United States would, however, be shipped "at a more modest rate over the next few years than previously planned" because of other demands on U.S. supplies. In

Djilas' Freedom," *New York Times*, 13 January 1957, 22; "Djilas Is Convicted; Gets 7 Years More," ibid., 6 October 1957, 1, 5.

    78. Dulles to Eisenhower, 25 April 1957, Dulles Telcons.
    79. Interview with Mates, September 1988.

fact, Dulles had already instructed the Department of Defense (but not the Yugoslavs or the press) that no more than ten planes were to be shipped each month, until November, when an additional determination on aid was to be made. Nonetheless, Senator Knowland quickly registered his opposition and his resolve to fight additional appropriations for Tito's government.[80]

Knowland made his remarks in the midst of the annual battle between the administration and the Congress over mutual security legislation. After raising the possibility of excluding Yugoslavia from the Mutual Security Program in favor of an exclusive reliance on PL 480 assistance, the administration, much to Riddleberger's surprise and annoyance, had included Yugoslavia in its 1958 requests. While acknowledging that the recent events in Poland and Hungary might have made the Congress more receptive to aiding Yugoslavia, the ambassador saw little reason to risk another bruising congressional battle.[81]

The administration had taken this step because Ambassador Mates had admitted that his country's economy had not improved as quickly as hoped and had asked for a continuation of the grant aid.[82] The president had agreed to the Yugoslav request because he continued to put great stock in the Mutual Security Program as an instrument of U.S. foreign policy. Eisenhower, in a letter to C. D. Jackson in April, eloquently expressed the view he wanted the American people to adopt on the whole foreign aid issue. He had championed the merits of mutual aid for years, Eisenhower explained, on the "basis of principle and moral law, but even more than this, on the basis of the best interests of the United States." Development and reform at home would be wasted unless such actions were supported "in the international field, by policies and procedures that create the proper kind of atmosphere in which America can be safe and prosperous." The average American family, "the housewife and her working husband," must not be misled by "demagogues" who equate a cut in mutual assistance with a tax cut and more prosperity at home. Such attitudes are "not only penny-wise and pound foolish, but are actually risking the security and safety of the country and all of its citizens." The case for

80. Jack Raymond, "U.S. Ban on Arms to Belgrade Ends," *New York Times*, 15 May 1957, 13; *DSB*, 10 June 1957, 36:939–40; Dulles to Riddleberger, 14 May 1957, *FRUS, 1955–1957*, 26:774.
81. Riddleberger to Dulles, 21 February 1957, RG 59, no. 1180, 768.5-MSP/2-2157.
82. Julius L. Katz, memorandum of conversation, 8 May 1957, RG 59, 768.5-MSP/5-857.

mutual assistance must be made not as a "philosophical exercise" but as a "down-to-earth, sink-or-swim, survive-or-perish" proposition.[83]

The president made this same argument, though with a more explicit connection to national defense, in a meeting with Senator Bridges in late May. Bridges, the ranking Republican on the Senate Appropriations Committee, had publicly criticized the mutual security program and the "do-gooders" who advocated assistance to such neutral nations as India and Yugoslavia. Eisenhower told Bridges that the only way to avoid war, "to save America in the long run from destruction—is through the development of a true collective system of defense." The president understood that not everyone agreed with his position, but he resented Bridges's derision of what he called his "life's work." Current estimates predicted the United States would suffer eighty-five million killed and wounded in just a single nuclear attack: "When you begin to think of things like that, you know there must not be war." The way to prevent war was to establish a deterrent, while keeping "the rest of the world from going Communistic." Eisenhower explained that the administration had designed the mutual security program to achieve the latter, to keep countries "from complete dependence on the other fellow." Yugoslavia was a case in point: Tito had successfully broken with the Kremlin, and the president did "not by any manner of means want Tito to find he had no place to go except back to the Soviets."[84]

The Yugoslavs, predictably, disliked Eisenhower's linkage between aid and the deterioration in the Soviet-Yugoslav relationship. They also objected to the rate of delivery and reduction in the quantity of material to be sent.[85] The Soviets, capitalizing on Tito's irritation with the United States, lessened the tension between Yugoslavia and the bloc by instructing the satellites to improve their relations with Tito, despite the latter's ideological shortcomings. Riddleberger assumed that both parties wished to return to the status quo that had existed before the Hungarian uprising, when relations were "cool but more or less correct."[86] The U.S. Embassy in Moscow agreed with Belgrade's contention that the two states "appear to have 'agreed to disagree' in ideological dispute." As the events in Hungary faded from public view,

---

83. Eisenhower to Jackson, 30 April 1957, Eisenhower Papers, PAP, Whitman File, Administrative Series, File: C. D. Jackson, 1956–57 (1).

84. Conversation between the President and Senator Styles Bridges, 21 May 1957, Eisenhower Papers, PAP, Whitman File, Diary Series.

85. Mark, memorandum of conversation, 16 May 1957, RG 59, 768.5-MSP/5-1657, and Riddleberger to Dulles, 17 May 1957, RG 59, no. 1585, 768.5 MSP/5-1757.

86. Riddleberger to Dulles, 29 May 1957, RG 59, no. 1631, 661.68/5-2957.

the issues uniting Yugoslavia and the Soviet Union once again became clear. Each state believed that more could be gained through a cordial rather than a quarrelsome relationship.[87]

By the end of May, the CIA discerned "at least a partial truce in the ideological and political war between Belgrade and Moscow." In a press interview given on the occasion of his sixty-fifth birthday, Tito attributed the thaw to a Yugoslav initiative that had resulted in a lessening of both Soviet and satellite criticism of his country. The CIA doubted that the rapprochement would ever reach the warmth of the previous year, but theorized that the Soviets felt enough in control of "national Communist pressures" in the satellites to conclude a public peace with Tito.[88]

Publicly, Tito continued to minimize the differences between his country and the Soviet Union, while providing oblique encouragement to the forces of change in Eastern Europe and to Dulles's support for him as a agent of that change. In a June interview with Edward R. Murrow, portions of which were broadcast in the United States as part of the *See It Now* series on CBS, Tito stressed that Yugoslavia and the Soviet Union were both building socialism, but by different methods. He declined to characterize the recent unrest in Poland as resulting from "national communism" but rather from "resistance towards the policy which was implemented during the time of Stalin." He cautioned the West that when changes occurred in countries like Poland, it should not "expect the restoration of the old regime to take place." Nor should the West attempt to influence such changes, because that would "only make these developments more difficult." Tito also defended the second Soviet intervention in Hungary as "unavoidable," lest the unrest there "bring about the new world war."

When Murrow asked Tito if he agreed with Khrushchev's recent statement that a future generation of Americans would live under socialism, Tito reinforced his moderate credentials by stating that "it is up to the American people to decide what system of society it will develop and what system it would prefer." While lamenting the lack of progress in bringing peace to the Middle East, Tito ridiculed the idea that the Soviets would gain influence in an area where "feudalism" still existed. He urged the West to concentrate on the economic development of the Arab states, rather than base its policy there on a

87. Richard H. Davis to Dulles, 11 June 1957, RG 59, no. 2679, 661.68/6-1157.

88. Knight W. McMahan, Acting Assistant Director Current Intelligence, to Deputy Director (Intelligence), "Communist Propaganda in Policy Perspective, 24–29 May 1957," 31 May 1957, Eisenhower Papers, PAP, Whitman File, Administrative Series, File: Dulles, Allen (3).

fear of communism. He characterized his own foreign policy as one of "co-existence," and urged other nations to adopt a similar outlook. Both socialism and capitalism should peacefully compete for influence, but Tito declared that "the internal developments of any country is a question for the people of that country to decide about."[89]

This interview had caused some concern within the administration, with Allen Dulles dispatched by the OCB to discover when CBS planned to air the film, and what questions had been asked of Tito. "If we can get the questions," F. M. Dearborn wrote to Robert Cutler, "it should not be too difficult to guess at possible answers."[90] After the broadcast, administration analysts optimistically decided that the differences between the Soviet Union and Yugoslavia were far greater than Tito admitted in his interview. Tito's assertion that "socialist states should be equal and sovereign" was not one the Soviets could ever accept, which ensured that Tito would remain outside the bloc. The nature of the Hungarian Revolution constituted another "fundamental" difference. The Soviets saw the rebellion as a "counterrevolutionary" conspiracy, while Tito viewed it as "a spontaneous mass demonstration" against the regime's Stalinist policies. Tito's criticism implied that the Soviet suppression of such a movement robbed them of any claim that they "represent the masses" and betrayed them as "a reactionary and counterrevolutionary force." Tito apparently viewed Poland under Gomulka as following a path similar to his own, but hoped that change there would be gradual and not provoke the Soviets to drastic action. Poland provided a good example of Tito's dilemma when he contemplated the satellites: "He wants them to become more independent, but he has to be very careful and anxious" lest they repeat the Hungarian experience.[91]

In August 1957, after Khrushchev had purged more of those opposed to his reforms from positions of leadership in the USSR and sent kind words to Yugoslavia on the second anniversary of the Belgrade Declaration, he and Tito met (at first secretly) in Romania. The two

89. Wayne Phillips, "Tito, on U.S. TV, Asserts He Backs Mao's New Line," *New York Times*, 1 July 1957, 1, 2; Transcript of Interview: President Tito–Edward R. Morrow, 26 June 1957, Eisenhower Papers, WHO, OSANSA, Records 1957–1961, OCB Series, Subject Subseries, File: Interviews with Foreign Leaders.

90. F. M. Dearborn to Robert Cutler, 24 June 1957, Eisenhower Papers, WHO, OSANSA, Records 1957–1961, OCB Series, Subject Subseries, Folder: Escapees, Refugees.

91. Comments on Morrow Interview with Tito, 28 June 1957, Eisenhower Papers, WHO, OSANSA, Records 1952–61, OCB Series, Subject Subseries.

men agreed once again to suppress their differences in the name of communist unity and cooperation and to support a number of common foreign policy positions. Secretary Dulles expressed no surprise at this, claiming in a news conference on 6 August that since the latest leadership changes in the Soviet Union, the United States had assumed the Soviets would make a new effort to "woo" Marshal Tito.[92] In a late August letter sent to reassure Congress Dulles explained that while their final communiqué pledged cooperation between the CPSU and the Yugoslav Communist Party, Tito also obtained "Soviet reaffirmation of the principles of the Belgrade declaration and Moscow Declaration." Tito, said Dulles, "has never denied that he is a Communist—a point made clear in his American television appearance"—but he has also always proclaimed his resolve to remain free of "Soviet domination."[93]

Riddleberger agreed that each side "for their own reasons" had decided to minimize their public dispute. Tito believed that Khrushchev, now free of internal opposition, would have to honor the Belgrade and Moscow declarations, or at least "is forced by his own policy to pretend that he does." His own accommodation with the Soviets would always be limited by his resolve to maintain Yugoslavia's independence, yet Tito's support for the solidarity of the "international workers movement" was a significant gesture. Riddleberger saw the continuation of Soviet-Yugoslav agreement on a number of foreign policy issues as predictable and advised it would only increase in the future.[94]

Over the next few months, Yugoslavia aligned itself more closely with Soviet than Western foreign policy, as Riddleberger had predicted, but also continued to look to the United States for aid. In the fall of 1957, Yugoslav state secretary for finance Avdo Humo came to Washington for financial discussions. Before the sessions began, Dulles expressed his concern that as the Yugoslav Communist Party and the CPSU increased their ties, the independence of the Yugoslav government would suffer. Yugoslavia's vote against the most recent UN resolution on Hungary, which called on the Kádár regime to cease its repressive practices, seemed to validate that concern. Yugoslavia appeared to depart from the "Soviet line" only in its refusal to extend diplomatic recognition to East Germany, but there were some indica-

92. "State Department Record of Remarks by Secretary Dulles At New Conference," *New York Times*, 7 August 1957, 10.
93. Dulles to Senator John Marshall Butler, 20 August 1957, RG 59, 611.68/8-2057.
94. Riddleberger to Dulles, 7 August 1957, RG 59, no. 200, 661.68/8-757.

tions that Yugoslavia was about to reverse that position as well. Dulles still held to his personal belief in Yugoslavia's independence, but warned Humo of his growing isolation in that position. Yugoslavia would have to be more cooperative, the secretary said, if the administration were to justify the continuation of aid in the face of so many other "deserving claimants."

Humo responded with Yugoslavia's familiar assertion that its policies had not changed, but that those of the USSR, as it moved away from Stalinism, had altered. He also related Khrushchev's view that Yugoslavia, far from being subservient to the Soviet Union, was "a satellite of the United States." The Soviet Union had not reformed as much as the Yugoslavs would wish, but even the most modest progress had to be encouraged, and this remained the basis of Yugoslavia's policy toward the USSR. Dulles demurred, charging that current Soviet foreign policy remained as aggressive as it had been in Korea, and that the suppression of the revolt in Hungary was even more "brutal" than the behavior of Stalin.[95]

Dulles's words had little effect. On 14 October, Mates informed State Department officials that Yugoslavia would establish diplomatic relations with East Germany within twenty-four hours. While Mates characterized this as Yugoslavia's attempt to facilitate a peaceful solution to the German question, the Department of State advised him that the United States would perceive the move as signaling Yugoslavia's abandonment of nonalignment and as a surrender to Soviet pressure.[96] In discussing Yugoslavia's action with Selwyn Lloyd, the British foreign secretary, the next day, Dulles explained that the United States did not plan to sever its ties with Yugoslavia but would again reduce the amount of military and economic aid being sent there. The West German government intended to break diplomatic relations with the Tito regime, and Dulles had not dissuaded them. Dulles believed that Yugoslavia's faith in the de-Stalinization campaign within the Soviet Union was misplaced; Khrushchev was "more versatile and actually more dangerous than Stalin." Mr. Lloyd agreed.[97]

But was this constant and by now predictable tinkering with aid likely to produce beneficial results? As the administration contem-

95. Leverich, memorandum of conversation, 2 October 1957, *FRUS, 1955–1957*, 26:781–86.

96. *FRUS, 1955–1957*, 26:786–87, editorial note.

97. William N. Dale, memorandum of conversation, 15 October 1957, *FRUS, 1955–1957*, 26:787–88.

plated its next move, State Department analysts voiced the familiar fear that a rapid termination of aid would force the Yugoslavs more deeply into the Soviet embrace and also call the success of the entire policy of the United States toward Eastern Europe into question. Nonetheless, by late October, the State Department deemed the suspension of jet aircraft deliveries to Yugoslavia after November to be the wisest course (spare parts for other military items would still be sent), coupled with the adjournment of PL 480 and MSA negotiations and other development project discussions. The United States planned to inform the Yugoslavs within the next week or two of the decision to suspend economic aid, then a short time after that of the decision to suspend aircraft deliveries. Nothing would be done however, until after the Federal Republic of Germany had terminated relations with Tito's government, so that the Yugoslavs would not assume the United States was retaliating for this single act. The United States still hoped to maintain good relations with Yugoslavia, but reasoned that the alignment of Yugoslav policies with those of the USSR had removed most of the justification for the United States aid program.[98]

When informed of the government's proposals, Ambassador Llewellyn E. Thompson advised from the embassy in Moscow that the administration's action "will be pleasing to Soviets since it will doubtless greatly facilitate their efforts to tighten their hold on Yugoslavia." He believed that the suspension of aid would "lend credence" to Soviet charges that the West wanted to dictate policy to Yugoslavia and conditioned its aid on the proper political behavior of the recipient.[99]

Dulles had similar worries. He had approved the administration's proposed response, but cautioned his staff on 24 October that the United States should not be impulsive and should thoroughly reexamine its policy toward Yugoslavia. The United States had a "large investment" in Tito, and Dulles believed he could still "lead the satellite states to a greater degree of independence." Unless Tito himself had abandoned this ambition, the United States should not force him to rely more upon the Soviet Union. As a result of these comments, the State Department softened its approach somewhat and decided instead to inform the Yugoslavs only that the whole question of economic assistance had to be restudied in light of recent Yugoslav

98. C. Burke Elbrick to Dulles, 18 October 1957, *FRUS, 1955–1957*, 26:788–90; Frederick Jandry to Murphy, 22 October 1957, ibid., 790–92; Dulles to Riddleberger, 22 October 1957, ibid., 792–73.

99. Llewellyn E. Thompson to Dulles, 24 October 1957, *FRUS, 1955–1957*, 26:793.

actions and that negotiations therefore could not proceed as planned.[100]

In addition to being handicapped by its own indecisiveness, the administration also had to contend with the fluctuations in the Yugoslav-Soviet relationship. The Soviets, in preparation for the fortieth anniversary celebrations of the Russian Revolution, had circulated a draft copy of a declaration on "socialist solidarity," which they intended to have the delegates from the socialist countries sign while they were in Moscow. After reading the document, Tito announced that a recurring back ailment would prevent him from attending the meetings. Kardelj, who headed the Yugoslav delegation to Moscow, viewed the draft statement as another Soviet attempt to force Yugoslavia to renounce nonalignment and rejoin the bloc. The Yugoslavs ultimately refused to sign, despite the Soviets "displeasure" at Tito's absence and their defiant stance.[101]

While these events were taking place, the tension between Yugoslavia and West Germany lessened. The Yugoslavs had "miscalculated the force of the West German reaction" over their decision to recognize East Germany and had signaled a wish to prevent a further deterioration in relations. In response, the Federal Republic had agreed that it would maintain its consulates in Yugoslavia and continue economic and credit relations. Murphy also speculated that the recent announcement made by the Yugoslavs of Tito's inability to travel to Moscow demonstrated his unwillingness to become involved in the power struggles in the Soviet Union and "may also reflect an awareness that he may have gone too far in his rapprochement with the USSR." On balance then, Murphy advised Dulles that "some of the major objectives of the modifications in US aid which we proposed may already have been at least partly realized." He therefore recommended that Riddleberger (who was in the United States for an extended period on other State Department business) return to Belgrade and request a meeting with Tito to ascertain the exact nature of the USSR-Yugoslav relationship. In the interim the United States would continue its suspension of aircraft deliveries and its postponement of PL 480 negotiations. Dulles agreed.[102]

100. Notes of the Secretary of State's Staff Meeting, 24 October 1957, *FRUS, 1955–1957*, 26:794–95.

101. Elie Abel, "Tito Will Not Go To Moscow Fete," *New York Times*, 30 October 1957, 1, 10; Memorandum of Discussion at the 342d Meeting of the NSC, 31 October 1957, *FRUS, 1955–1957*, 24:177–78; Kardelj, *Reminiscences*, 134–35; Mićunović, *Moscow Diary*, 315–25.

102. Murphy to Dulles, 30 October 1957, *FRUS, 1955–1957*, 26:799–801; "U.S. Sending Envoy to Gauge Tito Stand," *New York Times*, 31 October 1957, 1, 8.

Late in November the Soviets released the text of the declaration promulgated at the Moscow celebrations, which had so offended the Yugoslavs. As correspondent Elie Abel wrote in the *New York Times*, the points at issue were indeed obvious: the document declared the Soviets to be the head of the worldwide socialist movement and denounced those countries with ties to the imperialist West. Abel recorded a Yugoslavia official as saying that hopes for a genuine accommodation with the Soviets had lessened as the "fundamental" nature of the differences between the two states had again surfaced. While the CIA did not see the document itself as "very ringing [or] very important," Allen Dulles viewed Yugoslavia's refusal to sign it as significant.[103]

When Ambassador Riddleberger met with him on 6 December, Tito, unhappy with Washington's constant reassessments of Yugoslavia's worthiness to receive military aid, revived the suggestion he had first made in his letter to Eisenhower in August 1956 and requested of Riddleberger that the United States military aid program be quietly terminated. Yugoslavia would simply purchase whatever equipment and spare parts it needed. The ambassador agreed that might be the best solution to the present impasse.[104] Tito resisted Riddleberger's efforts to draw him into a detailed discussion of the recent declaration issued in Moscow and warned the West not to overemphasize Yugoslavia's refusal to sign. However, Riddleberger reported that Tito viewed his country's prospects as "somber . . . caught as it is between two blocs."[105]

Ambassador Mates met with Murphy a few days later to propose that representatives of the two countries meet in Belgrade to settle the details for the aid program's cessation.[106] On 11 December, Dulles informed Riddleberger that the United States would accede to Yugoslavia's requests and make arrangements for the termination of the military assistance program.[107]

As Ambassador Riddleberger later recalled: "Both countries, I

---

103. William J. Jordan, "Yugoslavs Hold Red Bloc Policy Is Unacceptable," *New York Times*, 23 November 1957, 1, 2; *FRUS, 1955–1957*, 24:186–87, editorial note.

104. Riddleberger to Dulles, 6 December 1957, *FRUS, 1955–1957*, 26:803–7; Elie Abel, "Tito Assures U.S. He's Independent of Moscow Bloc," *New York Times*, 9 December 1957, 1, 9; Russell Baker, "Tito Calls on U.S. To End Arms Aid," ibid., 10 December 1957, 9.

105. Riddleberger to Dulles, 6 December 1957, *FRUS, 1955–1957*, 26:803–7.

106. R. B. Hill, memorandum of conversation, 9 December 1957, *FRUS, 1955–1957*, 26:807–8.

107. Dulles to Riddleberger, 11 December 1957, RG 59, no. 569, 768.5-MSP/12-1157.

think, had reached the point where they were happy to see military aid discontinued." The whole process had become "frightfully complicated," and Tito was always unhappy with the procedures that compelled him to supply details on the Yugoslavs' use of the equipment provided. Riddleberger remembered that Dulles had anticipated the termination of the program and had previously asked him if the United States could end it without jeopardizing its political objectives in Yugoslavia. Riddleberger had replied in the affirmative, provided the administration allowed the Yugoslavs to take the initiative.[108]

U.S. attempts to influence the U.S.-Yugoslav relationship through the suspension of military aid, begun in the wake of the Soviet visit to Belgrade in 1955, reached their climax in 1957. But it was Yugoslavia, not the United States, which took the action necessary to alleviate the almost constant tension then in existence between the two countries. Tito, after two years of uncertainty concerning the U.S. military assistance program, finally asked for its termination. Despite his erratic "yo-yo" relationship with the Soviet Union, his fears about Yugoslavia's security had dissipated enough to enable him to act on his resolve to adhere to neither bloc. He also could not allow the economic ties his regime cherished with the West to be jeopardized because of the now less than essential military aid program.

The Eisenhower administration, acknowledging its inability to control Yugoslav behavior and sobered by the Hungarian rebellion, still hoped to salvage something from its support of Tito and Dulles's views on the appeal of national communism. The president thus readily agreed to end what had clearly become a counterproductive program. The continuation of economic ties, plus Yugoslavia's need for spare parts to maintain its U.S.-supplied equipment, would guarantee the United States a less controversial but still useful connection with the Tito regime. The wedge still had a role to play, but only as a long-term and relatively low yield political strategy.

---

108. Riddleberger, Oral History, Princeton, 65.

CONCLUSION

1958–1960
THE WEDGE STRATEGY ASSESSED

The Eisenhower administration's last full review of its Yugoslav policy, completed in 1958 and designated NSC 5805, reflected the changes that had occurred since Truman and then Eisenhower had first considered the place of Yugoslavia in the United States's Cold War strategy. Since Tito's break with Stalin in 1948, the United States had furnished his government with over $1.5 billion in military and economic assistance. The military aid had been terminated at Tito's request, although the Yugoslavs still hoped to purchase spare parts and equipment. Yet support for Yugoslav independence remained "an integral part of the broader U.S. policy which has as its objective the eventual attainment of complete national independence by all of the Eastern European satellites." Yugoslavia's role, dubbed as that of an "exhibit" earlier by Dulles was indeed symbolic: to stand "as a constant reminder to the satellite regimes, serving as a pressure point both on the leaders of those regimes and on the leadership of the USSR."

This NSC policy statement reaffirmed the administration's intention to orient "the Tito regime in the direction of political and economic liberalization and closer Yugoslav ties with the West in general and Western Europe in particular," but not at the cost of jeopardizing Yugoslavia's "potential for weakening the monolithic front and internal cohesiveness of the Soviet bloc." For the present, aid had "served the minimum U.S. objective of keeping Yugoslavia independent of the Soviet bloc." The United States would therefore continue its economic assistance program and allow the Yugoslavs to purchase military equipment, "as long as satisfactory U.S.-Yugoslav political relations continue to exist." According to an International Cooperation Administration (ICA) appendix attached to the NSC review, past economic assistance had been classified as "Defense Support," but future assistance would be classified "as Special Assistance to indicate that it is being provided primarily in pursuance of U.S. political objectives."[1]

The long-term nature of these objectives became even clearer in May when the administration adopted NSC 5811/1, "U.S. Policy Toward the Soviet-Dominated Nations in Eastern Europe." Although the Soviets had met the challenge to their authority posed by the Hungarians in 1956, the NSC expected "an atmosphere of change and ferment more highly charged than under Stalin" to persist throughout the area. The discontent and hostility to Communism that had prompted the unrest in 1956 had not disappeared; the hatred caused by the USSR's suppression of the Hungarian revolt, coupled with Poland's continued success in maintaining a measure of autonomy, would only encourage dissent. Yugoslavia served as a constant and additional spur to nationalist sentiment.[2]

For the short term, the NSC, in debating NSC 5811/1 agreed as a body that the United States should promote the weakening of the Soviet bloc and encourage "the peaceful evolution of the dominated nations toward national independence and internal freedom," while recognizing the continued likelihood of "the close political and military control of the Soviet Union." But the means to be used engendered rather heated debate within the Council and reflected the lessons that at least Dulles and Eisenhower had learned concerning the perils of the wedge strategy. While the minutes of the NSC deliberations remain partially classified at this writing, it appears that the means the JCS proposed to the Council to implement NSC 5811/1 included "passive resistance" as well as "violent uprisings, rioting and guerrilla operations," provided the United States was also ready to cope with the Soviets' response. The JCS based these recommendations in part on the belief that independence could not be secured by the satellites

1. NSC 5805, "U.S. Policy Toward Yugoslavia," 28 February 1958, plus attachments, Eisenhower Papers, WHO, OSANSA: Records 1952–1961, NSC Series, Policy Papers Subseries, File: NSC 5805/1, "Policy Toward Yugoslavia."

2. NSC 5811/1, "Statement of U.S. Policy Toward the Soviet-Dominated Nations in Eastern Europe," 24 May 1958, *FRUS, 1958–1960*, 10(1):18–31.

without a fight. Dulles disagreed, declaring that "the best hope of bringing about an acceptable evolution toward greater freedom for the satellites is the exertion by the satellites of constant pressure on the Soviet Union and on their own regimes in the hope of effecting a change in the thinking of the Soviet rulers." How to do so is a "delicate matter . . . but the example of Hungary showed that the elements that we most depended upon had been liquidated by the resort to violence." In Dulles's opinion the JCS plan was "dangerous" and had to be deleted from the document. Eisenhower agreed.[3] Although the remainder of the discussion on this issue and the relevant portions of the policy itself are classified, Dulles's words indicate how much he and the president had reconsidered their approach to change in Eastern Europe.

Relations between the United States and Yugoslavia quickly improved after the military aid issue had been settled. At an NSC meeting in April, Dulles expressed his gratitude to Tito, who "had actually got the Administration off the hook," by asking to discontinue a program he knew "was an embarrassment to the Administration in its relations with the Congress and with various groups in the United States."[4] In January 1958, Yugoslav vice-president Vukmanović-Tempo, with whom administration officials had had difficult negotiations in the past, publicly praised the United States for its policy of noninterference in Yugoslav affairs and its generous economic assistance. He called the U.S.-Yugoslav relationship a model for cooperation between states with different social systems and stages of development. In an obvious contrast, Vukmanović-Tempo expressed only hope for an improvement in the Yugoslav relationship with the Soviet Union.[5]

As Vukmanović-Tempo implied, the rancor between the two communist states continued unabated. In an address to the Seventh Congress of the League of Communists of Yugoslavia (LCY) in April 1958, Tito claimed that the Yugoslavs and the Soviets had settled their differences to the extent that "mutual respect exists, and that there is no interference by one in the internal development of others—as was stated in the Belgrade Declaration." In fact, the Soviets had already denounced the "revisionism" in the Yugoslav party's new ideological program, which reflected the domestic and foreign policy changes Tito

3. Memorandum of Discussion at the 366th Meeting of the National Security Council, 22 May 1958, *FRUS, 1958–1960*, 10(1):12–18.
4. *FRUS, 1958–1960*, 10(2):325, editorial note.
5. Elie Abel, "Yugoslav Lauds U.S. Relationship," *New York Times*, 11 January 1958, 1, 3.

had made since his break with Stalin. After a "rabble-rousing" speech by Yugoslav vice-president Aleksander Ranković, the ambassadors of the Soviet and Eastern European countries stalked out of the Congress. Historians have since labeled this round of disagreements "The Second Soviet-Yugoslav Dispute."[6]

The quarrel between the Yugoslavs and Soviets over the LCY program illustrated how little and how much had changed since 1948. In the document the Yugoslavs, still in the throes of their Titoist heresy, continued to argue for an equal rather than a subservient relationship between the Soviet Union and other socialist states. They claimed that the Soviet leadership, in making their dramatic revelations at the Twentieth Party Congress in 1956, had recognized the need for a new direction. The Soviets responded by labeling the Yugoslavs as unrepentant for the "mistakes of a nationalist character" made in 1948 and citing their theories as "contrary to the principles of Marxism-Leninism."[7]

All of this seemed to serve U.S. interests. Ambassador Karl L. Rankin advised the State Department from Belgrade that while the current split was not as intense as that in 1948, the Yugoslav people believed that "drift towards Soviets initiated by Khrushchev-Bulganin visit in 1955 has now been stopped if not reversed." Popular support for the Tito regime, tarnished by Tito's stance on the Hungarian rebellion and the recognition of East Germany had increased because of this latest Yugoslav-Soviet quarrel.[8]

Shortly after the LCY Congress, the CPSU delivered an ultimatum to the Yugoslavs to accept ideological conformity or suffer the consequences. The Soviet Union also suspended a promised $285 million in credits to the Tito regime. More ominous, the Soviets implemented a harsher policy toward the satellites and in June 1958, Radio Moscow announced that Imre Nagy and several others had been tried and executed. The United States quickly denounced the "murder" of these "Hungarian patriots" and held the Soviets responsible for "this latest

6. Campbell, *Tito's Separate Road*, 41–42; Clissold, *Yugoslavia and the Soviet Union*, 71 and as quoted in on 275; for a full account see Vaclav L. Benes, Robert F. Byrnes, and Nicolas Spulber, eds., *The Second Soviet-Yugoslav Dispute: Full Text of Documents, April–June 1958* (Bloomington: Indiana University Press, 1959). The Communist Party of Yugoslavia (CPY) changed its name to the League of Communists of Yugoslavia (LCY) after the last party congress in 1952.

7. Clissold, *Yugoslavia and the Soviet Union*, 72, 276–78.

8. Belgrade (Robert B. Hill) to Department of State, 16 February 1959, RG 59, no. 350, "Yugoslavia in 1958—A Political Evaluation," 768.00/2-1659; Karl L. Rankin to Dulles, 30 April 1958, RG 59, no. 1467, 661.68/4-3058.

crime against the Hungarian people and all humanity." Dulles, when asked at a news conference if Nagy's execution had any connection to the current Yugoslav-Soviet dispute replied: "It could have a relationship and be a suggestion to President Tito that, if he is not more compliant, he may sooner or later suffer a like fate."[9]

Privately, Dulles surmised that the Kremlin leadership was divided over the course of Soviet-Yugoslav relations. The secretary could not imagine, for example, that Khrushchev, who had initiated the policy of rapprochement with Yugoslavia, had now reversed himself. He was probably yielding to others who still feared Yugoslavia's effect on the satellites. In any case, the Soviet refusal of aid for Yugoslavia provided a propaganda opportunity for the Western powers, who could use it to demonstrate the fraudulent nature of the Soviet Union's claims that it demanded no concessions in return for assistance.[10] A National Intelligence Estimate prepared in early July correctly added another explanation for the Kremlin's behavior: Communist Chinese pressure on the Soviets to adopt a "tough line" in bloc and international affairs.[11]

Despite the obvious deterioration in Yugoslav-Soviet relations, the Eisenhower administration had to press its usual case to secure economic assistance for Yugoslavia during the Congress's annual MSA debate. In his testimony before the Senate Foreign Relations Committee in late March, Dulles repeated his oft-stated contention that Yugoslavia was and would remain independent of the Soviet bloc.[12] Knowland and Bridges mounted their predictable fight as well, but the Soviet suspension of aid to Yugoslavia in May seemed to prove the administration's case. As Dulles told one senator whose support he enlisted, the "attitude of the Soviets toward Yugoslavia is the most useful demonstration we have of the fact they really can't tolerate a national Communist party—it also shows how if you have courage you can get away with it."[13] The secretary prevailed; the MSA bill once again included assistance for Yugoslavia. In August, the United States announced that it would also assist Yugoslavia with various develop-

9. Campbell, *Tito's Separate Road*, 42–43; Elie Abel, "Soviet Said to Bid Yugoslavia Obey or Face Penalty," *New York Times*, 12 May 1958, 1, 5; *DSB*, 7 July 1958, 39:7.

10. NSC Meeting no. 368, 3 June 1958, Eisenhower Papers, PAP, Whitman File, NSC Series, File: NSC Meeting no. 368.

11. NIE, SNIE-11-8-88, "Implications of Current Soviet Conduct," 8 July 1958, *FRUS, 1958–1960*, 10(1):171–75.

12. Allen Drury, "Dulles Appeals for Aid to India and Yugoslavia," *New York Times*, 25 March 1958, 1, 13.

13. Dulles to Senator Smith, 3 June 1958, Dulles Telcons.

ment projects, in some cases replacing aid withdrawn by the Soviets.[14] The Yugoslav government continued to purchase various kinds of military equipment from the United States as well, particularly spare parts for jet aircraft.

When Ambassador Mates left his post to return to Yugoslavia in the summer of 1958, Dulles suggested that Eisenhower grant him a farewell interview, in view of the "strained relations between Yugoslavia and the Soviet Union" and Yugoslavia's continuing struggle to maintain its independence "against Sino-Soviet bloc pressures."[15] Eisenhower met with Mates at the end of June and stressed his hope that neutral countries like Yugoslavia would work with the West on such crucial issues as arms control. Mates gave his assurance that Tito was committed to such issues, even though conditions in Yugoslavia were difficult. His country had suffered "material losses" in the cause of peace, the outgoing ambassador told the president, but peace could not be purchased "by submitting to subjugation."[16] When Yugoslavia's new envoy, Marko Nikezić, presented his credentials in late October, Eisenhower voiced his continuing support for Yugoslavia's independence.[17]

By the end of 1958, administration analysts had concluded that the latest dispute between the Yugoslavs and the Soviets demonstrated the resolve of the Yugoslav Communist Party to define its own version of socialism. The Soviet Union, by contrast, remained unable to accept the Yugoslav course without endangering its own status in the international communist movement and its control in Eastern Europe. In short, Yugoslavia's independence still constituted a disruptive force within the communist world. Internally, Yugoslav policies had moderated and Western contacts had increased, as a result of both Soviet pressure and U.S. encouragement. Nonalignment had even become a virtue, in that the administration agreed that it had great appeal to intellectuals in Eastern Europe and therefore served as another source of division within the bloc.[18] Even Tito's ties to neutral states in Asia

14. Allen Drury, "Foreign Aid Voted by House, 259-134," *New York Times*, 15 May 1958, 1, 12; Paul Underwood, "U.S. to Help Build Yugoslav Projects," ibid., 19 August 1958, 1, 3.

15. Dulles to Eisenhower, 19 June 1958, Eisenhower Papers, PAP, Whitman File, International Series, File: Yugoslavia (1).

16. Memorandum of conversation, 25 June 1958, Eisenhower Papers, PAP, Whitman File, International Series, File: Yugoslavia (1).

17. "Yugoslavs Get Pledge," *New York Times*, 28 October 1958, 9.

18. Roy Melbourne to Lay, 16 December 1958, with enclosure, NSC 5805/1, OCB Report on Yugoslavia, 10 December 1958, Dec. Docs., 1987, Microfiche no. 78, Doc. nos. 1198 and 1199.

and Africa represented a "net gain for the West," since when visiting those areas Tito praised the United States for its policy of providing assistance "without strings."[19]

Despite the cordial nature of the U.S.-Yugoslav relationship, Tito's twin roles as communist and neutral caused a few final controversies during Eisenhower's tenure. After Nikita Khrushchev's visit to the United States in 1959, Yugoslavia again wondered why Tito could not come to Washington, or Eisenhower stop at Belgrade on his proposed visit to Europe in November and December of that year. The Yugoslavs considered it essential that the past ten years of good will between the United States and Yugoslavia be crowned by a meeting of Tito and Eisenhower.[20] The Eisenhower administration did not share that conviction. In October Dulles's successor, Secretary of State Christian A. Herter informed the Yugoslavs that the president's schedule was too heavy to allow a Tito visit at that time; nor would Eisenhower include Belgrade in his European itinerary. Although the Tito government reacted with surprise and anger,[21] the administration doubtless believed it too soon after Khrushchev's visit to entertain another controversial communist head of state. Eisenhower may also have deemed it too risky to include Yugoslavia in a tour that already featured visits to India and Spain, the two other states most often cited by members of Congress who opposed mutual security aid to countries not openly on the side of the West.

Tito finally met Eisenhower when he came to the United States in the fall of 1960 for the United Nations' General Assembly meetings. The UN session, designed as a disarmament forum for world leaders, posed a number of problems for the administration. The last big power summit meeting, held in Paris in May, had collapsed in the wake of the Soviets' downing of the U.S. reconnaissance plane known as the U-2. Early in September, Khrushchev had informed Ambassador Thompson that he had little hope of any improvement occurring in U.S.-Soviet relations while Eisenhower remained in the White House.[22] Yet Eisenhower and his advisers feared that the nonaligned bloc represented by Tito, Nehru, and Egyptian leader Gamal Abdul

19. Hill to Dulles, 16 February 1959, RG 59, no. 350, 768.00/2-1659.

20. "Tito Vows Replies to Soviet Attack," *New York Times*, 8 March 1959, 13.

21. "Eisenhower Schedule Precludes Visit by Tito," *New York Times*, 10 October 1959, 9; editorial, "As Belgrade Sees It," ibid., 28 November 1959, 20; Paul Underwood, "Kardelj Refuses a Harvard Offer," ibid., 29 November 1959, 2.

22. Thompson to Christian A. Herter, 8 September 1960, *FRUS, 1958–1960*, 10(1):549–52.

Nasser might use the UN sessions to press for another big-power summit.[23]

In their rather anticlimatic meeting in New York City (in his memoirs Eisenhower referred to it as "innocuous"), Tito and Eisenhower discussed a range of issues from arms control to economic development.[24] When Eisenhower twice remarked that he hoped Yugoslavia's neutralism was "neutral on his side," Tito merely repeated his standard explanation that neutralism did not imply passivity but "meant not taking sides." Most of the two leaders' conversation concerned arms reduction and the hope for world peace, with Tito suggesting that despite the enmity that China felt for both the United States and Yugoslavia, no disarmament agreement could succeed without Chinese participation. Eisenhower replied that "the hatred in the United States for the leaders of Red China was so strong that any eager politician that suggested recognition had better start swimming for London." The two men said little about the Soviets, although Tito remarked "with a smile" that before his accidental meeting with Khrushchev in the UN lobby that morning, it had been some time since he had seen the Kremlin leader. The meeting ended with mutual expressions of friendship and an invitation from Tito for Eisenhower to come to Brioni.[25]

Although he made no mention of it in his meeting with the president, Tito and four other nonaligned leaders did send a letter to Eisenhower and Khrushchev, which contained the draft of a UN resolution calling on the two men "to renew their contacts" in the cause of peace. Eisenhower labeled the suggestion "an effrontery" and rejected it on the grounds that the Soviets had given no indication of their willingness to enter into substantive talks.[26] In a meeting with British and Australian leaders, Eisenhower questioned why the world had not responded with "shock and resentment" to the neutral nations' request. He expressed particular surprise at Nehru's "joining in this, since Nehru certainly understands the Communist tactics." Eisen-

---

23. Peter Lyons, *Eisenhower: Portrait of a Hero* (Boston: Little, Brown, 1974), 872–73.

24. C. Douglas Dillon, Memorandum of Conference with the President, 22 September 1960, and Goodpastor, Memorandum of Conference with the President, 5 October 1960, Eisenhower Papers, PAP, Whitman File/International Series, File: Yugoslavia (1); Dwight D. Eisenhower, *Waging Peace* (Garden City, N.Y.: Doubleday, 1963), 583.

25. Bohlen, memorandum of conversation, 22 September 1960, Eisenhower Papers, WHO, Office of Secretary, International Series, File: Yugoslavia (1).

26. Letter from Certain Heads of State to the President, 29 September 1960, with enclosure, "Draft U.N. General Assembly Resolution," *FRUS, 1958–1960*, 2:370–71; Eisenhower, *Waging Peace*, 586–88.

hower dismissed the other signatories, including Tito, as men he "does not have much use for." Khrushchev scorned the proposal as well, and the five signatories eventually withdrew it.[27] While Eisenhower had willingly joined with Dulles in using Tito and his state as a wedge against the Soviets, he clearly did not share his late secretary of state's enthusiasm for Tito himself.

Although drawn into Yugoslavia's affairs only because of the Second World War and the Cold War that followed it, the United States quickly became one of the Tito regime's severest critics. America's distaste for Yugoslavia's internal and external policies never disappeared and Tito's commitment to socialism never wavered, but the nature of the two states' relationship slowly changed. After the Tito-Stalin split of 1948 the Truman and Eisenhower administrations saw opportunities for the West in closer ties with Yugoslavia's outcast regime. Tito's defection in and of itself weakened the Soviets' military power and discredited their tactics in Eastern Europe. If assisted by the West, Tito also could serve as a beacon to the satellite states and provide the United States with the wedge it needed to dislodge the Soviets' control there. A Yugoslavia dependent on the West for military assistance might also choose to join NATO, or at the very least engage in joint defense planning with the Western alliance.

Both administrations claimed that they would demand no concessions from Yugoslavia in return for aid, but each expected Tito to cooperate with his benefactors and their foreign policy. Tito did not fulfill these expectations, despite threatened and actual aid suspensions. And although he resumed relations with the Soviet Union, Tito did not respond to its attempts to make Yugoslavia subservient to Soviet policy either. His resolve to remain both a communist and a neutral proved stronger than either side's attempts to control him. Yet the Truman and Eisenhower administrations continued to be willing to assist him and to battle their critics in the public and the Congress on his behalf, revealing a willingness to forgo ideological conformity to gain a substantial geopolitical advantage.

However, this flexibility was often difficult to exercise; there were too many contradictions involved in a democratic state sustaining a communist one in order to achieve an eventual end to communism. As Ambassador Allen had warned in the early 1950s, it was Tito's independence that at first attracted the United States to him, but that

27. Goodpastor, memorandum of conference, 2 October 1960, *FRUS, 1958–1960*, 2:375; *FRUS, 1958–1960*, 2:398–99, editorial note.

independence was often as hostile to the West as to the East. The dilemmas inherent in a wedge strategy so dependent on a communist regime became more pronounced as the Eisenhower administration made the wedge a central part of its approach to the Cold War. Dulles, determined to shatter and democratize the Soviet bloc, persisted in seeing Tito as a agent of liberation despite the latter's constant avowals of devotion to socialism. Eisenhower, less enamored of the Yugoslav leader, always appeared more interested in the military aspects of Tito's defection and more conscious of his adherence to communist ideology. But neither man fully explored the consequences of radical change in Eastern Europe or the feasibility of a state like Yugoslavia joining NATO until the Hungarians attempted the first and Tito's unshakable commitment to socialism made the second undesirable.

After the Hungarian revolution, Eisenhower and Dulles emphasized their support for evolutionary rather than violent change in Eastern Europe. Tito's actions during that crisis and his on-again-off-again relations with the Soviets also forced the administration to acknowledge that neither Tito's nationalism nor his communism had altered. If Tito's value as a wedge demanded that he remain part of the communist world, if his usefulness, in Dulles's words, was mostly as an "exhibit," so be it.

An independent but still communist Yugoslavia may not have been all that Truman and Eisenhower had hoped to achieve by coming to Tito's aid in his quarrel with Stalin; however, the resolve shown by both administrations to sustain him in power despite the nature of his system illustrates the amount of continuity that existed within the Democratic and Republican approaches to containment. If the containment policy, as Kennan once argued, was designed to resist Soviet imperialism, then Truman's battle to sustain Tito's independence represented one of that policy's greatest successes. The willingness of Eisenhower and Dulles to use Tito's commitment to national communism and to tolerate, even grudgingly, his nonalignment, demonstrates that they, like Truman, based their foreign policy on geopolitical rather than ideological concerns.

INDEX